Data Interoperability Community of Interest Handbook

Michael M. Gorman

Whitemarsh Information Systems Corporation
2008 Althea Lane
Bowie, Maryland 20716
Tele: 301-249-1142
Email: Whitemarsh@wiscorp.com
Web: www.wiscorp.com

ISBN 978-0-9789968-0-2

Printed in the United States of America

10 9 8 7 6 5 4 3 2 1

Table of Contents

Figures

Tables

Preface

Why was this book necessary? That is a good question and is answered here. Data Interoperability within enterprises almost always involves databases. Databases are almost always multi functional. Hence, database, as an IT discipline which started in the middle 1960s, has always been a cross-functional or community effort. The work products of these Communities of Interest are the specifications (i.e., metadata) of the databases, the missions, organizations, functions within which the databases operate, and the specifications of the information systems from these communities that feed data into or employ data from these databases.

Communities of Interest are not just the right approach for these efforts. They have been the only approach for the past 50+ years. Highly efficient, and broadly successful Communities of Interest are work-product centric, author anonymous organizations. Individual contributions are subservient to the produced data interoperability standard. This book is a handbook for successful Data Interoperability Communities of Interest. That is, those that are work-product centric, author-anonymous. To be successful, Communities of Interest operate under a formal set of rules and produce highly engineered, thoroughly integrated work products.

The Congress of the United States (a Community of Interest for America) operates under an elaborate set of rules. These rules were adapted for members of ordinary societies by GEN Henry M. Robert in 1915. These are now commonly called *Robert's Rules*. Notwithstanding they also require a "Sergeant of Arms." For sure not to shoot members, but to enforce good order. From the United States Senate website[1], "The Sergeant at Arms and Doorkeeper, elected by the members, serves as the protocol and chief law enforcement officer and is the principal administrative manager for most support services in the United States Senate." Even with such an individual, some sessions in both houses of the U.S. Congress seem not to be in good order.

Over the years, I have participated in a number of Communities of Interest. These range from committees to develop programs for Boy Scout Troops, to informal groups within various employments, and a number of times during Whitemarsh consulting assignments. As the years have passed, the financial impacts of decisions made by Communities of Interest have become greater. For example, it is common for the decisions made by the ANSI INCITS H2 Technical Committee on Database, a Community of Interest especially focused on the ANSI standard database language, SQL, to have tens-of-millions of dollars implications.

---

[1] The website address is:
<http://www.senate.gov/reference/office/sergeant_at_arms.htm>

Such decisions should be made not only with the utmost technical precision but also with the utmost bureaucratic care. Proper formulation, notice, discussion, voting, and on some occasions, appeals are all absolutely essential.

Some Communities of Interest in which I have participated seem like "professional" hockey games. That is, three 20 minute periods of continuous fighting interrupted by short intervals of skating around the rink. When serious discussions and decisions within a Community of Interest need to take place, consuming 50% of the time settling who votes, how votes are taken, what determines success or failure, if or when you can abstain, when papers are produced, how minutes are created, and all the rest is clearly a waste of time and effort. All of that should be predetermined by the rules and procedures of good order.

The purpose of this book, therefore, is to set down a set of bureaucratic and procedural rules for accomplishing the scope and program of work of Communities of Interest. Hereafter, I just refer to these organizations as Communities of Interest. In addition, this book also provides clear procedures for accomplishing the Data Interoperability Community of Interest's technical work. While it was clear to me via all the Community of Interest meetings that the bureaucratic policies and procedures were needed, it was however a complete surprise that the technical policies, procedures and product specifications were also needed. They too are provided in this book and are very much further detailed with materials from the Whitemarsh website[2].

I hope this book brings value to your Community of Interest efforts. Suggestions for revision are always welcome. Send me email.[3]

Michael M. Gorman
November 2006

[2] www.wiscorp.com

[3] The email address is: Whitemarsh@wiscorp.com

Acknowledgments

There were four main sources for the material in this book. First is the Multi-Lateral Interoperability Program[4]. This is a military Command and Control (C2) community of interest exclusively focused on data interoperability that was founded within NATO (North Atlantic Treaty Organization). The MIP organization has been operational for more than 10 years across 26 nations. Simply stated, this organization has created a first class Information Exchange Data Model for Command and Control. Not surprisingly, it is called C2IEDM. The scope and the purpose of the MIP organization are set down in the opening section of Chapter 1 of this book. Only very minor edits were performed on their text. If the text is compelling as to the mission and goals of data interoperability, then it is because the need for and concepts surrounding data interoperability transcend organizations and nations. The most significant contribution of these materials has been the engineering of this style of community of interest. While the MIP material has been edited for use in this book, the intention was to remain true to their data interoperability Community of Interest engineering.

The second source for material is an even older community of interest: The International Committee of Information Technology Standards (INCITS, www.incits.org). This organization is at least 40 years old and operates under the auspices of the American National Standards Institute (ANSI). This uniquely American, volunteer-based, organization is responsible for developing IT standards for SQL, COBOL, FORTRAN, Optical Digital Data Disks, C, C++, Metadata, Radio Frequency Identification (RAID), and the like. The INCITS organization operates almost exclusively through Communities of Interest. The author of this book has been the Secretary of the Database Languages Committee, H2, since its very first meeting in April 1978. The organizational and operational materials from INCITS have been invaluable in the construction of the "bureaucratic" component of this book. Similarly, while the INCITS material has been edited for use in this book, the intention was to remain true to its information technology standard's Communities of Interest engineering. Thus, similarity to the original text is no accident.

Just having a complete policies and procedures manual to govern meetings, documents, decisions and appeals to decisions does not automatically bring peace, order, and harmony. That is achieved by a chair who understands that his role is to progress the standard and doing that requires peace, order and harmony. For 26 of the 28 years, the chair of H2 has been Dr. Donald Deutsch. That SQL is clearly one of the most accepted IT standards in the world is due to

[4] The MIP website is located at: www.mip-site.org.

his firm hand and calm demeanor. Don, my "ANSI boss," and close friend for more than 40 years is therefore great fully acknowledged. Because the engineering and operations of H2 are excellent, a number of H2 documents have been employed to construct key content in several chapters.

The third source of material has been the Office of the CIO of the United States Army. During the time, September 2003 through December 2004, this author, and two other individuals, Bruce Haberkamp and Jim Blalock worked almost continuously on building an enterprise[5]-wide Data Management Program that could achieve data interoperability across the U.S. Army. A workshop based on a prototype of these efforts was conducted in December 2003. It was very successful. Dr. Edward Siomacco (COL, U.S. Army Ret) authorized and encouraged the workshop. These efforts resulted in sections within two Army documents. The data management paragraphs of Army Regulation 25-1, and an entire data management chapter in the Department of Army Pamphlet (DA PAM 25-1-1). These materials provided the three distinct levels to the Data Interoperability Program: Program, Project, and Community of Interest.

The fourth sets of materials have been from the Whitemarsh Corporation's extensive development of data management related methodologies, metadata engineering, and a metadata repository that can accomplish the program and scope of work for a Community of Interest. These materials have been in constant use and refinement since the middle 1970s. Organizations that have employed these materials are listed under Clients on the Whitemarsh website. During 2005 and 2006 Whitemarsh constructed the materials necessary for a Community of Interest. These materials contributed to the technical processes of constructing the data interoperability products.

---

[5]. As defined within this book, an enterprise is merely a term to relate to a collection of organization units that have common collections of data, processes, activities within a business or a company and sometimes beyond corporate affiliations as in the case of data interchanges. Ideally, there is also a common governance of these items. An enterprise is therefore not just a synonym for business or a company. Rather, it is intended to convey a common data, process, and activity view across the organizational units sharing that view. A Data Interoperability Program is presumed to work across enterprises. Specific Communities of Interest work within enterprises and with respect to data interoperability, represent a shared governance. Some Communities of Interest work across corporate boundaries as in the case of the ANSI committee of the U.S. State Motor Vehicle Departments. Maryland drivers who speed in Nebraska see notations on their Maryland driving record.

Collectively then, the organizational engineering from the MIP program, the bureaucratic structures and processes from INCITS, the firm and guiding hand of a "Don Deutsch," the programmatic levels from the U.S. Army, and the technical materials from Whitemarsh have been brought together to create this book. All during the engineering and construction of his book, Hank Lavender, a retired USAF Colonel and graduate of the Air Force Academy, and also a senior database management consultant to the U.S. Department of Logistics's Defense Logistics Standards Management Office, and a long time friend and a professional colleague, has been ever ready to read a chapter, and even whole manuscripts and provide back immediate and very constructive comments.

Within the MIP program thanks goes to Gene Simaitis and Francisco Loaiza of the Institute for Defense Analysis, to COL Stuart Whitehead, and to Mike Morris. These four along with countless others have made the MIP data model, the C2IEDM, the premiere Command and Control data model throughout the world.

A common thread to all of these Army data interoperability initiatives has been the Office of the CIO under the command of LTG Stephen Boutelle. It was his program actions that funded the development of the data interoperability materials within the Army regulations, and that funded the workshop that demonstrated that the guidance in this book works efficiently and effectively.

A review and very valuable guidance have been received from David Allen of the Office of the Assistant Secretary of Defense, National Information Infrastructure, Office of the CIO.

A critical review and encouragement have been received from Andreas Tolk of the Old Dominion University. These individuals and many others in the data communities such as Robert Seiner of The Data Administration Newsletter, Terry Moriarty, Kevin light, and Karen Lopez of the ever responsive Data Management Discussion Group, Ron Ross for the material on Resource Life Cycle Analysis, and the DAMA community at large have all impacted the quality and validity of this book. Once a year all the "data folks" get together at the DAMA-Metadata International Conference. Tony Shaw and his great staff from Wilshire Conferences are responsible for making every year the best yet.

It is largely because of the hundreds of staff years from all these four acknowledged organizations and all the individuals cited above that this book represents an integration, editing, and publication effort rather than an original creation effort. In short because of all these efforts, this book is equivalent to a book you would read after it has been continuously revised over many years.

1

The Demand for Data Interoperability

The application of data in the early 21st century is demanding. It covers a wide spectrum of scenarios that range from conventional to crises responses, and to asymmetric operations. Unilateral capability is important but most planning is made on the assumption of alliance and coalition operations in scenarios that are difficult to predict and which often arise at short notice. Thus, the nature and composition of data to meet requirements may be quite specific but should be based upon general and flexible capabilities.

To achieve this, an assured capability for the interoperability of data is essential. The successful executions of fast-moving operations need an accelerated decision-action cycle, increased tempos of operations, and the ability to conduct joint operations. Executives require timely and accurate information. Also, supporting business information systems[6] need to pass information within and across language boundaries. Moreover, tactical information must be provided to the operational and strategic levels of command.

The aim of a Data Interoperability Community of Interest, hereafter referred to just by Community of Interest, is to achieve data interoperability at all levels in support of combined and joint operations. Because data interoperability is almost always cross-functional, and cross-organizational, achievement of the highest level of data interoperability requires institutionalized, cross-functional, and cross-organizational semantics.

---

[6]. In the context of this book, a Business Information System is generic term for an information system that most commonly employs a database management system and a database. Simply put, a business information system is an application of IT technology in support of a collection of end users. The term is thus distinguished for example, from a computer's Operating System such as Windows or Unix, or a Database Management System such as Oracle, or "office" systems like Microsoft's Word, Power Point or Excel.

The catch phrase for this within the U.S. DoD is *factory to foxhole.* Specialized, parochial semantics are direct inhibitors to data interoperability.

The concept for the overall end state is to have multiple and disparate organizations operate as a single, synchronized team in accomplishing its assigned mission. In order to achieve that synergy, a common understanding is required. The interoperability contribution to this end state is to facilitate the timely flow of accurate and relevant information.

The perspective of this book is that there is a collection of operational Communities of Interest within an enterprise's Data Interoperability Program, and this book is a component of day-to-day operations of all the subgroups[7] within the Data Interoperability Program. If it is the case that there is only one community of interest, then the entire organizational structure could consist solely of that community of interest and its contained technical committees. Consequentially, there would be no need for the Data Interoperability Program Committee and any of its contained subgroups. Other areas of this book could be similarly organizationally collapsed and/or streamlined in such a case.

1.1 Formal Interpretation of this Book

Formal interpretation of this book may be obtained upon request to the Data Interoperability Program Committee[8]. It is their responsibility to determine the meaning of any content and to render decisions about the effect of such interpretation. Any request for interpretation will be addressed by Procedures Board Committee at the first meeting following receipt of the request. The Data Interoperability Program Committee will maintain a record of all requests including the substance of the request and the interpretation provided. This

[7]. Within the context of this document, *subgroup* is a generic term that refers to any constituted data interoperability program organizational entity including the Data Interoperability Program committee, its contained boards, Communities of Interest, its contained technical committees. This term is employed within the context in question, and applies universally to all data interoperability program organizational entities.

[8]. From the publishing perspective of this book, if a reader of this book finds that content is missing, misstated, or could be stated or described differently, suggestions are always welcome. Send them to Whitemarsh@Wiscorp.com. The ultimate goal of this book is to assist in the engineering of Communities of Interest that operate efficiently and effectively. Feedback will enhance future editions.

record of interpretation will be periodically distributed to all members of the Data Interoperability Program Committee as well as all subgroup officers, and will serve as a basis for future revisions of this document.

Appeals to any interpretation made under this procedure may be made directly to the Community of Interest by requesting in writing that the issue be reviewed at its next scheduled meeting of the Data Interoperability Program Committee.

1.2 Objective of this Book

The objective of this book is to facilitate the identification, development, and evolution of data interoperability standards. These standards are produced within Communities of Interest that, in turn, operate within an enterprise's Data Interoperability Program. Data interoperability standards from one Community of Interest are themselves almost always semantically interrelated with other data interoperability standards from other Communities of Interest. A key function of certain subgroups within the overall Data Interoperability Program is semantic harmonization across data interoperability standards. Without harmonization data interoperability standards ultimately become the specifications of just another "stovepipe" database. The centerpiece product in a Data Interoperability standard is the Information Exchange Data Model. Surrounding this product is the multiple classes of metadata. Throughout this book, the word, standard, is used as a shorthand for the complete specification of a Data Interoperability standard. If a Community of Interest just creates a file of SQL DDL for the Information Exchange Data Model and calls it a Data Interoperability standard, they greatly short change the effort, and will likely fail to achieve the goal of data interoperability.

1.3 Communities of Interest

From the Wikipedia, "a Community of interest is a community of people who share a common interest or passion, such as rugby fans on Rugby365.com, or music lovers on MP3.com. These people exchange ideas and thoughts about the given passion, but may know (or care) little about each other outside of this area. Participation in a community of interest can be compelling, entertaining and create a 'sticky' community where people return frequently and remain for extended periods."

Within the context of this book, a Community of Interest is the organizational implementing mechanism through which data interoperability is achieved across collections of data. In almost all organizations, data is cross functional. Consequently, data interoperability communities of interest under whatever names they have been called have existed for 30 or more years.

Within information technology, Communities of Interest is really a new name for an old concept. Charles Betz indicates that these groups have been called Communities of Practice, Consortia, Steering Committees, Advisory Committees/Councils, Coordinating Committees, or Interest Groups.

Communities of Interest exist within the context of an organization's data interoperability program. Each community of interest is likely focused on a particular functional area or a collection of functional areas. For example, if there is a data interoperability community of interest for Order Processing, then while functionally narrow, it may embrace a collection of organizations and individuals that deal with creating interoperable order processing data. Such a community might exist because each participating organization has a different order processing system.

Other more naturally existing data interoperability communities of interest exist with data operational data store (ODS) database, data warehouse (both wholesale and retail) projects, or master data projects (including reference data). These classes of projects have always been cross functional, and thus, the groups of individuals from the different participating organizations have always functioned as communities of interest.

This book then is really a new book about an old concept. The objective is to provide a formalization to these cross-functional data interoperability groups so that when these groups come into existence they can operate more smoothly, efficiently, and effectively. Less smoke and mirrors: more real work.

1.4 Organization of this Book

The book begins with this chapter and then proceeds to Chapter 2 which explains the need of data interoperability environments. There is then an overall archtiecture for the book: The Knowledge Worker Framework. Frameworks are merely mechanisms for depicting, understanding, and explaining a complex subject. Some frameworks are durable and persistent while others are temporal. The Knowledge Worker Framework, which was described in the early 1980s by

Matthew Flavin is throughly explained in materials from the Whitemarsh website, is for the knowledge worker rather than for the process worker. The key columns for the framework are:

- Mission (Chapter 4)
- Database Object (Chapter 5)
- Business Information System (Chapter 6)
- Business Event (Chapter 7)
- Business Function (Chapter 8)
- Business Organization (Chapter 9)

Figure 1 depicts the Knowledge Worker Framework. Explained in a left-to-right fashion, every enterprise has a mission, and without a mission there is no reason for the enterprise. Database object classes and the resulting database objects represent the "data proof" that the mission is accomplished. Business information systems are the "IT mechanisms" through which the mission-based data is collected and stored in databases. Business events are the business information system triggering mechanisms that are set within calendar and business cycles. Functions, often called in this book, Business Functions, are the human-centric processes that are performed and that on occasion trigger the business events. Finally, organization, also called Business Organization in this book, are the bureaucratic constructs of collections of persons who perform business functions.

The order, left to right, represents the least political to the most political. Where, that is, place is not in the framework because in today's network environments, "where" can be anywhere and often is virtual. In the case of this

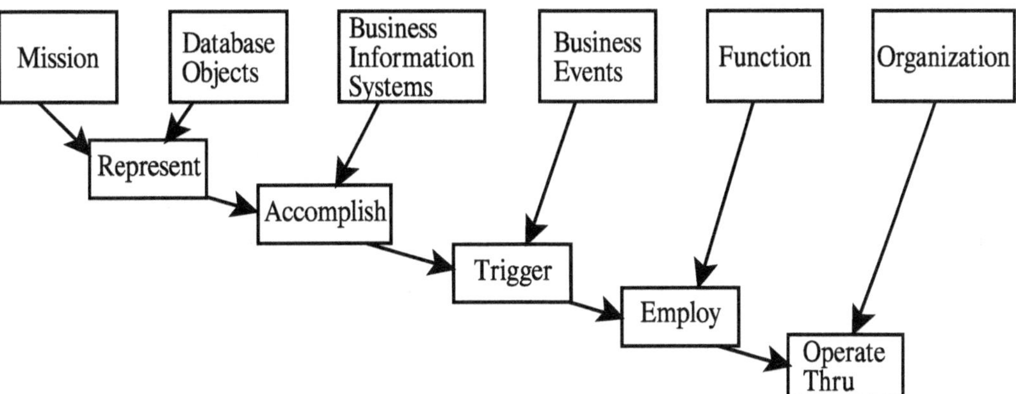

Figure 1. Interrelationships among Knowledge Worker Framework components.

book, the mission is to build interoperable data environments. As this mission is accomplished, products are constructed. In this case the products are database objects but are not real-data-based products. Rather, they are metadata-based products. To construct these metadata-based products, business information systems are executed. In this case, the building of data interoperability specifications, the business information systems are metadata-based information systems. These metadata-based information systems are activated during the accomplishment of the functions associated with the creation of data interoperability specifications. Finally, functions are accomplished by persons operating within positions of the organizations participating in the communities of interest.

Stated from right to left, organizations operate through functions which, when performed, trigger business events that activate business information systems that add, delete, or modify the data of the database objects in the fulfillment of data interoperability missions.

It is because interoperable data environments are needed, are specified, exist within organizations, and are employed by persons as they perform their functions in support of accomplishing some aspect of the data interoperability mission that this framework, the Knowledge Worker Framework, is ideally suited to these purposes.

The metadata repository that is to contain the complete specifications of data interoperability environments is described in Chapter 3. It's a high-level data model and is further specified in Chapter 5. The data model's corresponding process model is specified in Chapter 6.

The positions that should be established are described in Chapter 10. Chapter 11 provides the specifications for key documents and guidance for document creation. Chapter 12 enumerates the types of data interoperability projects that should be undertaken. The final chapter, Chapter 13, provides a set of rules that govern the establishment of communities of interest, the conduct of meetings, voting, the collection of fees and other necessary activities that reduced the need for a real Sergeant of Arms.

In general, Chapters 4 through 13 represent the policies, products, processes, projects, procedures, positions, organizations, and rules for instituting and operating a Data Interoperability Program through its contained Communities of Interest.

This book is intended to be a day-to-day cookbook for any subgroup within a Data Interoperability Program. The form of the book's content is sometimes narrative paragraphs, and other times hierarchal lists and/or specifications. The intention was to create the material in the best use-form. In short, this book contains: the what, the when, and the how to accomplish data interoperability's specification, implementation, and evolution.

To that end, this book is organized into three overall parts:

- Part 1, that is, Chapters 1, 2, introduction and rationale chapters.
- Part 2, that is, Chapters 3 through 8, is the infrastructures chapters for establishing data interoperability programs and their communities of interest.
- Part 3, that is, Chapters 9 through 13, are the governance chapters. The parts, chapters and descriptions are provided in the table that follows.

Data Interoperability Community of Interest Handbook Organization		
Part	**Chapter**	**Description**
1. Introduction and Rationale	1.Demand for Data Interoperability	This chapter presents the overall rationale for the demand for data interoperability, its value proposition, the objective of the book and its organizational framework.
	2. Rationale for Data Interoperability	This chapter presents the rationale for a community of interest. Included in the rationale are its key reasons for existence, the role of shared policy, and the need to focus on database objects[9] classes as the foundation stones for shared data.
2. Infrastructure	3. Metadata	This chapter sets forth the requirements for metadata with the objective that the reader concludes that to have any reasonable hope of being successful in data interoperability there must first be success with metadata.

[9]. A database object is a Whitemarsh crafted term that refers to "object oriented" features contained within databases that are managed by database management systems. The ANSI INCITS H2 Technical Committee on Database has gone a long way in defining database object classes within the SQL language. In this book and in Information Technology in general, "class" implies type and the string without "class" implies instance. Thus, there is the class of sandwich, Peanut-Butter and Jelly. It would therefore be referred to as a Peanut-Butter and Jelly sandwich "class." But "my" Peanut-Butter and Jelly sandwich that I hold in my hand is just that, a Peanut-Butter and Jelly sandwich. No "class."

Data Interoperability Community of Interest Handbook Organization		
Part	**Chapter**	**Description**
	4. Mission	Chapter 4 presents the overall mission of data interoperability. Missions describe the objective in idealized terms without the "who" (Positions and Organization), or the "how" (functions).
	5. Database Objects	Chapter 5 present the "what." That is, the metadata products that need to be created during the existence of a data interoperability project. In this case these products are the specifications necessary to then implement so as to enable data interoperability throughout an enterprise's operations.
	6. Business Information Systems	Chapter 6 identifies the business information systems, which, in the case of a Data Interoperability Program, are actually metadata information systems that enable members of the various Data Interoperability Programs to create, evolve, and maintain the products set out in Chapter 5. Again, once the metadata-based products of Chapter 5 are created, they, as specifications, are implemented and made operational through normal information technology processes. Over the years the implementation technology of these metadata-based products has and will change. In years gone by, the implementation technologies were shared tapes that were transported across distances to then run on different computers. This implementation technology was replaced by computers residing in commonly employable networks. Thereafter, these were replaced by client-server environments with enterprise-based proprietary networks. Today, there are the Internet and web-based services. Tomorrow? All during these technology evolutions the fundamental set of metadata-based products and the processes to create the products have largely remained the same. Some things, needs and processes are constant.
	7. Business Events	Chapter 7 presents the business events that occur along the road to creating the metadata-based products of Chapter 5. Also presented are the bureaucratic business events that occur while carrying out the scope and program of work of a Data Interoperability Program.

Data Interoperability Community of Interest Handbook Organization		
Part	**Chapter**	**Description**
	8. Business Functions	This chapter presents the business functions, that is, the processes that are to be undertaken by the positions within the organizations to build the products necessary for a successful data interoperability mission. Of necessity, these processes are not completely detailed. Additional detail is available from various methodology products from the Whitemarsh website.
3. Governance	9. Business Organizations	This chapter presents the various organizations that should exist for a robust Data Interoperability Program. If your program is merely a single Community of Interest, then the organizational structure should be collapsed into just the organization, Community of Interest. The chair and officers of that one Community of Interest would necessarily have to assume the responsibilities, authorities and duties of the total program. If thereafter additional Communities of Interest emerge, then the additional layers within the organization could be created and set into place.
	10. Positions	This chapter presents the various positions that should exist across the subgroup organizations. In this book "position" applies to members as well as functional positions such as officers, editors, and the like. Included as well in this chapter are the processes for applying for membership, withdrawal of membership, and member status review.
	11. Documents	This chapter presents a sketch of the kinds of documents or "large" products that are built from the collections of metadata products set out in Chapter 5. A strawman collection of documents is identified. These were drawn from the U.S. Federal Government's Department of Defense's Architecture Framework (DoDAF). Every other enterprise that has an IT methodology would need to examine, retain, or replace the set of documents described in this Chapter.

Data Interoperability Community of Interest Handbook Organization		
Part	**Chapter**	**Description**
	12. Projects	This chapter presents the various projects involved in Data Interoperability Programs and Communities of Interest. A project is creation, evolution, or employment of a collection of metadata products accomplished through a set of functions performed by one or more positions within one or more organizations in support of the data interoperability mission. Projects must be identified, staffed, allocated resources, and monitored for both timeliness and quality.
	13. Rules	This chapter contains a detailed set of rules that govern the operation of any subgroup within a Data Interoperability Program. Rules are needed because the consequences of decisions from any Community of Interest decision are likely to have significant monetary and other resource effects. Adding one table to an existing database design costs about $32,000. Adding the extract from that table to 10 different systems is likely to cost a similar amount. Thus, every decision is costly. Decisions need to be made in a very rigorous, reliable, and a repeatable manner with strict rules, appropriate notices, sufficient times for implementation, and the like.

Table 1. Chapters organization by part sequence.

Now, if all of this sounds like a lot of work, it really is and isn't. It is a lot of work if you and your organization are not accomplishing it now. But it isn't a lot of work when you compare it to the collective set of activities that are performed and products that are built to remedy data interoperability chaos.

Accomplished well, these activities have a negative real-dollar cost and a negative time expenditure. At first, there will be more time and money spent ramping up the effort. But once done, the time and money expenditures that were formerly budgeted can be reduced well in excess of this ramp up cost.

Has this been proven? Of course it has. Chapter 3 contains just a few examples. In one 1980s example, multiple versions of a particular class of business information system were being built, individually, for a cost of about $400,000. After these practices were put into place, these same systems were being created for about $100,000. The cost for the ramp up was about $125,000. So, the first use of these policies and procedure was projected to cost about $525,000. But the second was to cost 60% (of the $400,00), and there after, 40% (of the $400,00). But due to rigorous metadata and excellent systems engineering management, the first system came in at 80% of the $525,000; the second system came in at 40%; and thereafter, the systems came in at 20%. That actually meant that there was almost a positive ROI on the first use. Actually, the cost was just $20,000 over the custom system cost.

Has this strategy and fundamental organization been used outside of IT? Of course it has. Just look at the organization, operating procedures, and results from any well run fire department. Within these departments there are well-defined missions for each class of fire or emergency; clearly identified objects that are employed and interrelated one with another; clearly delineated systems that are employed to report fires, dispatch equipment, manage fire suppression, and report and evaluate on results; well-defined events that are the consequence of functions and that employ systems; all manner of human functions that are performed, and finally, detailed and experience honed organizations to perform all manners of fire activities. Similar examples abound for almost every highly organized complex activity. In virtually 100% of these organizations chaos occurs only when the missions through to organizations are not well engineered and rigorously followed. Chaotically engineered and organized activities that produce quality, efficient and cost-effective results are almost always accidental.

1.5 Executing this Book

The chapters of this book, as illustrated through the Knowledge Worker Framework depicted in Figure 1 above, are set out as a way to engineer and constitute a data interoperability program, to establish communities of interest, and to establish data interoperability projects. This stands in stark contrast to the planning and executing the every day activities to actually build the interoperable data environments. So, if you are not part of the engineering and construction crew but part of the using-crew this section is for you.

Consider a house. You do not start by building the front door, then the hallway, then the dining room or living room, and then the downstairs half-bath, the kitchen, rec-room, and backdoor. And then, build the stairs, the upstairs hallway, the bedrooms, and the bathrooms. Rather, these are "use-ways" once the house is built.

Consequently, either an entirely different book would have had to be created or an alternative manner of executing the contents of this book had to be set out. The latter were chosen.

Section 1.4 identifies the engineering and construction of the house. This section identifies the use-sequence. Sometimes the sequence is the same. Other times it is different. Represented here is the day to day execution of data interoperability programs, organizations, and projects once instituted. As Figure 1 depicts the engineering sequence of key chapters, Figure 2 depicts the "execution sequence" for the chapters. Rules, Chapter 13 is missing from this figure because rules are "called" from many if not all the other chapters. In actuality, "rules" are invoked when decisions cannot be made except through the application of a precise rule set.

The suggested way to read and use this book is set out in the table that follows Figure 2. Each description cell contains guidance as to the reading of the chapter

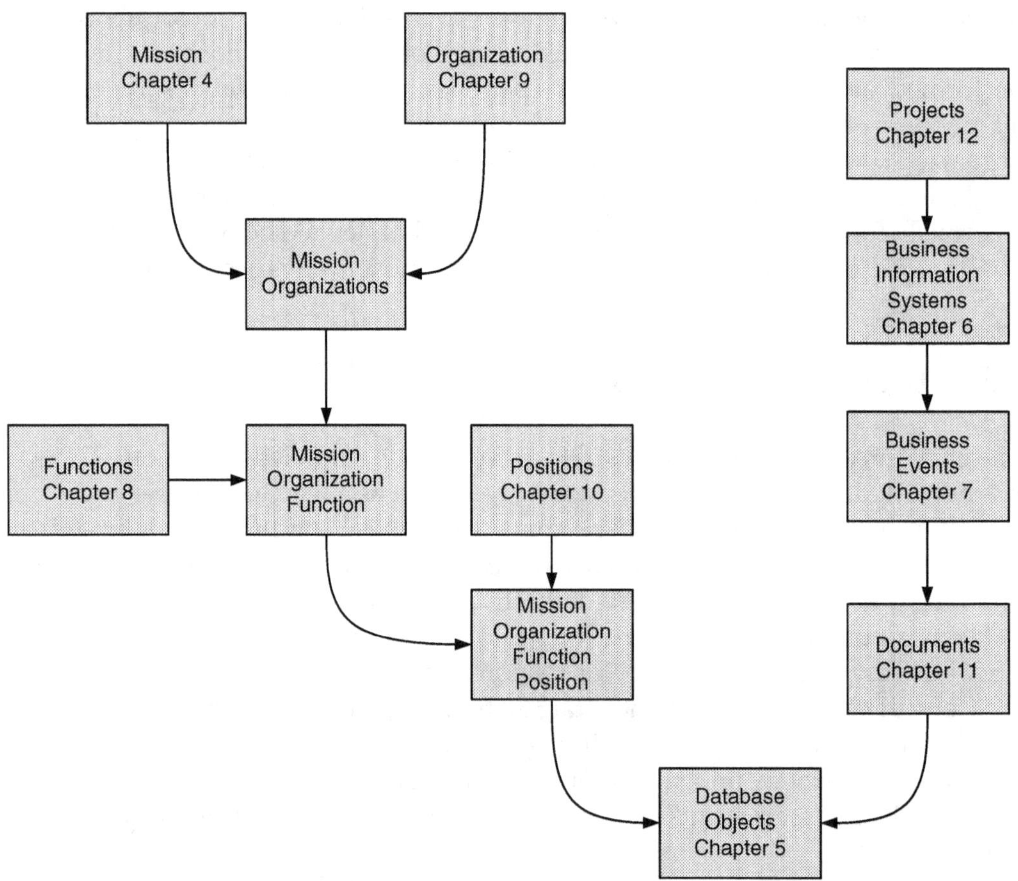

Figure 2. Data interoperability specification build sequence.

and also a use-based description of the chapter. The first three rows of this table, Demand, Rationale, and Metadata that represent those chapters all need to be read, accepted, and in the case of the metadata repository, deployed. Row 4, Mission, when accomplished will then produce metadata that is stored in row 3's metadata repository.

In the execution sequence, missions are first specified through a boot-strap ad hoc organization. If there is a go-ahead for a data interoperability program then the organizations are created as necessary. It may be a full data interoperability program and its subcommittees along with several communities of interest, or it may be a single community of interest that performs all the necessary functions. Then, as the functions are performed by the persons in various positions within specific projects, the various milestones are accomplished as a consequence of building the various metadata products.

Data Interoperability Community of Interest Handbook Use Sequence	
Chapters (short title)	**Description**
1. Demand	This chapter provides the overall objective of the book and the use of communities of interest to achieve data interoperability then you should not proceed to Chapter 2.
2. Rationale	This chapter presents the overall key reasons for data interoperability the concept of "data is executed policy," a comprehensive definition of metadata, and the identification and engineering of database objects which are the foundation stones for data interoperability. If data interoperability is merely viewed as vast seas of unintegrated, redundant and semantically conflicting tables over which the DBMS is merely an access method, then you will never achieve data interoperability. In contrast, there is a value proposition for data interoperability. If there is not general agreement on its value proposition or an analogous value proposition then you should stop and not proceed to Chapter 3.
3. Metadata	This chapter presents the value from having the appropriate metadata infrastructure. If that metadata infrastructure is not achieved, then having more than just point-to-point interfaces between systems is largely impossible. If an organization does not have an integrated, end-to-end, nonredundant metadata infrastructure, then even if all the collections of point-to-point interfaces are centrally managed, they will just be another server-farm of stand-alone databases, but this time of metadata. If there is

Data Interoperability Community of Interest Handbook Use Sequence	
Chapters (short title)	**Description**
	any improvement, it's marginal. Centralized data brokering of centrally defined collections of point-to-point interfaces is not the mission of a quality Data Interoperability Program. The goal must be first an end-to-end integrated metadata model, and then the loading into a metadata database the appropriate metadata from all systems and databases participating in a nonredundant and integrated manner so that true semantic harmony including precision and granularity can be achieved. That is the true mission of data interoperability. If you cannot agree on the engineering and organization of metadata, or on the creation of formal policies, procedures, and organizations for the creation, maintenance and use of metadata, then stop, do not proceed to Chapter 4.
4. Mission	This chapter presents the missions that must be accomplished in any Data Interoperability Program. These missions should be reviewed and if necessary be refined before any other real work is attempted. Missions are hierarchically organized descriptions of the idealized target or objective of the effort. If you cannot agree on the destination, then do not start the journey. When a data interoperability project is actually started, then the missions related to the areas involved in interoperability are created. These too are then reviewed and revised. Agreement by participants is critical as these become the basis for data sharing. Shared missions beget shared data. Once you have identified shared missions, proceed to create the necessary organizations that build the Information Exchange Data Models and that support the information systems that feed and/or retrieve data from the shared spaces.
9. Organization	This chapter presents the types and kinds of organizations that should be established to be successful. Each organization is defined and the types of positions that should be established are identified. As stated above, if there is only a single Community of Interest, then these organizations do not have to be established. Rather, each organization type should be reviewed and the key functions and duties of the organization should be reflected, if appropriate, in the single Community of Interest. Each of these organizations should be reviewed and modified to make sure they fit into your overall organizational structure. When a data interoperability project starts and after the missions are created then you can know whether this is a single Community of Interest

Data Interoperability Community of Interest Handbook Use Sequence	
Chapters (short title)	**Description**
	effort or whether there has to be a Data Interoperability Program infrastructure created as well. Each organization has to be established, chartered, and staffed. A metadata management support infrastructure has to be procured or activated. Staff has to be obtained, assigned, and trained. Once the Community of Interest is set into place then the first meetings can start.
10. Positions	This chapter presents the positions that must be established in any of the organizations that are created via Chapter 9. Each position and its duties are generally described. Given your organization, are the positions properly named? Should their duties be enhanced or streamlined? These are all-important issues that should be addressed. Along with the organizations the various positions have to be created and staff assigned to the positions. The actual skills required are implied by the missions, functions, organizations, and positions. All the activities within these positions are common, every day IT activities that should be readily known or learned by professionals. Detailed process specifications, training courses and the like are all contained on the Whitemarsh website.
8. Functions	This chapter presents the functions, but at a high level that needs to be performed by each of the organizations set out in Chapter 9 in support of achieving either the overall Data Interoperability Program and/or any of the Communities of Interest. The functions that are to be performed are every day IT tasks and are fully defined and described in any number of University courses on data modeling, software development, configuration management, unit and system testing and documentation.
12. Projects	This chapter identifies and describes the types of projects that are to be accomplished in the development of any data interoperability standard. Each of these project types should be examined and evaluated to ensure that it is complete. Missing components should be added. Unnecessary components should be deleted. Each project should identify the appropriate milestones and the required metadata products, and ultimately the functions that need to be performed by the positions within organizations to achieve the data interoperability mission. Now that the missions are done, organizations created, positions filled, and staffs are ready to perform tasks, the data interoperability projects can be

Data Interoperability Community of Interest Handbook Use Sequence	
Chapters (short title)	**Description**
	instituted and accomplished. Each project has its own process model implied in the various sections. Chapter 4 builds the products identified in Chapter 5 according to the specialized work breakdown structures set out in Chapter 8. The level of interoperability achieved depends on the level of the enterprise on which it is focused. The higher the level the higher the level of interoperability and the more useful the work products.
6. Information Systems	This chapter presents the scope of the metadata systems and processes for building these metadata products. You need to assess that you have the right tool set to build the products, that the right processes are being used, and most of all that these metadata products are related to all the other metadata products so that there is one end-to-end, integrated, and nonredundant set of metadata products. When this is accomplished, then manufacturing additional metadata products from already existing ones becomes quite simple. Information systems in the context of the Information Exchange Data Models are the vehicles necessary to feed or access data within the databases regardless of how the data is either obtained and/or retrieved. These information systems have to have extract and/or load processes built within them and then be employed for the purposes of testing the quality of the exchanged data.
7. Events	This chapter presents the milestones that are to be accomplished in the achievement of the program and scope of work of the Data Interoperability Program and of any Community of Interest. Are these the right milestones for standards in your organization? If not, then change them so that you can ensure that data interoperability standards are properly constructed so as to gain maximum acceptance. Each of these milestones should be accomplished through the application of the functions outlined in Chapter 8. The resource assignment strategies should be set into place to ensure that the right quantity of staff is assigned to the functions, positions, and organizations to achieve the milestones.
11. Documents	This chapter provides a strawman set of documents or products that represent collections of metadata products from Chapter 5. Each product should be examined to determine if it is appropriate for your IT organization. If there are different ones, then make modifications accordingly. The goal is to have a complete set of products across all the critical IT dimensions. It is clear that a given metadata product from

Data Interoperability Community of Interest Handbook Use Sequence	
Chapters (short title)	**Description**
	Chapter 5 is employed multiple times and serves different rolls in the development of complete IT specifications for a complete data interoperability solution. As Community of Interest projects are accomplished, certain "bureaucratic" documents such as progress reports, annual reports, finance reports and also the actual Information Exchange Data Model standards have to be created. These reports will take time to accomplish. If there is a robust infrastructure of metadata, then these reports will mainly be processes of metadata extraction and formulation into the sections of the different administrative reports.
5. Objects	This chapter identifies and describes the actual metadata products that are to be built in order to achieve the data interoperability milestones. Examine each product and determine if you know how to build it. Do you have the proper metadata tools in place to ensure that not only are the metadata products built but that you know how to build the products? There are copious materials on the Whitemarsh website that assist in this regard. Creating the metadata objects is really a critical step. Short cuts should not be taken, for example, not creating missions, organizations, etc. and proceeding directly to data models. It is within the context of the enterprise metadata and the information systems metadata that the Information Exchange Data Models have real life and value. Experience has shown that when the metadata is built at the enterprise and information systems levels that the Information Exchange Data Models almost always have an increased level on the interoperability maturity scale. When this is accomplished then there will be a lessened need to create data exchange bridges between Information Exchange databases.

Data Interoperability Community of Interest Handbook Use Sequence	
Chapters (short title)	**Description**
13. Rules	This chapter provides the individual set of rules that should be observed by the various positions within the different organizations. As stated above, every decision by a community of interest has 10s of thousands of dollars of implications. Some decisions will cost millions of dollars. Each such decision, therefore, should be made with the maximum precision and good-order. Delivery of documents that form the basis for decision making, sufficient review time, proper motions, questions, discussions, and votes are all critical for a well engineered and operating organization with such an important mission. Hopefully, this chapter will never have to be accessed because there is a 100% consensus on every issue. But just in case there isn't, this chapter contains the necessary rules through which decisions can be made.

Table 2. Chapters and description by execution sequence.

Supplementing all the material in this book is a large quantity of books, courses, methodologies, and also a metadata repository software system from Whitemarsh. This book, in conjunction with these materials should make the creation and operation of Data Interoperability Communities of Interest a practical, rational, and accomplishable set of activities.

This book does not contain "the only way" to accomplish interoperable data environments. Rather, it is "a way." The data and process chapters contain detailed specifications. Again, these detailed specifications represent "a way," not "the way." There is a similar quantity of detail in the mission, organization, function, and position chapters. These too represent "a way," not "the way." The ultimate goal of the book is to convey a sufficiently detailed strategy such that, if followed, would lead to success. Alternatively, if another approach is desired, then the detail in this book provides good benchmarks for testing comprehensiveness and completeness.

2

Rationale for Data Interoperability

2.1 Key Reasons for Data Interoperability

In order to put forward a good rationale, the purpose or value of a Community of Interest has to be set down. From the point of view of this book the reasons are to:

- Increase the level of conflict free policy execution.
- Increase the level of confidence in decision making.
- Reduce the risk in decision making.
- Reduce the cost of preparation and research prior to decision making.

The first section of Chapter 1 clearly states the mission of data interoperability: the ability to make collective decisions faster and with greater confidence. Chapter 2 also states that there is a need for data interoperability because of shared missions. Chapter 2 also presents the metadata models necessary to capture the complete specifications necessary to know exactly what data can and should be shared. Simply put, the data subset representations of shared missions need to be exchanged. Since mission descriptions can be 50 pages or more in length, a more precise identification of what is to be shared and the basis for sharing needs to be specified.

Chapter 1 also clearly infers that it is not the fixed, random, or even ad hoc exchanges of data between information systems, or between end-users and information systems that ultimately are critical and important. Rather, it is the common, shared, and consensus-based understanding of data that has to be set out in each of the systems that ultimately control the data that is captured, stored in databases, and then shared. If such an environment exists then not only will the routine business process drive data exchanges be improved but so also will be the random and ad hoc access of data through information systems because semantics and value domains will be reliable and repeatable.

Given common, shared and integrated metadata, then business managers and decision makers can integrate databases through traditional or service oriented architecture environments with the confidence that the responses come from a network of nonredundant, integrated, synchronized, and semantically homogeneous databases and information systems.

2.2 Shared Policy is Basis for Common Understanding

The basis for the common, shared, and consensus-based understanding of data is policy. After all, data is the "what" that remains after *policy* is executed. Thus, *Data is Executed Policy*. When an organization creates policies, it necessarily creates as its companion, procedures. Together, policy and procedures are set into place to the run the business. As the business runs, data, the consequence of policy execution, is created and stored in databases. These databases become the persistent memory of the organization.

"Data" specifications are thus policy definitions. Similarly, process specifications are procedure definitions. Consequently, all data (i.e., policy) specifications are metadata. All process (i.e., procedure) specifications are also metadata. A metadata database (e.g., Whitemarsh Metabase) is a database for all Policy and Procedure Specifications. The metadata model diagrams in Figures 6 through 11 are high level graphical depictions of shared policies and procedures.

Any policies and procedures which are not specified or transformed to metadata, and which do not result in database data, are not only just anecdotes, they also cannot lead to trustworthy enterprise persistent memory. Similarly, these non specified policies and procedures cannot lead to trustworthy data interoperability.

Policies exist in meaningful configurations that map onto the common sense-based transactions of the business. These transactions are all tied to one or more of the resource life cycle nodes. The processes that support the capture, storage, modification, and access of the data are accomplished by the business information systems.

2.3 Comprehensive Definition of Metadata

A quick response to the question, What is Metadata, is that it is data about data. However, that's too cute. More formally, the string, metadata, is divided into *meta* and *data*. "Meta" in the Oxford Dictionary means, "something of a higher or second-order kind." The word, data, however is not employed within this paper in its strictest sense, that is, a data item like *Birth date = 03/22/1941*, but in more general sense so as to include unstructured data like text and diagrams.

For the purposes of this book, the scope of metadata is restricted to the world of Information Technology. Consequently, metadata are the materialized artifacts that define the requirements for, the specifications of, design of, or even executing characteristics of an IT system, or component of that system. "System" here is used in a very broad context. Thus, included within the scope of systems are databases, application systems, and their technology environments. Therefore, metadata is what is one or more levels of abstraction removed from the actual databases, applications, or their technology environments. In a computing environment, metadata would therefore include:

- Requirements.
- Functional descriptions.
- Work plans.
- Database designs through to schema DDL (data definition language).
- Application system designs possibly through to computer program source code libraries.
- Technology environment designs through to actual installation artifacts.

But within this context, would not include:

- Actual databases with data records of employees, invoices, products, and customers.
- Executing application systems.

- Operating systems and other systems software such as DBMS and Web browsers.

- Telecommunications Networks.

- Computers.

These are not metadata because they are "real," while the previous list represents artifacts about the reality. But once the information system is executing, metadata may be created that describes the characteristics of the operating environment. That class of metadata would include for example:

- Computer system execution schedules.
- Computing resource consumption requirements.
- Quantity of records in particular files.
- Quantity of users by time of day for particular processes.
- Job completion and/or error messages.

2.4 Database Objects: Foundation Stones for Shared Policy

The data specifications within which transactions are created and exist are database object classes. The domain of data of a database object class should relate perfectly to the domain of data of a coherent policy existing within the enterprise. It is on the foundation of quality database that there can be quality data interoperability. That is because:

- Each database object class's data structure (typically database tables) is the data representation of a policy's definition.

- The database object class's processes through which data rows are added, deleted, and modified are the mechanisms necessary for policy execution, that is, the policy's procedures through which database objects are transformed from one valid state to another.

- A fully defined policy that includes both its complete definition and its necessary steps for coherent execution.

- Interrelated collections of rows across multiple tables of one database object class and across multiple collections of rows across multiple database object classes form more comprehensive policies.

When data is seen as executed policy, and is realized through database objects, then quality databases support the following within the enterprise:

- Business information systems that are a coherent union of the policy that, in turn, support the execution of procedures that represent the accomplishment of the policy. Because of shared policy, data can be more easily shared across systems whether in scheduled or ad hoc manners.

- Consistent collection and/or modification of policy instances through the life cycle of the policy. These policies, applied enterprise-wide, ensure that all systems and databases participating in a community of interest are similarly updated.

- Consistent execution of policies whenever, wherever, and however deployed as the essence of the policy, and the totality of its critical procedures are encapsulated within the database object class itself.

- Minimized redundancy and consistent policy implementations across distributed environments as the database object class can be distributed through encapsulated strategies.

- Comparable instances of deployed policies that are independent of hardware architectures and operating systems.

2.5 Engineering Database Objects

What forms the basis of a database object? Simply, it is a business' policies and procedures. While policies can exist without procedures, the converse is not true. This ontological priority dictates that procedure is dependent on policy. They go together like hand and glove. The glove (procedure) serves no useful purpose without the hand (policy).

A database object is a person, place, or thing that has internal consistency, and is transformed from one valid, predefined state to another through well defined rules. The minimum value states are null and valued. The internal behavior of a database object class as its objects transform from one state to another is immaterial to its user. Database object classes conform to the requirements of business rather than the converse. Database objects are the corporate memory of the enterprise. All the rest are anecdotes.

Policies and procedures, that is, database object classes, bring order, consistency, and predictability. The larger the enterprise, the greater the dependence on policies and procedures. Data is the evidence of policy execution. An employee's record is proof that policies have been carried out. Procedures are the techniques, methods, or processes by which policies are carried out. For example, if an enterprise's policy is to be profitable, then its balance statement, produced by processing all the general and subsidiary journals is the measure of adherence to the policy. If policy is met, the enterprise must be profitable.

The procedures are named, and their data actions are associated with specific subsets of the named data structure. The names of the procedure sets represent data structure transformations from one recognizable state to another. Each state represents a determined value set within the business. Procedures include, for example: establishing an employee requisition, accomplishing employee hiring, and performing employee assignment.

Enterprise-database is an organizational operating condition in which there are both defined policy coherence and integrity, as well as consistency in policy transformations throughout the enterprise irrespective of functional and organizational style and irrespective of policy transformation technology (that is, computers, operating systems, programming languages, and database management systems).

Enterprise-database is the expression, population, use, and manipulation of all database objects. Enterprise-database begins first with quality-database object classes founded upon the policies and procedures surrounding their specification, implementation and evolution.

Value proceeds not first from the database object, but from the database object class. The consequences of quality-database object classes are "real" database objects. The information technology assets of the enterprise are both its database objects and its database object classes.

Finally, an enterprise is interoperable only to the extent to which its metadata is nonredundant, not conflicting, and integrated. To believe otherwise or to believe that, for example, the only thing that has to happen to database objects is they are transformed to XML in order for an enterprise to be interoperable. This flies in the face of common sense and simple logic. Is it "record" or "record?" Is it seam or seem? Is it 2.79 MPH or 2.79 KPH? Is it rounded or precise? Is it a running total or an amount at that instant? Data alone doesn't provide the answer. Data and semantics do, but only in context in an integrated, non-conflicting, and a nonredundant manner.

2.6 Value Proposition for Data Interoperability

Many arguments can be made for data interoperability including increased consistency, data quality, timeliness and the reasons cited in Chapter 1. While these are all important, they are very difficult to measure mainly because databases and information systems are too expensive to set up in controlled experiment modes: One clearly bad, another clearly good. The one argument that can be made very clear and compelling and one that "management" can readily see is the cost argument.

From a study done about the U.S. Department of Defense's STRATCOM (Strategic Command) standardization initiative, a collection of information systems and databases were identified. They were examined for redundancy, conflict, and overlap. The goal was to minimize these characteristics. The result was that 35 systems were reduced to just six. The quantity of lines of code was reduced from 20 million to just 12 million, and the quantity of databases were reduced from 23 to just 12. The total quantity of database columns was reduced from 18,000 to just 2,200. As to costs, there was a reduced operational cost of 20% and there was a redirection of 26% of all staff billets.

In 1995, another study performed at the U.S. DoD's Air Force showed that the average cost of a data interface between two systems costs about $350,000 per year. Extrapolated to the Air Force as a whole, the cost was $167 million per year.

A general approach to data interoperability is to create interfaces between two different systems. If each system exchanges data with the other, that's two interfaces, and the organization owner of each system needs to then budget $350,000 each year. When the quantity of systems goes to 15, then the quantity of one-way interfaces of every system to every other system goes to the formula: N*(N-1)/2 or 105. If every interface is two-way, then that would be 210 interfaces. That would then be about $80 million per year. Now, not every system interfaces with every other system, nor are all the interfaces two way. So, the $80 million cost is the outside estimate.

The inside cost number would be that every system has just one interface with its successor system. That would then be 14 interfaces for a yearly cost of about $5 million. Assuming an average between the two, the cost would be about $37.5 million per year. If, in this example, there was a common information exchange data model, then there would be just 15 one-way or 30 two-way interfaces.

Assuming the average, that is, 23 total interfaces, then the cost would be about $8 million per year. That's a savings of about $30 million per year in just interface development and maintenance costs.

In a mid 1990s study of an entire collection of databases, supporting systems and the exchange of data among systems, it was determined that about 200 individual databases all contained data that could be traced to just four original source databases. Instead of different systems sourcing their data from 200, just four data sourcing strategies need to be created. Since this potential disaster was discovered before all interfaces were created to the 200 data sources, there were no real savings, just a large cost overrun avoided.

Using typical metrics for a management information system, the savings by totally eliminating one system is significant. Table 3 tabulates the savings.

Cost Avoidance	
Characteristic	**Value**
Average MIS is 200 Tables	200
Function points of software per table	80
Each function point costs	$400
Initial MIS Cost (200 * 80 * 400)	$6.4 million
Life cycle costs for evolution & maintenance 5x more	$32 million
Total Life Cycle Cost	$38.4 million

Table 3. Typical life-cycle costs for a moderate sized Management Information System.

The only real way to get a handle on the costs of an existing network of database object classes and information systems is to identify and capture the information necessary for the meta models contained in Figures 6 through 11. This metadata will provide a rough network topology of what resource life cycle nodes are addressed by which systems and database object classes. Clearly, if through this analysis, a given database object class is being created by more than one system, then there is a consolidation opportunity. Additionally, if systems and database object classes are mapped to multiple resource life cycle nodes, then there are partitioning opportunities that will then enable simplification and possibly eventual consolidation of partitioned information systems allocated to the same resource life cycle node.

2.7 Measuring the Level of Data Interoperability

A very critical question regarding the specifications associated with the development of Information Exchange Data Models is the level of interoperability that should be represented by the standard. The cost of not having data interoperability can be quite significant.

For example, in a mid 1990s study by the United States Air Force, they determined that a lack of data interoperability was costing it approximately $167 million per year in expenses to develop and maintain system interfaces.

The stories regarding the U.S. Gulf War I during 1991 are legend. Battle plans had to be stored on 3.5 inch disks and then flown by helicopter to different military organizations so that they can be read, transformed and then used.

In the early 1990s, the C4ISR architecture working group began to address the interoperability issue in earnest. C4ISR stands for Command, Control, Communications, Computers, Intelligence Surveillance, and Reconnaissance. A key deliverable from this architecture working group was LISI (Levels of Information Systems Interoperability).

The Levels of Information Systems Interoperability is model, generated in 1998, has five levels (zero as worst, and four as best) as follows:

Levels of Information Systems Interoperability	
Level	**Description**
4	Distributed global information and applications. Simultaneous interactions with complex data. Advanced collaboration, e.g., interactive Common Operational Picture updates, and event-triggered global database updates.
3	Sophisticated collaboration, e.g., Common Operational Picture.
2	Heterogeneous product exchange. Basic collaboration Group Collaboration, e.g., exchange of annotated imagery, maps with overlays.

Levels of Information Systems Interoperability	
Level	**Description**
1	Homogeneous product exchange e.g., FM voice, tactical data links, text files, transfers, messages, e-mail.
0	Manual Gateway, e.g., diskette, tape, hard copy exchange.

Table 4. Levels of Information Systems Interoperability.

From the 1998 report,

> The LISI Interoperability Maturity Model provides a common basis for requirements definition and for incremental system improvements. The LISI Interoperability Maturity Model identifies the stages through which systems should logically progress, or "mature," in order to improve their capabilities to interoperate. LISI considers five increasing levels of sophistication regarding system interaction and the ability of the system to exchange and share information and services. Each higher level represents a demonstrable increase in capabilities over the previous level of system-to-system interaction.

In the eight years since the release of the LISI process, its goals and objectives have largely been unrealized despite recommendations by the C4ISR Working group.

Rather than let the underlying concepts from this valuable approach disappear, Andreas Tolk at Virginia Modeling Analysis & Simulation Center (VMASC), Old Dominion University along with members of that center has extended the LISI into an LCIM (Levels of Conceptual Interoperability Model). While the LISI model focuses on the system view within an enterprise, the Levels of Conceptual Interoperability Model (LCIM) was developed to focus on the importance of data and their exchange between systems regarding interoperability. As such, it is applicable in various domains, from ontological applications via web services to data model replications. The LCIM model has an analogous but different set of levels. These are depicted in Figure 3.

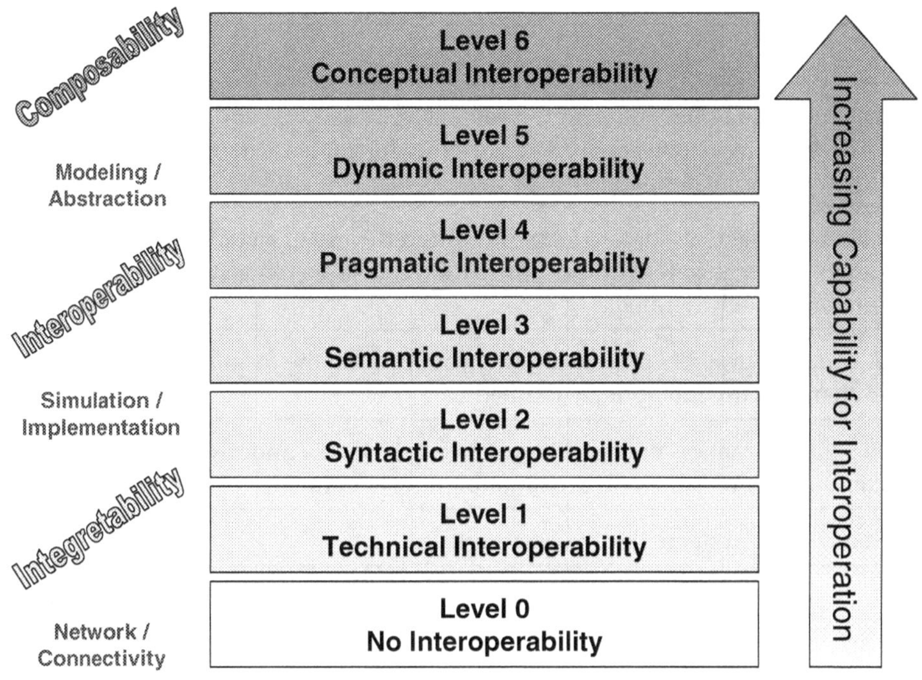

Figure 3. Levels of Conceptual Interoperability Model.

Specifically, the level, where again zero is the lowest and six is the highest, are described in the following table.

Levels of Conceptual Interoperability Model	
Level	**Description**
6	The conceptual data models underlying the data across systems are aligned. This requires that conceptual models be documented as "fully specified but implementation independent models," enabling their interpretation and evaluation by other engineers.
5	Systems are able to comprehend the state changes that occur in each other system's assumptions and constraints over time; thus, the effect of the information exchange is unambiguously defined.

Levels of Conceptual Interoperability Model	
Level	**Description**
4	The meaning of the data and the context of its use are "understood" by the participating systems, and the context in which it is exchanged is unambiguously defined.
3	The meaning of the data is shared through the use of a common reference model and the content of the information exchange requests are unambiguously defined.
2	A common protocol to structure the data is used; the format of the information exchange is unambiguously defined.
1	A communication infrastructure is established, underlying networks and communication protocols are unambiguously defined.
0	Stand-alone systems have no shared data.

Table 5. Levels of Conceptual Interoperability.

A brief comparison was conveyed at the September 2006, Fall Simulation Interoperability Workshop in Orlando, FL. Leslie Winters of the U.S. DoD Joint Forces Command wrote in the paper, "Next Generation Data Interoperability: It's all About the Metadata" that:

> There is a relationship between the LISI and LCIM. The conclusion one may draw is that enterprise level systems interoperability with conceptual interoperability of data can support and promote unified interoperability of an organization. This is because high levels of interoperability from a systems and data perspective will lead to the shared understanding that is required from the organizational perspective in an organization that is dependent on IT.

This interrelationship is shown in Figure 4. In general, the missions, organizations, function, database objects, and business events metadata that are recommended to be collected, along with the engineering of the data interoperability program and its subgroups, and the Communities of Interest and its subgroups are all geared to create interoperable data environments that are very high on the LCIM scale. The specific LCIM questionnaire and evaluation strategies are not included in this version of the book.

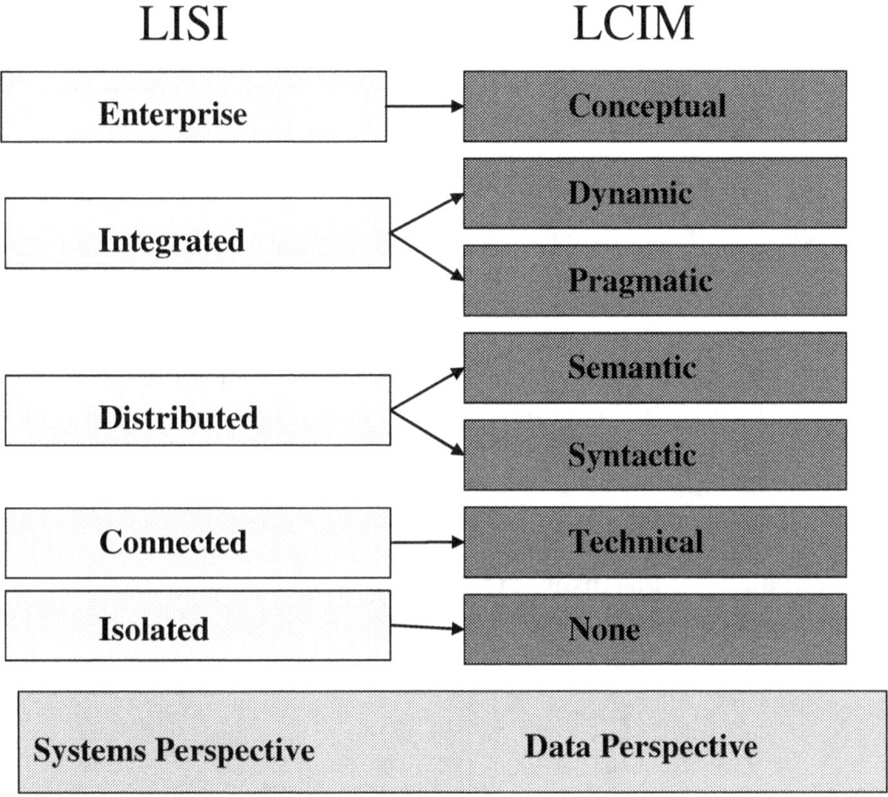

Figure 4. Interrelationship between LISI and LCIM.

2.8 Summary

The key point in all these analyses and strategies is that there has to be common-mission-based Communities of Interest from multiple organizational areas. Once enterprise missions are discovered and the organizations allocated, the Communities of Interest are readily apparent. The initial objective of these Communities of Interest is to identify the appropriate resources, their life cycles, and to then discover and allocate database object classes and information systems.

All the Communities of Interest then need to consolidate their findings and present an enterprise-wide picture of the overall topology of database object classes and information systems. From that basis, the real work of the community of interest can begin. That is, configuring the most efficient and effective set of data interoperability specifications that:

- Increase the level of conflict free policy execution.
- Increase the level of confidence in decision making.
- Reduce the risk in decision making.
- Reduce the cost of preparation and research prior to decision making.

The sections on the levels of conceptual interoperability are very important. They provide ways to assess the level of interoperability that can be expected from any data interoperability implementation strategy. If the target is tactical or syntactic level, then while that may be achieved, it would likely be a surprise if levels higher than that are also accomplished. While lower levels seem easier and less costly to achieve, that is, in the long term, a false conclusion. If an integrated metadata environment is installed and operating, then creating a new interoperable data and system is easier and quicker if these are based on already defined and re-usable semantics and processes.

3

Required Metadata Infrastructure

3.1 Scope, Meaning, and Value of Metadata

No one would ever question why a business needs its finance books. Analogously, a metadata infrastructures is the business's information technology's books. If you cannot run a good business without the former, you cannot run a good information systems environment without the latter.

Organizations are increasingly distributed. That is, there are multiple companies and business units. Each of these has its own financial set of books. Ultimately, however all these books have to be brought together so that a consolidated balance sheet can be produced. To have financial interoperability, that is, the ability to produce a consolidated balance sheet, there must first be consistency and common definitions on the meaning, granularity, and precision of financial information. Similarly, there needs to be interoperability across many classes of IT data within the enterprise to then have consolidated inventories, sales, staffing statistics, distribution systems, and other forms of corporate assets. And again, the collection of common meanings and the specifications of granularity and precision of all this corporate data are represented as metadata. Thus, you cannot have data interoperability without first having a good foundation of metadata. The two go hand and glove: quality metadata precedes quality data. And quality metadata across the enterprise precedes efficient and effective data interoperability.

A significant portion of the time and costs associated with resolving the Year 2000 problem can be directly attributed to a lack of a quality metadata environment within information systems organizations. The fact that one information systems organization within an enterprise had virtually no Year 2000 problem while another organization within that same enterprise was running their information systems shop "24x7" was no accident. The former had a long history of metadata management and the latter believed that metadata was a wasted overhead expense.

Vital to data interoperability is control over semantics. The controls are mainly in the area of the definitions that form the basis of the interfaces to standard processes (e.g., computing net profit) and the standard data definitions (e.g., the meaning of profit).

It is not necessary, however, to control the interfaces to the end user. Just how a data entry screen or report looks to different people is immaterial so long as the enforced semantics (rules of meaning and usage) are the same.

Semantics can either be created, stored and updated/evolved during the very process of IT systems and database development or afterwards as a hindsight remembrance effort. In the development of large data processing projects dealing with enterprise-wide, indispensable business functions, hindsight remembrance efforts, that is, the documentation of the design requirements and resulting information system specifications are seldom accomplished such that they are timely, accurate, or complete. That is disastrous for the following three reasons:

- Only the momentous facts that are remembered are recorded.

- As systems are specified, the lower-level design details are redundantly developed, often in conflicting manners.

- As system components are maintained, the efforts are crippled because of the undocumented business knowledge that is essential to understanding.

More important than when to create and capture the metadata that comprise the complete semantics of databases and application systems is the orientation employed during the creation and capture process. If the orientation is IT-system centric, then metadata stovepipes are the most likely consequence. All the semantics will have been defined with the IT system as the outer scope. If, however, there is an enterprise-wide viewpoint in place such that data and process definitions are defined with the enterprise in mind, then the inevitable efforts required to make data interoperable will be greatly lessened.

As is often the case, in the event that stove-pipe systems already exist that are now being required to interoperate, it is very critical to have an enterprise-view of semantics under which the existing systems are analyzed, mapped, and enabled for data interoperability. If only the semantics of the interchanges are captured, then the effort is just another set of creating more stovepipes. But in this case, virtual stovepipes.

Systems are required to interoperate because they share an aspect of one or more missions. Data from one system is required to support the inferred mission being accomplished by the other system. Whole collections of systems that are required to share data must therefore have broadly shared missions. Missions are detailed in terms of both data and functions. Organizations perform functions that access, create, update, or delete the data. Common mission areas are the outer boundaries of the shared data. To only collect the semantics of the shared data without first identifying the shared mission, functions, and organizations is to greatly short change the effort. If through analysis there is no shared mission, then there cannot be shared data.

A shared mission does not require shared and/or simultaneously occurring activities. For example, a sales organization has staff in the field meeting with customers, determining customer product needs, delivery requirements, purchasing and payment habits, the level of required customer support and the like. Most of these activities, that is, product development, purchasing, payments, and customer support, are likely to be performed by organizations outside the direct mission of Sales and Marketing. Notwithstanding, Sales and Marketing needs up to date data from all these areas. Consequently, there is a shared mission: Total Customer Management. Because of this shared mission, there needs to be shared semantics. Shared data can cross multiple mission areas especially if missions are hierarchically defined.

Without fully knowing the shared mission, functions, and data, the likelihood of having productive data sharing is greatly reduced. If the determination of the scope and domain of the shared missions occurs after all the systems are built, then the effort will take longer, and more work will be required to resolve the differences and redundancies that occurred because the IT systems were created within stovepipes.

3.2 Metadata and the Knowledge Worker

Knowledge workers require policies and procedures to effectively accomplish their work. Policies are specifications of what is done. Procedures are specifications of how something is done. Both classes of specifications are metadata because they are specifications of the thing being accomplished and the way it is actually accomplished. Policies and procedures are often supported by information systems and databases. All this metadata, that is, the specifications of policies (things) and procedures (the way things are done), must be set within a metadata infrastructure for the knowledge worker. This infrastructure must accommodate both top-down and bottom up efforts. Eventually, if accomplished bottom-up, but with a goal of then building all the metadata that would have occurred had the effort been top-down, the future efforts of building new systems, eliminating redundant systems, or evolving systems will become much easier, faster, and more cost-effective because there will already be an over arching set of shared missions, data, functions and organizations.

The set of metadata, eventually resulting across the six models, are set out in Table 6. Note that the order, left to right, is not an accomplishment order, but a "political order." That is, from the least political to the most political.

Business Metadata Domains Within the Knowledge Worker Framework						
	Knowledge Worker Domain					
Metadata Domains	Mission	Database Objects	Business Information Systems	Business Event	Business Function	Business Organization
Missions The essential missions that define the very existence of the enterprise, and that are the ultimate goals and objectives that measure enterprise accomplishment from within different business functions and organizations.	✔				✔	✔
Organizations The organizations that accomplish the aspects of missions with databases, information systems and through functions	✔			✔	✔	✔
Functions The procedures that are performed by groups as they accomplish the various missions of the enterprise					✔	

Business Metadata Domains Within the Knowledge Worker Framework						
	Knowledge Worker Domain					
Metadata Domains	Mission	Database Objects	Business Information Systems	Business Event	Business Function	Business Organization
from within different enterprise organizations.						
Resource Life Cycles Resources, that is, the facilities, materiel, staff, etc. of the enterprise. How these resources are sequenced, interrelated, and how they are supported through databases and information systems.		✔	✔			
Information Needs The information (a.k.a. query results or reports) needed by various organizations in their functional accomplishment of missions through databases and information systems.			✔			
Database The data is needed by functional proponents, how is it defined within data architectures and databases and how and where are those databases deployed and then used by business information systems in support of mission accomplishment.		✔				

Business Metadata Domains Within the Knowledge Worker Framework						
	Knowledge Worker Domain					
Metadata Domains	Mission	Database Objects	Business Information Systems	Business Event	Business Function	Business Organization
Data Models The data models of the enterprise which consist of data elements, that is, the context independent semantic templates of data, which are configured into models of "real" data (the consequence of policy execution) determined to be needed by functional experts in support of enterprise missions. These data model specifications are then configured into implemented databases that ultimately operate within various organizations as they perform the functions needed by enterprise missions.		✔	✔			
Business Information Systems The business information systems, including where they are, how they are related to mission, organization, function, and databases. Through which business and calendar cycle they are accomplished, and what the impact is on these business information systems when policy (a.k.a., data) is required or changed.			✔			

Business Metadata Domains Within the Knowledge Worker Framework						
	Knowledge Worker Domain					
Metadata Domains	Mission	Database Objects	Business Information Systems	Business Event	Business Function	Business Organization

Table 6. Metadata domains set against knowledge worker areas.

3.3 Data Interoperability Framework

The set of metadata models, objects within those models, and processes that cause those models to materialize exist within an overall framework for data interoperability. Figure 5 depicts that framework. Fundamentally the figure shows that all activities are accomplished through projects. That means that every activity is planned, budgeted, has deliverables, and is able to be audited, reviewed, and as necessary executed again. Broadly there are three significant classes of projects:

- Enterprise Architecture
- Information Systems Architecture
- Data Architecture

Supporting those three are Business Terms and Data Integrity Rules projects, which are projects that can be "called" from within any of the other three overarching classes of projects.

Within each major class of project there are subordinate projects that accomplish, for example, missions or organizations, or functions. Each class of project has its own general data model and process model. The data model represents the products, and the specifications of the constructed products. The process model represents the activities (manual and automated) that need to be performed to create, updated, delete, and/or otherwise employ the represented data. The table that follows identifies the set of data interoperability architecture

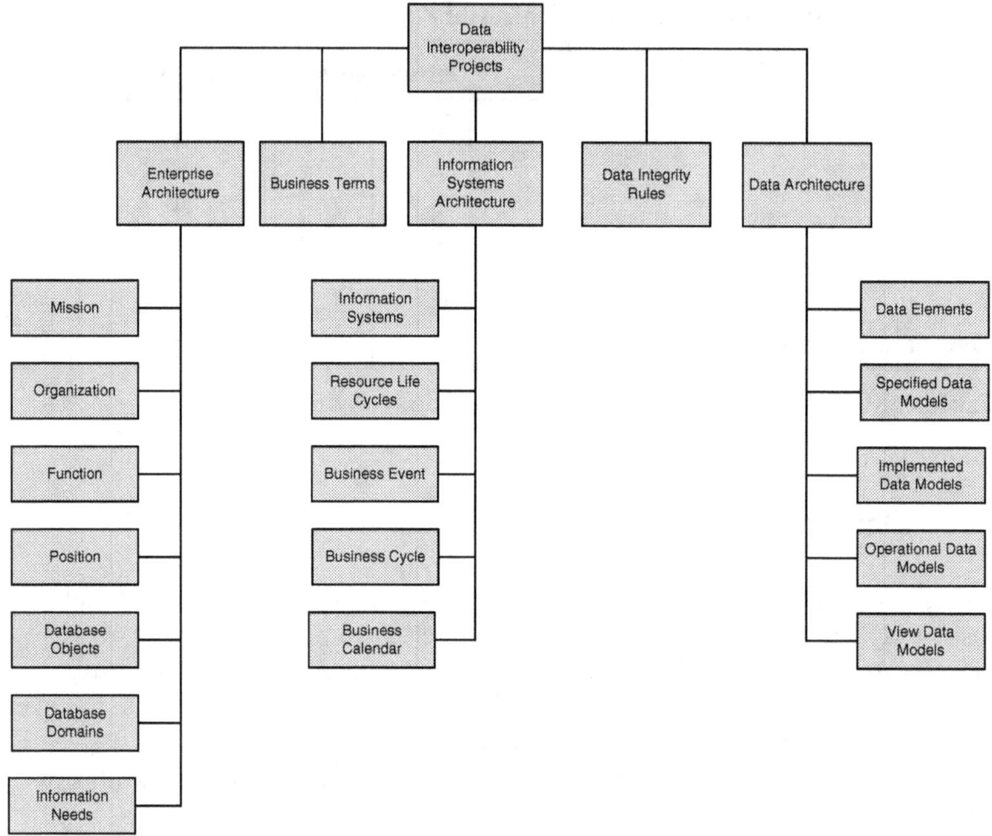

Figure 5. Data Interoperability Framework.

components, high-level and a more detailed-level diagrams that show the interrelationships among the architecture component metadata, and then, the sections within Chapters 5 and 6 that provide further description and/or specification. All these descriptions and specifications are necessarily at a high level because the complete specifications, which, while they exist, comprise many thousands of pages.

Data Interoperability Framework				
	Figures		Specifications	
Architecture Component	High Level	Metadata Entities	Chapter 5, Data	Chapter 6, Process
Business Calendar	10	12	5.1.1	6.3.1
Business Cycle	10	12	5.1.2	6.3.1
Business Events	10	12	5.1.3	6.3.1
Business Terms	n/a	n/a	5.1.7	6.2.8
Data Elements	11	14	5.1.9	6.4.1, 6.4.2, 6.4.3, 6.4.4, 6.4.4, 6.4.5, 6.4.6, 6.5.3
Data Integrity Run/a	n/a	n/a	5.1.8	6.2.9
Database Domains	6	17	5.1.10	6.2.5
Database Objects	9	13	5.1.11	6.2.6
Function	6	17	5.1.4	6.2.3
Implemented Data Models	11	15	5.1.12	6.5.2 6.6.1
Information Needs	7	16	5.1.13	6.2.7
Information Systems	10	12	5.1.5	6.3.1
Mission	6	17	5.1.14	6.2.1
Operational Data Models	11	18	5.1.15	6.5.1 6.6.2
Organization	6	17	5.1.6	6.2.2
Position	6	17	5.1.16	6.2.4
Projects	18	19	5.1.17	6.2.10

Data Interoperability Framework				
	Figures		Specifications	
Architecture Component	High Level	Metadata Entities	Chapter 5, Data	Chapter 6, Process
Resource Life Cycles	8	20	5.1.18	6.3.2
Specified Data Models	11	21	5.1.19	6.5.4
View Data Models	11	22	5.1.20	6.2.3

Table 7. Cross reference among architecture components, figures, and references in Chapters 5 and 6.

3.4 Required Metadata Models

The high-level meta models that enable the collection of the metadata necessary to support efficient and cost-effective data interoperability, are presented in the next six figures. Each subsection contains the rationale why this class of metadata is required for data interoperability. These models are:

- Mission, Organization, Function and Position (Figure 6).
- Information Needs (Figure 7).
- Resource Life Cycle Management (Figure 8).
- Database Objects (Figure 9).
- Business Information Systems and Business Events (Figure 10).
- Data Model Management (Figure 11).

Third normal form versions of these models are provided in Chapter 5. Process models are provided in Chapter 6. In the Figures 6 through 21 the lines with arrowheads represent relationships lines. A line with a single arrow head is a one-to-many relationship with the arrowhead resting on the "many" end. If the line has two arrow heads then that is a many-to-many relationship. If the line is circular then that is a recursive or hierarchical relationship. Finally, if there are two one-to-many relationship lines between two entities then that signifies a network relationship that serves to represent bills-of-materials.

3.4.1 Mission, Organization, Function and Position

Missions, organizations, functions, positions, and database domains metadata interrelationships are depicted in Figure 6. This collection of metadata to represent the context into which all data models and process models are placed.

Missions are multi-level and are needed to identify the joint domains under which data is to be shared. Shared missions imply shared data. If there are shared missions but no shared data, then the nonshared data necessarily exists in stove-pipe data structures. Such structures should be eliminated.

In environments where literal data sharing is not possible, then the data should at least exhibit shared semantics. As an extension to the Sales and Marketing example from above, the salesmen in the field may have locally loaded, stored, and processed databases through which customer management occurs. If that local data has its own stovepipe semantics versus the shared data semantics, then when the salesman needs a data refresh, there will have to be downloading, transformation, and then loading of the salesman's database. Or, if the salesman needs a question answered from the home office, most likely the salesman will ask the question in terms of the data structures, names and value domains from the laptop's databases. Confusion would certainly occur if the semantics are all stovepipe-based semantics versus the shared-data semantics.

Organizations are also multi-level and are cross-referenced with missions. If certain missions are shared, then there should also be joint organizations that will administer the shared missions. Positions, within the context of organizations are needed to then know what activities have to be performed to accomplish the shared missions. Finally, functions are needed so that it can be known what activities are affected by the shared data that exist across organizations within their common missions.

Functions represent the human activities that are performed by individuals acting in certain positions. These functions can be performed within the context of multiple sets of mission-organization pairs.

Positions are categories of work activities that are performed by persons. A position may exist within multiple mission-organization pairs. within the context of those organizations.

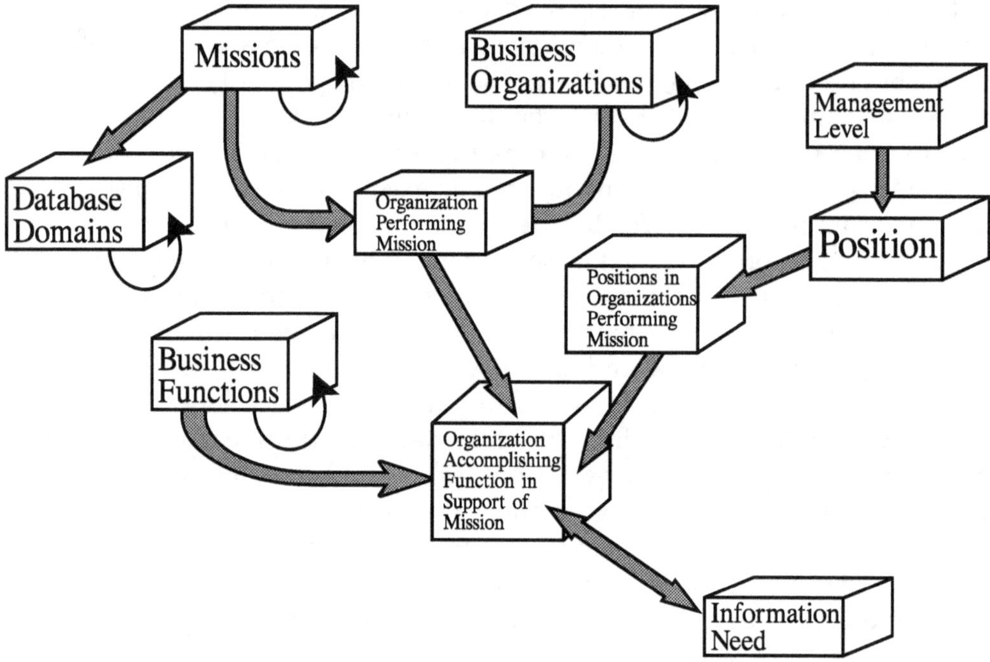

Figure 6. Metadata model for capturing mission, organization, function, position and database domain.

3.4.2 Information Needs

Information needs, depicted in Figure 7, are required because these spell out the specifications of the data that is being required to be shared across the functions performed by the organizations, in accomplishing the common missions. Specifying information need requirements is the first step in determining the information exchange data models. Without knowing the common information needs there is no basis for the information exchange data models. Information need's information also includes the initial characteristics of the needs such as the granularity, frequency, and form of the shared data requirement.

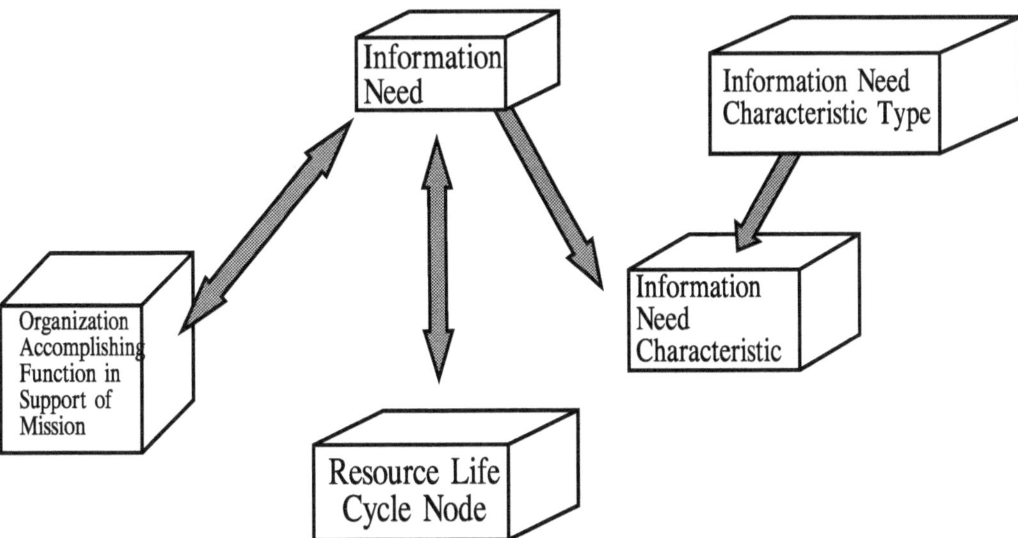

Figure 7. Metadata model for capturing information needs.

3.4.3 Resource Life Cycle Management

Resources (e.g., facilities, assets, staff, and programs), and resource life cycles (major state changes in the life of a resource), and resource life cycle intersections (Resource Life Cycle Node Structure) are needed to set the overall context of the database object classes (major policy-based data groupings) and business information systems. Resources and their life cycles are mapped to information needs that are made available to the functions performed by organizations in the pursuit of missions. Without resources there is no unifying focus for the existence of the database object classes and information systems. Additionally, resource life cycles enable the identification of redundant, conflicting, and missing database object classes and information systems. Finally, these provide a cross check on the adequacy of the information needs.

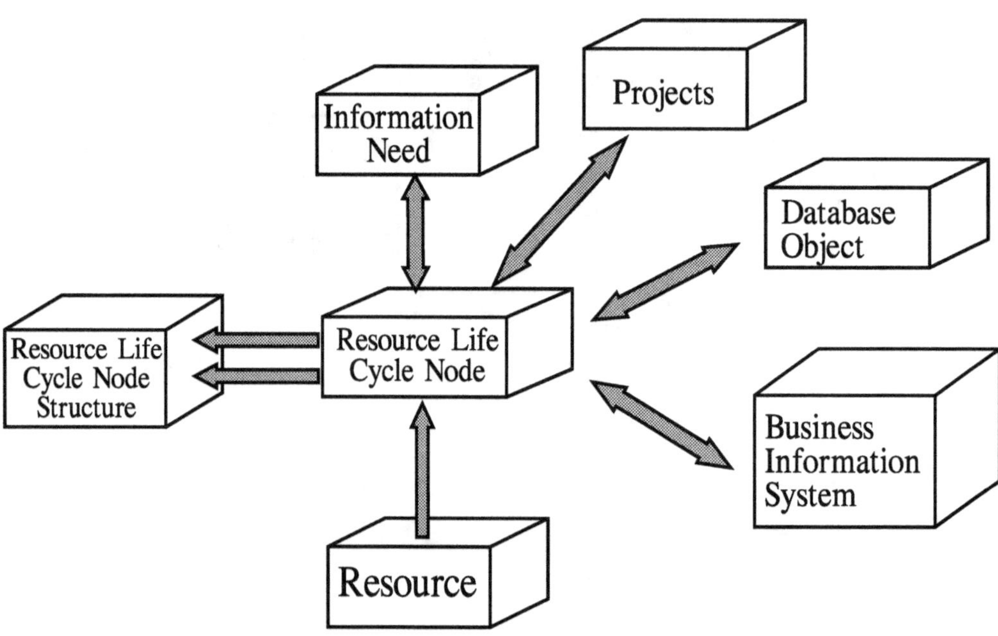

Figure 8. Metadata model for capturing resource life cycle information.

3.4.4 Database Objects

Database object classes are required because each database object class represents the complete specification of a major policy area represented within the domain of a database. Each database object class is supported by its state changes, its table-based transformation processes to ensure integrity of change, and finally by the database object information systems that cause the database object to be changed from one valid state to another.

It is necessary that database object classes be completely specified prior to being implemented so that the policies that the database objects represent are correct with respect to granularity and precision. Databases that contain database objects from database object classes must do so in a semantically correct manner. Otherwise, subsets of database objects are not able to be exchanged in a meaningful way. If some databases contain database objects at a different level of

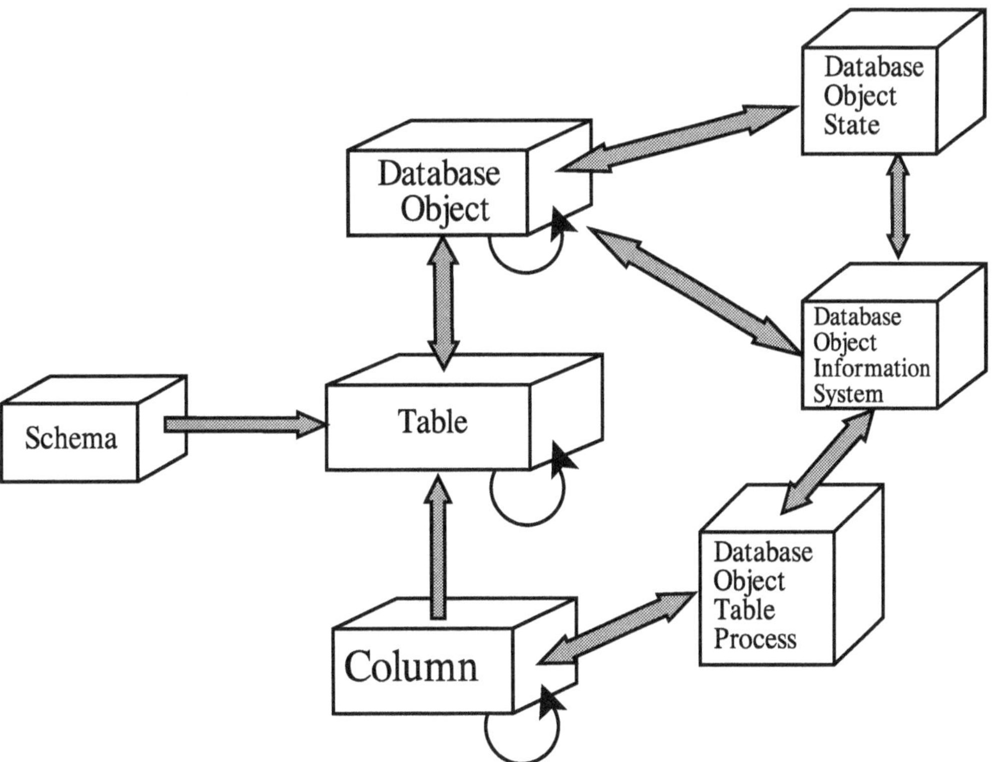

Figure 9. Metadata model for capturing database object specifications.

granularity and precision, the transformation from the base granularity and precision must be specified so that value transformations can be determined as correct. If this contextual setting is not accomplished, creating data interoperability environments will be difficult, time-consuming, and expensive.

3.4.5 Business Information Systems and Business Events

Business information systems along with their business and calendar cycles need to be determined to know when data is collected, which business information system performs the collection, and how the collections are set within calender

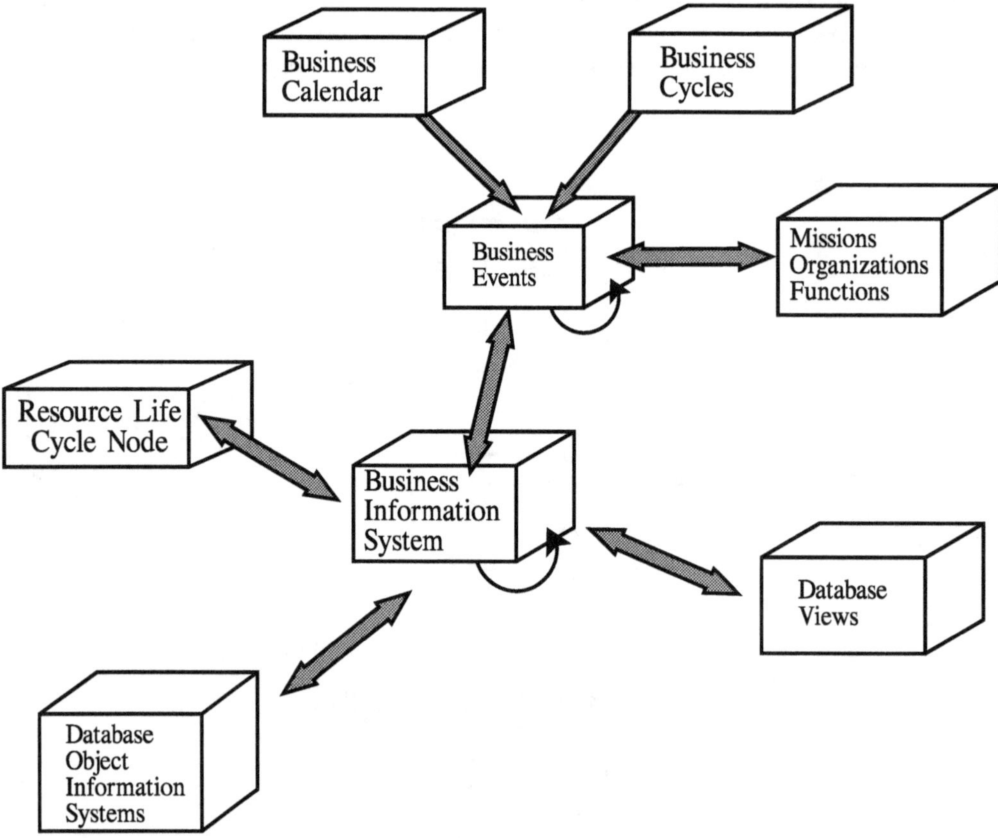

Figure 10. Metadata model for capturing business information systems and business events.

and/or business cycles. Here a calendar cycle takes on its common meaning. A business cycle can be by seasons such as the holiday season, the school year, and the like. Or a business cycle could be its financial year, tax year, or in the cases of some businesses, their year is 13 4-week months. Business information systems are triggered by their corresponding calender and business event cycles. Each such triggering is known as a business event. Without setting business information system activities within calendars and business cycles it will be difficult to know the currentness of the data that has been collected or to be accessed.

Business information systems are set within resource life cycle nodes of resources. Business information systems, when executed, cause the execution of the database object information systems, which, in turn, cause the state changes of database objects.

3.4.6 Data Model Management

Data model specifications, illustrated in Figure 11, should be organized into four levels, then set within the context of ISO 11179 data elements, and finally intersected with the information systems that access it. The data element level contains the semantics of all business facts. These facts are set within ISO 11179 data element concepts and value domains. Data element concepts are in turn set within contexts of concepts and conceptual value domains.

Names of the data element concepts, data elements, and down through to attributes of entities and columns of databases need to be established within taxonomies of well-developed words that set out semantics. Once set out, the semantic hierarchies enable automatically constructed names, definitions, and abbreviations. While the automatic nature is of value, more valuable is all the business fact semantics that are now controlled and managed.

The specified data models act as standardized templates through which actual data models can be manufactured. If constructed this way, and if all the attributes of the entities are mapped to ISO 11179 data elements, there is then an umbrella of enterprise-wide data semantics that exists within which database schemas support data interoperability.

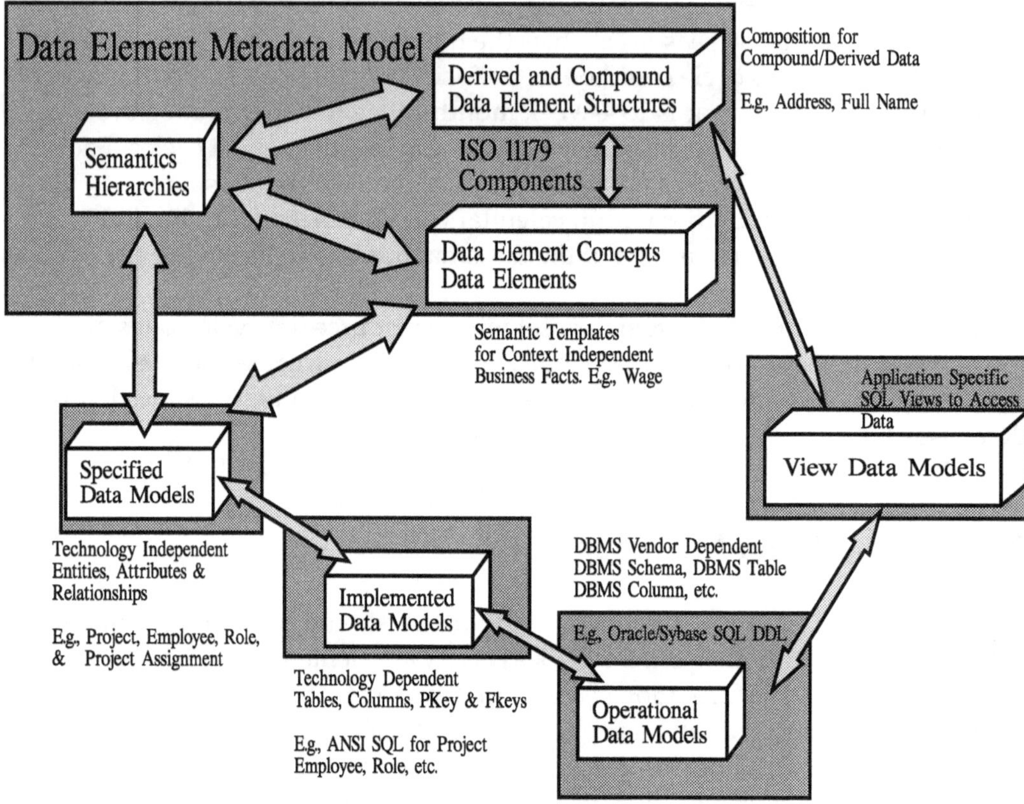

Figure 11. Metadata model for capturing data elements and four levels of data models.

Implemented data models are database schema models of tables and columns. Each collection of tables and columns is mapped to a database object class, and is either an entire database object class or a proper subset of one. Implemented data models are mapped back to their ancestors' data model templates of subjects, entities and attributes. The relationship between implemented and specified data models is through the mapping of an attribute to a column. This enables the multiple use of a whole or partial entity within the same implemented data model table, and across multiple implemented data model schemas.

Operational data models are the database schema models of data interoperability. Rows of data from one or more operational data model tables (called DBMS Tables) are what is exchanged between business information systems. Every business information system maps to one or more operational data model schemas. The relationship between operational and implemented data models is through the mapping of a column to a DBMS column. This enables the multiple use of a whole or partial table specifications within the same operational data model tables, and across multiple operational data model schemas.

Finally, view models represent the specification of the data exchange between a database through the database management system to the information system.

The reason there needs to be three levels of data models, a view model, and the ISO 11179 data element model are to then support an efficient and effective data interoperability environment. Without all these interrelated data models, the database designers and analysts will have to rely on memory, note cards, Visio diagrams, or other devices to know the precise details of data interoperability specifications. Even more important, these interrelated data models can exist within a multi-user, federated and distributed metadata repository that, in turn, supports a universal source of metadata specifications. Without these models, data interoperability specifications will be more expensive, redundant, conflicting, and will lead to more stovepipes. But this time the stove pipes will be metadata stovepipes.

The key benefits associated with metadata management include:

- Assist top management in identifying the resources required to build an information system.
- Provide discipline and control for the design process.
- Provide a structured approach to conceptual design.
- Enhance the application development process through the utilization of prior work.
- Provide a management facility for monitoring database projects.
- Allow for the nonredundant storage of data definitions and business policies that produce greater consistency throughout the enterprise.
- Increase the speed and accuracy in decision making because time and resources will not have to be expended determining just what the data and processes mean.

3.5 Industry Demand

The goal of all Whitemarsh efforts over the past 25+ years has been to assist clients in the development of quality database environments. That is, environments where data interoperability is common. To this end, Whitemarsh, starting in late 2003, began a formal definition of a strategy for achieving data interoperability. This strategy is manifest in courses, seminars, workshops, the Whitemarsh metabase CASE/Repository system and, of course, this book. Starting in the first half of 2006 Whitemarsh has been delivering a Data Interoperability Strategy Seminar. This seminar introduces the key topics and scenarios involved in creating interoperable data environments. The ultimate goal of the seminar is to teach the steps necessary to build shared data systems.

The key topics of the Data Interoperability Strategy seminar include the characteristics of data interoperability and the two classes of data interoperability errors that commonly occur. Identified as well are the problems that commonly occur such as complexity and latency.

Also presented in this seminar are the levels of data interoperability than can be achieved. These levels closely parallel those of a capability maturity model, and these levels can be assessed within an organization in generally the same manner as can software or data maturity.

The seminar then presents an overall framework for data interoperability and shows how common frameworks such as Zachman, Enterprise Architecture, and the Knowledge Worker affect the achievement of data interoperability.

The seminar then describes the key technological components of any really first-class interoperable data environment and provides examples of each including why these technological components are so important.

The seminar presents the overall contract and construction of a metadata repository environment critical component to a success strategy. Described as well is the necessary data interoperability environment including governance, infrastructure, Communities of Interest, key processes, success measures and the necessary training and tools.

The seminar then details the various scenarios that must occur to achieve a data interoperability environment including enterprise architectures, information systems plans, data model engineering, and, then both reverse and forward engineering. Collectively these scenarios cause the creation of and enable the maintenance and evolution of data interoperability environments.

The seminar then concludes with the key measures and returns on investment, and an overall summary and "way ahead," and most important, a questionnaire that polls the attendees on the strategies covered and the level of importance these concepts should receive in their corporate homes. The questionnaire is provided below. A percent is associated with each level of importance.

Data Interoperability Strategy Survey (2006). Respondents are about 20% of all attendees.				
	Percent			
Questions	**Strongly Agree**	**Agree**	**Disagree**	**Strongly Disagree**
Organizations would benefit from a comprehensive data management program including courses, methodologies, workshops, etc.	68	30	2	0
Organizations would benefit if databases (not DBMS) had consistent semantics for names for table columns across schemas.	78	20	0	2
Organizations would benefit from automatic Data Element, Attribute and Column naming and abbreviations built with consensus-based word lists and phrases (taxonomies).	53	47	0	0
Organizations would benefit from automatic Data Element, Attribute and Column definitions derived from contexts, value domains, etc.	50	42	8	0
Organizations would benefit if databases (not DBMS) had consistent semantics for value domains.	69	29	2	0

Data Interoperability Strategy Survey (2006). Respondents are about 20% of all attendees.				
	Percent			
Questions	Strongly Agree	Agree	Disagree	Strongly Disagree
Semantics should be inheritable from ISO 11179 Data elements to attributes, and from attributes to columns.	33	67	0	0
There is value in having data model templates that can be used in defining column collections within tables.	53	47	0	9
XML Schemas should be generated from a foundation of well designed and integrated data models.	51	45	4	0
Organizations would benefit from metadata repositories that support metadata integration and nonredundancy across projects, departments, etc. That is, define-once and use many-times.	82	18	0	0
Organizations would benefit from metadata repositories that are part of the everyday work process rather than a post implementation documentation effort.	86	12	2	0
End-users would benefit if they had access to metadata repositories for names, definitions, and the like.	82	16	2	0
Organizations would benefit from metadata repositories if the repositories could capture, report and support update of analysis and design work products in an	64	36	0	0

Data Interoperability Strategy Survey (2006). Respondents are about 20% of all attendees.				
	Percent			
Questions	Strongly Agree	Agree	Disagree	Strongly Disagree
integrated nonredundant manner.				
Project quality and work-speed would likely benefit if supported by comprehensive metadata repositories.	71	29	0	0
Organizations would benefit from metadata management strategies supported by both bottom-up reverse engineering, and top-down new database (not DBMS) manufacturing.	57	41	2	0
Average of Percent	64	34	1	1

Table 8. Survey questions and percent results across answer categories from data interoperability strategy seminars.

Data Interoperability Strategy Seminar Participant Organizations

Allstate Insurance
American Airlines
Bank of Montreal
Bill Chadwick Consulting
Blue Cross Blue Shield of Texas
BOM Financial Group
BTE Architects
Canadian Tire
Cap Gemini Energy
Caremark
CCC Information Systems
Chartwell, Inc.
Chevron Texaco
CIBC
Cingular
Citi Group
City of Toronto
CNA Insurance
Country Wide
Coventry Health Care
CUNA Mutual Group
Discover Financial Services
DOFASCO, Inc
East Neuk Associates
Elkay Manufacturing
Essential Futures
FedEx Services
Great Lakes Education Loan Services
HBC
HesselLink & Company
IBM Global Services
IESO (Independent Electrical System Operator)
J.P. Morgan Chase
Kohls Department Stores

Northern Trust
Railroad Retirement Board
RBC Financial Group
RR Donnelley
SentientPoint, Inc
Signma Systems
Solucient, LLC
Southwest Airlines
The Economical Insurance Group
The Burlington Northern and Santa Fe Railroad Company
U.S. Department of Homeland Security
United Airlines
Wallstreet Consulting
WEA Trust
WIS DoT
WPS Insurance

The high level metadata models enable IT organizations to have their own IT Intelligence Infrastructure. With this IT intelligence infrastructure, an IT executive can know that the data being used comes from a given system that is linked via metadata mappings to other systems that, for example run every night. Thus, statistics are less than 24 hours old.

The metabase's data model enables integration and nonredundancy across the complete set of Enterprise Architecture, and IT specifications that ultimately drive the construction of databases and information systems. This metabase's data model includes enterprise missions, organizations, functions, and the database and information system metadata used to represent state transforms of critical enterprise resources. The metabase's data model also enables the discovery of which resources are "naked," and which are updated by redundant and semantically conflicted systems and/or databases, etc.

Because of the set of meta entities that comprise business event, business event calendar, and calendar, you can know what processes run, in what sequence and what databases are updated. For example that feeder systems are run every day but the sales forecast is run Quarterly. Where are the most current numbers? The metabase can answer that question.

Because of the ISO 11179 Data element metadata meta-entities, you can trace data types and precision. If one column is "99" and another is "99v99" and if the "99v99" is rolled into the "99", then what happened to the "cents?"

Because of the Specified Data Model meta entities (subject-entity-attribute) you can trace granularity to make sure that the granularity is synchronized. Suppose one table has a primary key component of Year and Month. But another has Year, Month, and Day? Which is more precise? When you ETL data from the YMD rows into the YM table, does the YM table then represent last, rolling, highest, lowest, who knows?

4

Mission

4.1 Data Interoperability Mission

Data interoperability not only creates, implements, employs, and evolves both the necessary metadata specifications of data interoperability solutions, but also the resulting interoperable databases and business information systems so as to achieve maximum data interoperability with the least quantity of specialized extract-transforms-and-load infrastructures. In support of that mission there are two overall subordinate mission:

- Data Interoperability Program Management.
- Standards Development Management.

4.2 Data Interoperability Program Management

The Data Interoperability Program Management involves the policies and procedures associated with engineering and operating the overall data interoperability program within the enterprise. Included within the overall program management are:

- The program itself.
- Project and community of interest engineering and management.
- The identification, specification, and management of the various metadata products that are contained in various metadata development projects.
- The set of business events that track the progress of building data interoperability standards.

- The organizations and positions within the organizations involved in managing the Data Interoperability Program and in managing the metadata products.

- The functions necessary for accomplishing Data Interoperability Program activities.

- The overall IT deliverables that contain the metadata product specifications.

- The rules that govern the correct operation of the Data Interoperability Program.

Involved also are the creation and management of all data interoperability standards that are identified and developed.

The overall goal of the Data Interoperability Program is to instigate and manage data interoperability projects. While each data interoperability project must stand on its own, the collections of data interoperability projects need to fit within a broader scope of enterprise interoperability. Some projects rely on data that is created by multiple data interoperability projects. To ensue maximum interoperability across these multiple sets of shared data, one or more Communities of Interest will have as their domain the collective-shared domain of other Communities of Interest.

The Standards Development Board within the Data Interoperability Program committee ensures that the operations of the various Communities of Interest are in accordance with the Data Interoperability Program's scope and program objectives. Included in this are the creation and management of Data Interoperability Program master schedules, lists of Data Interoperability projects, adherence to schedules, and other programmatic administrative matters such as a central document register and databases, websites, budgets, financial reports, and completeness, and quality evaluations of Community of Interest developed and maintained standards.

4.3 Standards Development Management

Standards within the Data Interoperability Program are developed by Communities of Interest. Each Community of Interest builds metadata products that contain the specifications of the IT databases and business information systems that must be built, tested, and managed as they operate to achieve the mission of enterprise-wide data interoperability. Rigor is maintained through recognized system engineering practices, which are:

- Operations.
- Systems Engineering and Architecture.
- Data Modeling.
- Test and Evaluation.
- Configuration Control.

4.3.1 Operations

The purpose of operations is to model the relevant aspects of the Business Information Systems (operation's perspective) to the Community of Interest solution. The operational modeling discipline is concerned with understanding the program and doctrinal context within the Community of Interest solution, developing the operational requirements, developing the Community of Interest solution's operational structure, behavior and performance, identifying and modeling the operational information needs, and developing the operational test cases that will be used to validate the Community of Interest solution. The Operations Technical Committee provides operational advice to all other technical committees and operational support to technical groups on an as required basis. Specifically, Operations:

- Identifies user/operational requirements to support application information systems interoperability at the appropriate organizational levels in order to support multi-organizational, combined and joint operations.

- Identifies and prioritizes Information Exchange Data Models in order to achieve both horizontal and vertical exchange of information.

- Identify and develops possible new Information Exchange Data Models and recommend change proposals on existing Information Exchange Data Models.

- Defines data integrity rules for horizontal and vertical information exchange.

- Analyzes operational processes applied to exchange plans and orders, and to develop data integrity rules accordingly.

- Identifies and takes heed of lessons learned from other interoperability initiatives and deployments.

- Provides user and operational guidance to other the Community of Interest technical committees in the development and/or execution of work plans, and ensures that the data interoperability solution meets operational requirements.

- Validates operational aspects of the solutions developed.

- Develops detailed work plans to ensure the accomplishment of the Data Interoperability Program objectives.

- Defines the overall operational architecture for the Data Interoperability Program.

- Defines Measures of Success (effectiveness and performance) for operational tests and validation.

- Defines operational test cases and scenarios for operational tests and validation.

- Integrates with other Community of Interest technical committees, and other Communities of Interest as necessary.

4.3.2 Systems Engineering & Architecture

The purpose of the system modeling discipline is to model the relevant aspects of the Business Information Systems (system's perspective) to the Community of Interest solution. The system modeling discipline is concerned with: understanding the context to the system, developing the system's requirements, developing the system's structure, behavior and performance, management and operating procedures, exchange mechanism technical specifications, modeling the data that will be used by the system, defining data integrity rules on how to use the data and developing the technical and system test cases that will be used to verify the Community of Interest solution.

The main task of the System Engineering and Architecture Technical Committee is creating the high level Community of Interest system level requirements in response to the Business Information System information requirements, and allocating them to appropriate component of the solution. These system level requirements are derived from the evolving operational requirements. All of this should be in support of an interoperability data architecture which certainly is the collection of all the metadata components and artifacts that define the semantics, data structures, value domains and restricted value sets necessary to support common and consensus-based understanding across the user community of shared missions.

It is the task of the System Engineering and Architecture Technical Committee to explore emerging technology and evolving standards for application to future implementation specifications. In this regard the System Engineering and Architecture Technical Committee may recommend and conduct experimentation as required, subject to approval by Communities of Interest. Specifically, Systems Engineering & Architecture:

- Develops and maintains the Data Interoperability Architecture by creating the high level requirements in response to the application information system requirements and by allocating them to an appropriate component of the data interoperability architecture.
- Derives these system requirements from the evolving operational requirements.
- Defines technical solutions to address operational and procedural requirements.
- Derives the detailed requirements from systems level requirements and the previous baseline in areas of hardware, software, and communications for the evolution of the Data Interoperability Program.
- Derives the management and operating procedures for the Data Interoperability.
- Derives data integrity rules for the use of the Data Interoperability Program.
- Explores emerging technologies and evolving standards for application to future implementation specifications.
- Validates Data Interoperability implementation and system level test specifications.

- Develops, in collaboration with the Data Interoperability Project Committee, and under the guidance of the Data Interoperability Program Committee, an integrated system's engineering framework describing the engineering phases, milestones, artifacts and tools for a data interoperability project.

- Integrates with other Community of Interest technical committees, and other Communities of Interest as necessary.

4.3.3 Data Modeling

The purpose of data modeling is to transform stakeholders' information needs into data models that can be employed by business information systems and managed during the life of the Community of Interest solution. Data modeling is concerned with information modeling, data modeling, data management, and providing guidance for the actual implementation. The main task of the Data Modeling Technical Committee is to take the requirements for the Information Exchange Data Models identified by the Operational Technical Committee as well as other requirements allocated by the System Engineering and Architecture Technical Committee, and define the data architecture and develop a common interoperable data model that will allow automated information exchanges to occur. The Data Modeling Technical Committee is also responsible for overall data management and maintenance of the Information Exchange Data Models.

The Information Exchange Data Models capture the information and data modeling artifacts. These data models are also used as a standard to support organizational implementation of applications, and to support organizational data management activities outside of the Data Interoperability Program. The Data Modeling Technical Committee is the custodian for the common reference data, and for test and demonstration data. The Data Modeling Technical Committee provides data modeling advice to all other technical committees and data modeling support to technical groups on an as required basis. Specifically Data Modeling:

- Defines the data architecture and develops the implemented, operational, and view data models that will allow automated information exchange to occur.

- Creates in conjunction with other data modeling committees of different Communities of Interest common specified data models.

- Creates in conjunction with other data modeling committees of different Communities of Interest common data element models.

- Ensures that there is maximum and common use of data element and specified data models across all implemented and operational data models so as to ensure maximum data interoperability across the Information Exchange Data Models created by each Community of Interest.

- Provides data modeling advice to all other technical committees on an as required basis.

- Integrates with other Community of Interest technical committees, and other Communities of Interest as necessary.

4.3.4 Test and Evaluation

The test engineering discipline is concerned with the overall test philosophy and critical test issues. The objective is that, after the conduct of the collection of these activities, confidence will have been provided that the Community of Interest solution is a viable solution for interoperability. The Operational Technical Committee, System Engineering and Architecture Technical Committee and Data Modeling Technical Committees all perform aspects of the test engineering discipline; nevertheless, the Test and Evaluation Technical Committee has the overarching responsibility. Specifically, Test and Evaluation:

- Ensures that the test engineering discipline is performed in a consistent, complete and coherent manner.

- Produces and maintains an overall the Test and Evaluation Master Plan, including a Test and Evaluation Strategy, and a test schedule.

- Coordinates all aspects of Implementation Level Tests, System Level Tests, Operational Level Tests, demonstrations and exercises, and, if needed, during other exercises / demonstrations where the Information Exchange Data model is involved.

- Produces test specifications for the Implementation Level Tests, System Level Tests and Operational Level Tests.

- Ensures that the Implementation Level Tests, System Level Tests and Operational Level Tests verify and validate the status of interoperability among the organizations involved and the satisfaction of the requirements.

- Provides guidelines for organizations to execute the Implementation Level Tests and validate the test results of the Implementation Level Tests.

- Plans, conducts, monitors, assesses, evaluates and reports on all aspects of the System Level Tests with the assistance of the other technical committees.

- Plans, conducts, monitors, assesses, evaluates and reports on all aspects of the Operational Level Tests, with the assistance of the Operations Technical Committee.

- Develops a data collection and evaluation plan for System Level Tests and Operational Level Tests.

- Records data collection and evaluation results into the test-results database.

- Maintains problem reports with appropriate metrics required for a continuous assessment and resolution.

- Maintains system management and test metrics.

- Acts as custodian for test data.

- Proposes changes to the Data Interoperability Architecture as a result of the test analysis.
- Coordinates, conducts and supports the Data Interoperability Program Demonstrations.

- Integrates with other Community of Interest technical committees, and other Communities of Interest as necessary.

4.3.5 Data Interoperability Configuration Control

The Configuration Control Technical Committee specifies a common set of procedures, methods and processes for controlling the standard's configuration. The Configuration Control Technical Committee also provides configuration control advice to all other technical committees on an as required basis. Configuration control must extend to all aspects of the standard including all its metadata, generated DBMS schemas, and all attendant software. Specifically, Configuration Control:

- Defines a common set of procedures and mechanisms upon which all the Data Interoperability Program baseline products will be managed.
- Implements the procedures defined in the Configuration Management Plan.
- Records and reports the status of configuration controlled items.
- Coordinates the change implementation process of the products.
- Processes requests for waivers and requests for deviation.
- Prepares and reports activities to the Data Interoperability Project Committee.
- Controls distribution of all Data Interoperability Committee products.
- Maintains a current the glossary.
- Integrates with other Community of Interest technical committees, and other Communities of Interest as necessary.

4.4 Summary

Missions are the hierarchically organized text-based statements of the idealized outcomes. Missions are the ultimate targets or objectives. Mainly, missions are never achieved in any final form. Missions serve as the contexts for both organizations and functions. When missions are set down, and then when organizations and functions are also set down, there should be even coverage among them all. There should be no organization without a mission. There should be no function without an organization to accomplish it and a mission that is addressed. If there are any discrepancies between missions, organizations, and functions then these have to be resolved before proceeding. It is much easier, cheaper, and faster to fix these problems before any detailed specifications such as those contained in Chapters 5 and 6 are set out and turned into metadata repository designs and metadata repository system implementations.

Careful review of reports by the U.S. General Accountability Office clearly show that almost 95% of all the errors in IT systems are cause by factors outside of IT. Chief among these factors are missions, organizations, and functions. It is therefore critical that missions be properly specified. In addition to comparing missions against existing organizations and functions, a key indicator of completeness is to review the missions and then attempt to conclude whether the enterprise has been completely and comprehensively described. If not then there is likely something missing in mission specification. A similar review should then be done with respect to organizations, and then finally functions.

5

Database Objects

A database object class, simply stated, is a collection of schema-contained database tables that share a common policy area. The tables directly contained in the database object's data structure are valued (i.e., rows of data added, deleted, or modified) through database object table processes in a way that guarantees the integrity of the individual rows. Collections of rows across database object table collections are added, deleted, or modified to satisfy the requirements of a database object state. The information systems that achieve the state change are called database object information systems. Therefore, the complete specification of database object classes consist of its four components, which are:

- Database Object Structure: the set of data structures that map onto the different value sets for real world database objects such as an auto accident, vehicle and emergency medicine incident.

- Database Object Table Process: the set of processes that enforce the integrity of data structure fields, references between database objects and actions among contained database object tables, the proper computer-based rules governing database object table insertion, modification, and deletion. For example, the process to properly and completely capture, store and manipulate the data for an auto accident.

- Database Object Information System: the set of specifications and resultant system that controls, sequences, and iterates the execution of various database object processes that cause changes in database object states to achieve conformance to the requirements of business policies. For example, the reception and posting of data from business information system activities (screens, data edits, storage, interim reports, etc.) that accomplish entry of the auto accident information.

- Database Object State: The value-states of a database object that represent the after-state of the successful accomplishment of one or more recognizable business events. Examples of business events are auto accident initiation, involved vehicle entry, an involved person entry, and auto accident DUI (driving under the influence of alcohol/drugs) involvement. Database object state changes are initiated through named business events that are contained in business functions. The business function, auto accident investigation includes the business event, auto-accident-incident initiation, which in turn, causes the incident initiation database object information system to execute, which in turn, causes several database object processes to cause the auto accident incident to be materialized in the database.

The descriptions of database object classes above are for "real" database object classes, that is, first, the data structure for an auto accident, vehicle and emergency medicine incident. Then second, the database object table processes that store, delete, or modify the data for all the database tables associated with the accidents, vehicles, or emergency medicine incidents. Third, the state changes related to the identification of an accident, and, then the base data for the collection of accident tables, and, then the reports related to the object, and finally the overall disposition of the object. Fourth, and finally, the database object information systems that transform the vehicle object table rows from one valid state to another valid state. E.g., changing the "identified accident" state to the state in which all the base data is now stored in the accident tables.

Analogously, and in this Chapter, the database object classes that are specified are **metadata** database object classes. That is, once valued these metadata database objects are the specifications of data interoperability products. These are not actual products, but the specifications of actual products. These product specifications, when turned into actual products, that is, when actual IT databases and information systems are constructed there will then be a data interoperability environment across the enterprise.

This book therefore contains the specifications of these metadata database object classes. Users of this book will have to take these specifications and use them to either make a metadata CASE/Repository system, or to procure one. Once it is built or installed, then the use of it will cause the creation of "actual" data interoperability specification that, in turn, would be implemented to cause enterprise-wide data interoperability environments to exist. The entity-relationship data models for each of these database object classes is provided in Figures 12 through 22 at the end of this chapter. Third normal form versions of these models are provided in Chapter 5. In the Figures 12 through 22 the lines with arrowheads represent relationships lines. A line with a single arrow head is a one-to-many relationship with the arrowhead resting on the "many" end. If the line has two arrow heads then that is a many-to-many relationship. If the line is circular then that is a recursive or hierarchical relationship. Finally, if there are two one-to-many relationship lines between two entities then that signifies a network relationship that serves to represent bills-of-materials.

This chapter contains the data structures of these metadata database object classes. Chapter 6 contains the specifications of the database object information systems at a high level, and an enumerated set of database object table processes within each metadata object class. Each of the process models also references Figures 12 through 22. Some figures contain multiple database object classes. In the metabase systems, each of these figures represents a metabase functional module. In these figures, some of the tables are grey. That means that these tables are updated through a different metabase functional module. For example, data elements are created in the metadata repository functional module associated with data elements. Data elements are however referenced in the specified, implemented, operational, and view data models for contextual purposes.

5.1 Atomic Database Objects

The metadata database object classes corresponding to the identified meta entities are depicted in high level diagrams in Figures 6 through 11. A third normal form set of database object tables related to these metadata database object classes are presented at the end of this chapter as Figures 12 through 22.

The database object specifications that follow are for atomic database objects. Atomic database objects are those that are constructed generally to stand alone versus set within the products or deliverables of an overall systems development life cycle. These atomic products are set within a common system development life cycle in Section 5.2 . This system development life cycle is merely an example of where to fit these metadata products.

Each atomic database object is cross referenced to its main figure, that is, Figures 12 through 22. The corresponding processes supporting these database objects are provided in Chapter 6, Business Information Systems. These processes are listed within that chapter since database object table processes and database object processes are commonly implemented as business information systems that interact with database management systems as opposed to processes wholly contained within the database schema of the database management system.

5.1.1 Business Calendar

Business Calender, defined in Figure 12, should contain at least the following:

1. Business Calender administrative information
   a. Identification information
      i. Organization authors
      ii. Person authors
   b. Configuration management information
      i. Status (development, test, production)
      ii. Version (xx,yy.zz)

2. Business Calender object class tables
   a. Business Calender Structure
   b. Business Calender
   c. Business Calender Structure Type.

3. Business Calender inter-object relationships
   a. Business Calender Structure references Business Calendar Structure Type
   b. Business Calender Structure [active] references Business Calendar
   c. Business Calender Structure [passive] references Business Calendar.

4. Business Calender related objects
   Business Event references Business Event Calender

5.1.2 Business Cycle

Business Cycle, defined in Figure 12, should contain at least the following:

1. Business Cycle administrative information
   a. Identification information
      i. Organization authors
      ii. Person authors
   b. Configuration management information
      i. Status (development, test, production)
      ii. Version (xx,yy.zz)

2. Business Cycle object class tables
   a. Business Cycle Structure
   b. Business Cycle
   c. Business Cycle Structure Type

3. Business Cycle inter-object relationships
   a. Business Cycle Structure references Business Cycle Structure Type
   b. Business Cycle Structure [active] references Business Cycle
   c. Business Cycle Structure [passive] references Business Cycle.

4. Business Cycle related objects

   Business Event references Business Event Cycle

5.1.3 Business Event

Business Event, defined in Figure 12, should contain at least the following:

1. Business Event administrative information
   a. Identification information
      i. Organization authors
      ii. Person authors
   b. Configuration management information
      i. Status (development, test, production)
      ii. Version (xx,yy.zz)

2. Business Event object class tables
   a. Business Event

3. Business Event inter-object relationships
   a. None

4. Business Event related objects
   a. Business Event references Business Event Cycle
   b. Business Event references Calendar Cycle
   c. Business Event is referenced by Business Information System
   d. Business Event references Mission-Organization-Function

5.1.4 Business Functions

[Business] Functions, defined in Figure 17, should contain at least the following:

1. Business Function administrative information
   a. Identification information
      i. Organization authors
      ii. Person authors
   b. Configuration management information
      i. Status (development, test, production)
      ii. Version (xx,yy.zz)

2. Business Function object class tables
   a. Business Function

3. Business Function inter-object relationships
   a. Business Function contains business function

4. Business Function related objects
   a. Business Function is referenced by Mission-Organization-Function

5.1.5 Business Information Systems

Business Information Systems, defined in Figure 12, should contain at least the following:

1. Business Information Systems administrative information
   a. Identification information
      i. Organization authors
      ii. Person authors
   b. Configuration management information
      i. Status (development, test, production)
      ii. Version (xx,yy.zz)

2. Business Information System object class tables
   a. Programming language
   b. Level

c. Construction method
d. Status
e. Application type
f. Environment type
g. Predominant user class
h. DBMS Environment

3. Business Information System inter-object relationships
   a. Business information system references business information system

4. Business Information System related objects
   a. Business information system references Programming language
   b. Business information system references Level
   c. Business information system references Construction method
   d. Business information system references Status
   e. Business information system references Application type
   f. Business information system references Environment type
   g. Business information system references Predominant user class
   h. Business information system references DBMS Environment
   i. Business information system references Database object information system
   j. Business information system referenced by Business Event
   k. Business information system referenced by Business Information System View
   l. Business information system referenced by resource life cycle business information system
   m. Business information system referenced by business information system database object information system assignment
   n. Business information system referenced by business information system

5.1.6 Business Organizations

[Business] Organizations, defined in Figure 17, should contain at least the following:

1. Business Organization administrative information
   a. Identification information
      i. Organization authors

   ii. Person authors
   b. Configuration management information
      i. Status (development, test, production)
      ii. Version (xx,yy.zz)

2. Business Organization object class tables
   a. Business Organization

3. Business Organization inter-object relationships
   a. Business organization contains business organization

4. Business Organization related objects
   a. Business Organization is referenced by Mission-Organization

5.1.7 Business Terms

Business Terms, not defined in figure as it is pervasive throughout many of the meta entities, should contain at least the following:

1. Business Term administrative information
   a. Identification information
      i. Organization authors
      ii. Person authors
   b. Configuration management information
      i. Status (development, test, production)
      ii. Version (xx,yy.zz)

2. Business Term object class tables
   a. Business Term

3. Business Term inter-object relationships
   a. Business Term contains Business Term

4. Business Term related objects
   a. Business Term is referenced by <meta-entity attribute: description>

5.1.8 Data Integrity Rules

Data Integrity Rules, not defined in figure as it is pervasive throughout many of the meta entities, really a form of data integrity rules, should contain at least the following:

1. Data integrity rule administrative information
   a. Identification information
      i. Organization authors
      ii. Person authors
   b. Configuration management information
      i. Status (development, test, production)
      ii. Version (xx,yy.zz)

2. Data integrity rule object class tables
   a. Data integrity rule
   b. Data integrity rule pseudo code
      i. Data integrity rule contained items
         (1) Data integrity rule object class
         (2) Data integrity rule object
         (3) Data integrity rule object value
            (a) alphabetic value
            (b) numeric value
      ii. Data integrity rule inter-contained item operator
   c. On success action
   d. On failure action

3. Data integrity rule inter-object relationships
   a. Data integrity rule references data integrity rule

4. Data integrity Rule related objects
   a. Attribute references data integrity rule contained item
   b. Entity references data integrity rule
   c. Column references data integrity rule contained item
   d. Table references data integrity rule
   e. DBMS column references data integrity rule contained item
   f. DBMS table references data integrity rule
   g. View column references data integrity rule contained item
   h. View references data integrity rule

i. [ISO 11179] data element references data integrity rule contained item
j. Data element concept references data integrity rule contained item
k. Compound data element references data integrity rule contained item
l. Derived data element references data integrity rule contained item
m. Database object table process references data integrity rule
n. Data integrity rule references Enterprise Identifier

5.1.9 Data Element Model

[ISO 11179] Data Elements, defined in Figure 14, should contain at least the following:

1. [ISO 11179] data element administrative information
   a. Identification information
      i. Organization authors
      ii. Person authors
   b. Configuration management information
      i. Status (development, test, production)
      ii. Version (xx,yy.zz)

2. [ISO 11179] Data element object class tables
   a. Concepts
   b. Concept structure
   c. Concept structure type
   d. Conceptual value domains
   e. Conceptual value domain structure
   f. Conceptual value domain structure type
   g. Data element concepts
   h. Data element concept structure
   i. Data element concept structure type
   j. Value domains
   k. Value domain structure
   l. Value domain structure type
   m. Value domain values
   n. Value domain value structure
   o. Value domain value structure type
   p. Data types
   q. Compound data elements

r. Derived data elements
s. Data element classifications

3. [ISO 11179] Data Element inter-object relationships
   a. Concepts
      i. Concept contains concept structures
      ii. Concept is contained in concept structures
      iii. Concept structure type contains concept structures
   b. Conceptual value domains
      i. Conceptual value domain contains conceptual value domain structures
      ii. Conceptual value domain is contained in conceptual value domain structures
      iii. Concept value domain structure type contains concept value domain structures
   c. Data element concepts
      i. Data element concept contains data element concept structures
      ii. Data element concept is contained in data element concept structures
      iii. Data element concept structure type contains Data element concept structures
   d. Data element classifications
      i. Data element classification contains data element classification structures
      ii. Data element classification is contained in data element classification structures
      iii. Data element classification type contains data element classification structures
   e. Value domains
      i. Value domain contains value domain structures
      ii. Value domain is contained in value domain structures
      iii. Value domain structure type contains value domain structures
   f. Value domain values
      i. Value domain value contains value domain value structures
      ii. Value domain value is contained in value domain value structures
      iii. Value domain value structure type contains value domain value structures
   g. Compound data elements
      i. Compound data element contains compound data element structure
      ii. Compound data element is contained in compound data element structure

        iii. Compound data element structure type contains compound data element structures
    h. Data element concept references conceptual value domain structure
    i. Data element concept references concept structure
    j. Data element references data element concept structure
    k. Data element references value domain structure
    l. Compound data element contains data element
    m. Derived data element contains data element
    n. Value domain references conceptual value domain structure
    o. Value domain value references value domain structure

4. [ISO 11179] data element model related objects
    a. Concept references Enterprise Identifier
    b. Conceptual value domain references Enterprise Identifier
    c. Value domain references Enterprise Identifier
    d. Data element concept references Enterprise Identifier
    e. [ISO 11179] data element references Enterprise Identifier

5.1.10 Database Domains

Database Domains, defined in Figure 17, should contain at least the following:

1. Database domain administrative information
    a. Identification information
        i. Organization authors
        ii. Person authors
    b. Configuration management information
        i. Status (development, test, production)
        ii. Version (xx,yy.zz)
2. Database domain object class tables
    a. Database domain
3. Database domain inter-object relationships
    a. Database domain contains database domain
4. Database domain related objects
    a. Database domain references mission
    b. Database-domain database-object references database domain

5.1.11 Database Objects

Database Objects, defined in Figure 13, should contain at least the following:

1. Database objects administrative information
   a. Identification information
      i. Organization authors
      ii. Person authors
   b. Configuration management information
      i. Status (development, test, production)
      ii. Version (xx,yy.zz)
2. Database object object class tables
   a. Database object tables
   b. Database object information systems
   c. Database object states
   d. Database object information system states
   e. Database object table processes
3. Database object inter-object relationships
   a. Database object contains database object tables
   b. Database object contains information systems
   c. Database object contains states
   d. Database object state contains database object information system states
   e. Database object information system contains database object information system states
4. Database object related objects
   a. Database object table references table
   b. Database object table process references data integrity rule
   c. Database object references database domain

5.1.12 Implemented Data Model

Implemented Data Models, defined in Figure 15, should contain at least the following:

1. Implemented Data Model administrative information
   a. Identification information
      i. Organization authors

   ii. Person authors
  b. Configuration management information
   i. Status (development, test, production)
   ii. Version (xx,yy.zz)

2. Logical model object class tables
   a. Schema
   b. Tables
   c. Columns
   d. Relationships
      i. Primary Key
         (1) Primary key columns
      ii. Candidate Key
         (1) Candidate key columns
      iii. Foreign Key
         (1) Foreign key columns

3. Logical model inter-object relationships
   a. Schema contains table
   b. Table contains table subtypes
   c. Table contains columns
   d. Column contains columns
   e. Table contains primary key
   f. Table contains foreign key
   g. Table contains candidate key
   h. Primary key contains foreign key
   i. Primary key contains primary key columns
   j. Column contains primary key columns
   k. Foreign key contains foreign key columns
   l. Column contains foreign key columns
   m. Candidate key contains candidate key columns
   n. Column contains candidate key columns

4. Implemented Data Model related objects
   a. Column references [ISO 11179] data element
   b. Column references value domain structure
   c. Column references SQL data type
   d. Column references attribute
   e. Schema references Enterprise Identifier

5.1.13 Information Needs

Information Needs, defined in Figure 16, should contain at least the following:

1. Information Needs administrative information
    a. Identification information
        i. Organization authors
        ii. Person authors
    b. Configuration management information
        i. Status (development, test, production)
        ii. Version (xx,yy.zz)

2. Information object class tables
    a. Information Needs Types
    b. Information Needs
    c. Ranking
    d. Characteristic Type
    e. Characteristic
    f. Information Need Characteristic Assignment
    g. Mission-Organization-Functional Ranked Information Need Assignment

3. Information Needs inter-object relationships
    a. Information Need Type contains Information Need
    b. Information Need contains Mission-Organization-Functional Ranked Information Need Assignment
    c. Information Need contains Information Need Characteristic Assignment
    d. Characteristic Type contains Characteristic
    e. Characteristic contains Information Need Characteristic Assignment
    f. Ranking contains Information Need Characteristic Assignment

4. Information Needs related objects
    a. Mission-Organization-Functional Ranked Information Need Assignment is referenced by Mission-Organization-Function

5.1.14 Mission

Missions, defined in Figure 17, should contain at least the following:

1. Mission administrative information
   a. Identification information
      i. Organization authors
      ii. Person authors
   b. Configuration management information
      i. Status (development, test, production)
      ii. Version (xx,yy.zz)

2. Mission object class tables
   a. Mission

3. Mission inter-object relationships
   a. Mission contains Mission

4. Mission related objects
   a. Mission is referenced by Mission-Organization

5.1.15 Operational Data Model

Operational data models, defined in Figure 18, should contain at least the following:

1. Operational data model administrative information
   a. Identification information
      i. Organization authors
      ii. Person authors
   b. Configuration management information
      i. Status (development, test, production)
      ii. Version (xx,yy.zz)

2. Operational model object class tables
   a. DBMS Schema
   b. DBMS Tables

c. DBMS Columns
d. Relationships
    i. Primary Key
        (1) Primary key DBMS Columns
    ii. Candidate Key
        (1) Candidate key DBMS Columns
    iii. Foreign Key
        (1) Foreign key DBMS Columns
    iv. Secondary Key
        (1) Secondary key DBMS Columns

3. Operational model inter-object relationships
    a. DBMS Schema contains DBMS Table
    b. DBMS Table contains DBMS Table subtypes
    c. DBMS Table contains DBMS Columns
    d. DBMS Column contains DBMS Columns
    e. DBMS Table contains primary key
    f. DBMS Table contains foreign key
    g. DBMS Table contains candidate key
    h. Primary key contains foreign key
    i. Primary key contains primary key DBMS Columns
    j. DBMS Column contains primary key DBMS Columns
    k. Foreign key contains foreign key DBMS Columns
    l. DBMS Column contains foreign key DBMS Columns
    m. Candidate key contains candidate key DBMS Columns
    n. DBMS Column contains candidate key DBMS Columns
    o. Secondary key contains secondary key DBMS Columns
    p. DBMS Column contains secondary key DBMS Columns

4. Operational data model related objects
    a. DBMS Column references value domain structure
    b. DBMS Schema references database
    c. DBMS Column references data type
    d. DBMS Column references column
    e. DBMS Schema references Enterprise Identifier

5.1.16 Position

Position, defined in Figure 17, should contain at least the following:

1. Position administrative information
   a. Identification information
      i. Organization authors
      ii. Person authors
   b. Configuration management information
      i. Status (development, test, production)
      ii. Version (xx,yy.zz)

2. Position object class tables
   a. Position
   b. Management Levels
   c. Person
   d. Position Person
   e. Mission Organization Function Position

3. Position inter-object relationships
   a. Management Level contains Position
   b. Position contains Mission Organization Function Position
   c. Position contains Position Person
   d. Person contains Position Person

4. Position related objects
   a. Mission-Organization-Function Position is referenced by Mission Organization Function

5.1.17 Projects

Community of Interest Project, defined in Figure 19, plans should contain at least the following:

1. Project Plan administrative information
   a. Identification information
      i. Organization authors

    ii. Person authors
  b. Configuration management information
    i. Status (development, test, production)
    ii. Version (xx,yy.zz)

2. Project object class tables
   a. Project Plan tasks
      i. Task
      ii. Predecessors
      iii. Critical dates
      iv. Unit effort
      v. Deliverable unit quantity
   b. Project Plan milestones
   c. Project Plan employed resource information
   d. Project Plan deliverables
   e. Project Plan success factors

3. Project plan inter-object relationships
   a. Task references deliverable
   b. Task references previous tasks
   c. Milestone references feeder tasks
   d. Task references previous milestone

4. Project Plan related objects
   a. Project plan references project plan
   b. Project plan references Enterprise Identifier
   c. Project plan references Information Exchange Data Model

5.1.18 Resource Life Cycle Analysis

Resource Life Cycles, defined in Figure 20, plans should contain at least the following:

1. Resource administrative information
   a. Identification information
      i. Organization authors
      ii. Person authors
   b. Configuration management information

   i. Status (development, test, production)
   ii. Version (xx,yy.zz)

2. Resource Life Cycle Analysis class tables
   a. Resource Type
   b. Resource
   c. Resource Life Cycle Node Structure
   d. Resource Life Cycle Node Structure Type
   e. Resource Life Cycle Node Database Object Assignment
   f. Resource Life Cycle Node Business Information System Assignment
   g. Resource Life Cycle Node Information Needs Assignment

3. Project plan inter-object relationships
   a. Resource references Resource Type
   b. Resource Life Cycle Node references Resource
   c. Resource Life Cycle Node Database Object Assignment references Resource Life Cycle Node
   d. Resource Life Cycle Node Database Object Assignment references database object
   e. Resource Life Cycle Node Business Information System Assignment references Resource Life Cycle Node
   f. Resource Life Cycle Node Business Information System Assignment references Business Information System
   g. Resource Life Cycle Node Information Needs Assignment references Resource Life Cycle Node
   h. Resource Life Cycle Node Information Needs Assignment references Resource Life Cycle Node Information Need

4. Project Plan related objects
   a. Project plan references project plan
   b. Project plan references Enterprise Identifier
   c. Project plan references Information Exchange Data Model

5.1.19 Specified Data Models

Specified data models, defined in Figure 21, should contain at least the following:

1. Specified data model administrative information

a. Identification information
    i. Organization authors
    ii. Person authors
b. Configuration management information
    i. Status (development, test, production)
    ii. Version (xx,yy.zz)

2. Specified model object class tables
    a. Subject
    b. Entities
    c. Attributes
    d. Relationships
        i. Primary Key
            (1) Primary key attributes
        ii. Candidate Key
            (1) Candidate key attributes
        iii. Foreign Key
            (1) Foreign key attributes

3. Specified model inter-object relationships
    a. Subject contains subjects
    b. Subject contains entity
    c. Entity contains entity subtypes
    d. Entity contains attributes
    e. Attribute contains attributes
    f. Entity contains primary key
    g. Entity contains foreign key
    h. Entity contains candidate key
    i. Primary key contains foreign key
    j. Primary key contains primary key attributes
    k. Attribute contains primary key attributes
    l. Foreign key contains foreign key attributes
    m. Attribute contains foreign key attributes
    n. Candidate key contains candidate key attributes
    o. Attribute contains candidate key attributes

4. Specified model related objects
    a. Attribute references [ISO 11179] data element
    b. Attribute references value domain structure

c. Subject references Enterprise Identifier

5.1.20 View Data Model

View data models, defined in Figure 22, should contain at least the following:

1. View data model administrative information
   a. Identification information
      i. Organization authors
      ii. Person authors
   b. Configuration management information
      i. Status (development, test, production)
      ii. Version (xx,yy.zz)

2. View object class tables
   a. View
   b. View column
   c. View column structure
   d. View column structure type
   e. View column structure process
   f. View column DBMS column

3. View inter-object relationships
   a. View contains view columns
   b. View column contains view column structure
   c. View column structure type contains view column structure
   d. View column structure process contains view column structure
   e. View column contains view column DBMS column

4. View related objects
   a. View columns
   b. View column DBMS column references DBMS column
   c. View column references [ISO 11179] derived data element
   d. View column references [ISO 11179] compound data element
   e. View references business information system

5.2 U.S. Department of Defense Architecture Framework Deliverables

The U.S. Department of Defense expended considerable resources over the past years developing its Department of Defense Architecture Framework (DoDAF). This life cycle is a successor to another that was created during the 1970s and 1980s. The DoDAF is a general purpose framework, and has been used for multiple classes of architectures. Included for example are: weapon systems, force deployments, all manners and classes of hardware and software, and for information technology systems.

With the exception of two misnamed and misdefined architecture products, this collection of architecture products is very generalized. The two misnamed and misdefined products are the OV7 (logical data model) and the SV11 (physical data model). These two should be generalized "thing" based models where subsequently, in an IT specialization, these "things" might be computer hardware, files, or databases. The OV7 would a "thing type" and the SV11 would be a "thing instance," or "thing physical transformation." Then, within a database specialization of an IT specialization, these "things" could be data models.

As just stated, a specialized class of the generalized DoDAF architecture is an IT Systems engineering architecture. For those IT systems that then involve databases or which contain metadata data-based components, such as those described in Section 5.1, there could be a database specialization. The table that follows is such a specialization. The first column identifies the overall class of a set of products. The second column is the short name for the framework product. The third column is the name of the product. The fourth column is an overall description of the product. The fifth column identifies the metadata database objects from Section 5.1 that need to be built to achieve data interoperability. This table then represents a data interoperability specialization of the DoD's Architecture Framework.

U.S. Department of Defense DoD Architecture Frame Framework (Version 1, February 2004)				
View	**Frame-work Product**	**Frame Product Name**	**General Description**	**Metadata Database Objects**
All Views	AV-1	Overview and Summary Information	Scope, purpose, intended users, environment depicted, analytical findings	Mission, Database Domains
	AV-2	Integrated Dictionary	Architecture data repository with definitions of all terms used in all products	Business Terms, Data Element Model
Oper-ational	OV-1	High-Level Operational Concept Graphic	High-level graphical/textual description of operational concept	Mission, Database Domains, Functions, and Organizations
	OV-2	Operational Node Connectivity Description	Operational nodes, connectivity, and information exchange needs between nodes	Business Event, Business Calendar, Business Cycle, Business Information Systems, Organization, and Function
	OV-3	Operational Information Exchange Matrix	Information exchanged between nodes and the relevant attributes of that exchange	INFORMATION EXCHANGE DATA MODEL via physical data model, with Business Information Systems, Business Event, Business Calendar, and Business Cycle
	OV-4	Organization al Relationships Chart	Organizational, role, or other relationships among organizations	Organization, Function, and Business Event

U.S. Department of Defense DoD Architecture Frame Framework (Version 1, February 2004)				
View	**Frame-work Product**	**Frame Product Name**	**General Description**	**Metadata Database Objects**
	OV-5	Operational Activity Model	Capabilities, operational activities, relationships among activities, inputs, and outputs; overlays can show cost, performing nodes, or other pertinent information	Business Function, Business Events, Physical Data Model, and View Data Model
	OV-6a	Operational Rules Model	One of three products used to describe operational activity—identifies data integrity rules that constrain operation	Business Functions, Business Events, Physical Data Model, Views, Data Integrity Rules, Business Information Systems, and Database Objects.
	OV-6b	Operational State Transition Description	One of three products used to describe operational activity—identifies business process responses to events	Projects (To Be and As-is) That Identify Business Functions, Business Events, Physical Data Model, Views, Data Integrity Rules, Business Information Systems, and Database Objects.
	OV-6c	Operational Event-Trace Description	One of three products used to describe operational activity—traces actions in a scenario or sequence of events	Mappings Regarding Business Functions, Business Events, Physical Data Model, Views, Data Integrity Rules, Business Information Systems, and Database Objects.
	OV-7	Logical Data Model	Documentation of the system data requirements and structural business process rules of the Operational View	Data Element Model, Conceptual Data Model, and Logical Data Model.

U.S. Department of Defense DoD Architecture Frame Framework (Version 1, February 2004)				
View	**Frame-work Product**	**Frame Product Name**	**General Description**	**Metadata Database Objects**
Systems	SV-1	Systems Interface Description	Identification of systems nodes, systems, and system items and their interconnections, within and between nodes	Business Information Systems, Views, and Inter-view Mappings
	SV-2	Systems Communica-tions Description	Systems nodes, systems, and system items, and their related communications lay-downs	Not directly applicable to data interoperability communities of interest.
	SV-3	Systems - Systems Matrix	Relationships among systems in a given architecture; can be designed to show relationships of interest, e.g., system-type interfaces, planned vs. existing interfaces, etc.	Business Information Systems, View Models, and Physical Data Models
	SV-4	Systems Functionality Description	Functions performed by systems and the system data flows among system functions	Business Information Systems, Database Objects Model, and Logical Data Model
	SV-5	Operational Activity to Systems Function Traceability Matrix	Mapping of systems back to capabilities or of system functions back to operational activities	Business Information Systems, Business Events, Business Functions, and Optionally to Organizations and Missions
	SV-6	Systems Data Exchange Matrix	Provides details of system data elements being exchanged between systems and the attributes of that exchange	Business Information Systems, Views, and Inter-view Mappings

U.S. Department of Defense DoD Architecture Frame Framework (Version 1, February 2004)				
View	**Frame-work Product**	**Frame Product Name**	**General Description**	**Metadata Database Objects**
	SV-7	Systems Performance Parameters Matrix	Performance characteristics of Systems View elements for the appropriate time frame(s)	Not directly applicable to data interoperability communities of interest.
	SV-8	Systems Evolution Description	Planned incremental steps toward migrating a suite of systems to a more efficient suite, or toward evolving a current system to a future implementation	Projects Relative to the "To Be" and "As-is" That Identify Business Functions, Business Events, Physical Data Model, Views, Data Integrity Rules, Business Information Systems, and Database Objects.
	SV-9	Systems Technology Forecast	Emerging technologies and software/hardware products that are expected to be available in a given set of time frames and that will affect future development of the architecture	Not directly applicable to data interoperability communities of interest.
	SV-10a	Systems Rules Model	One of three products used to describe system functionality—identifies constraints that are imposed on systems functionality due to some aspect of systems design or implementation	Business Information System, Database Objects, Data Integrity Rules and Logical Data Model.
	SV-10b	Systems State Transition Description	One of three products used to describe system functionality—identifies responses of a system to events	Business Events and Database Objects

U.S. Department of Defense DoD Architecture Frame Framework (Version 1, February 2004)				
View	**Frame-work Product**	**Frame Product Name**	**General Description**	**Metadata Database Objects**
	SV-10c	Systems Event-Trace Description	One of three products used to describe system functionality—identifies system-specific refinements of critical sequences of events described in the Operational View	Mappings among Business Events and Database Objects
	SV-11	Physical Schema	Physical implementation of the Logical Data Model entities, e.g., message formats, file structures, physical schema	Physical Data Model and View Data Model
Tech-nical	TV-1	Technical Standards Profile	Listing of standards that apply to Systems View elements in a given architecture	Not directly applicable to data interoperability communities of interest.
	TV-2	Technical Standards Forecast	Description of emerging standards and potential impact on current Systems View elements, within a set of time frames	Not directly applicable to data interoperability communities of interest.

Table 9. U.S. Department of Defense Generalized Architecture Framework and data interoperability.

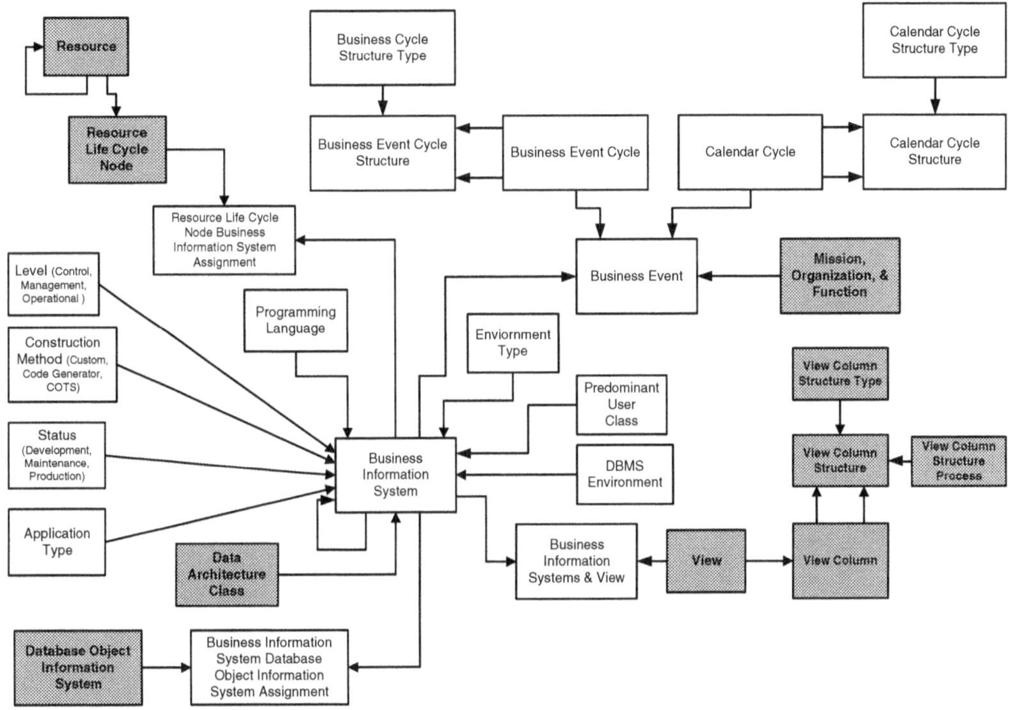

Figure 12. Business Information System data model.

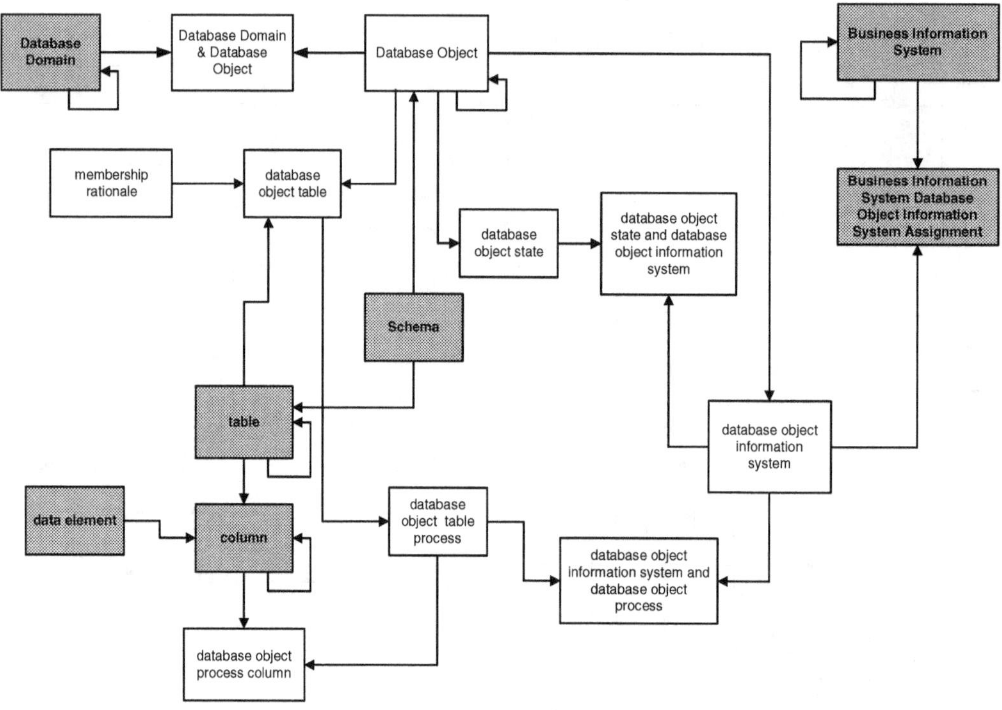

Figure 13. Database Objects data model.

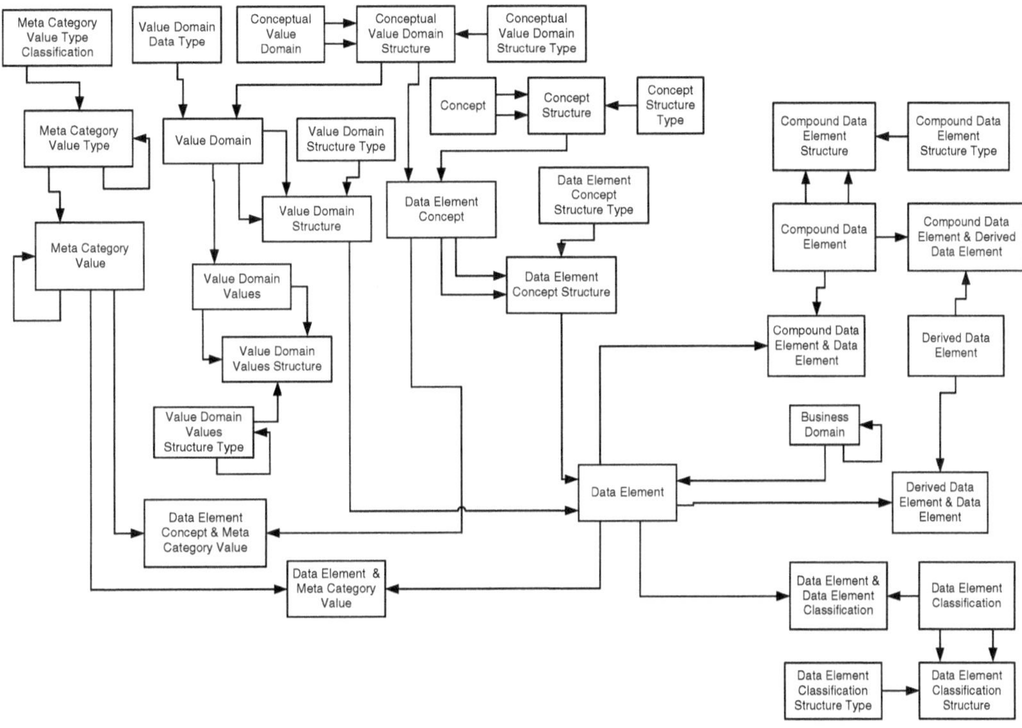

Figure 14. Data Elements data model.

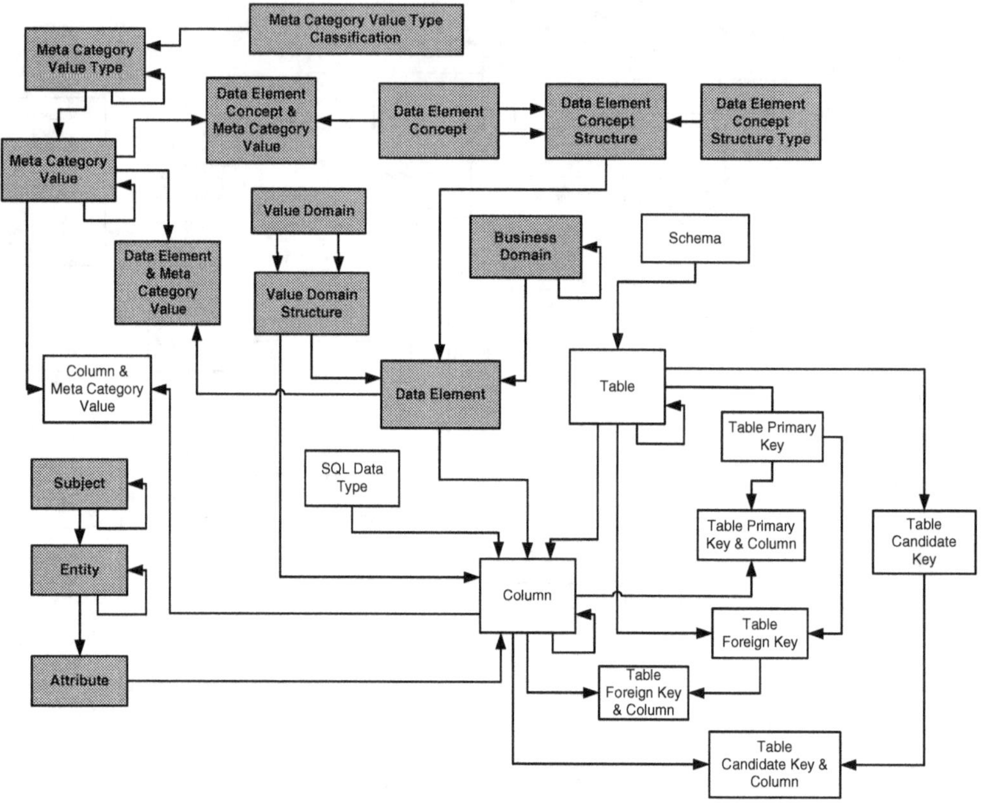

Figure 15. Implemented Data Model data model.

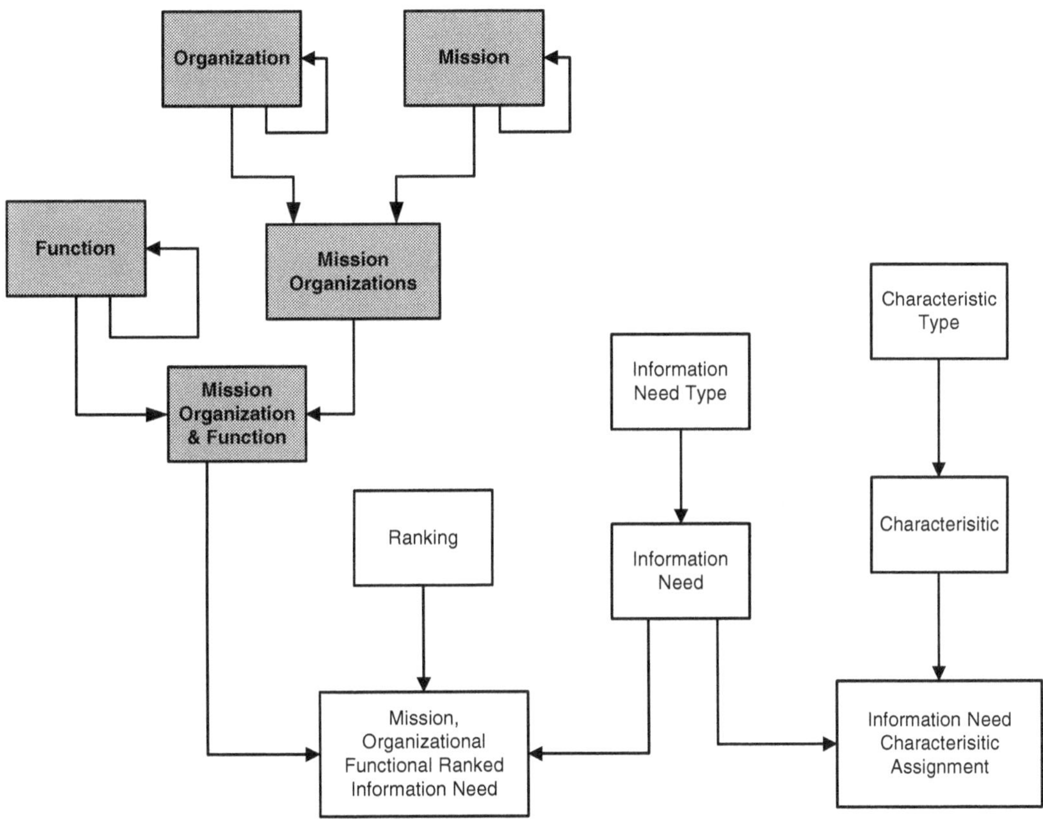

Figure 16. Information Needs Analysis data model.

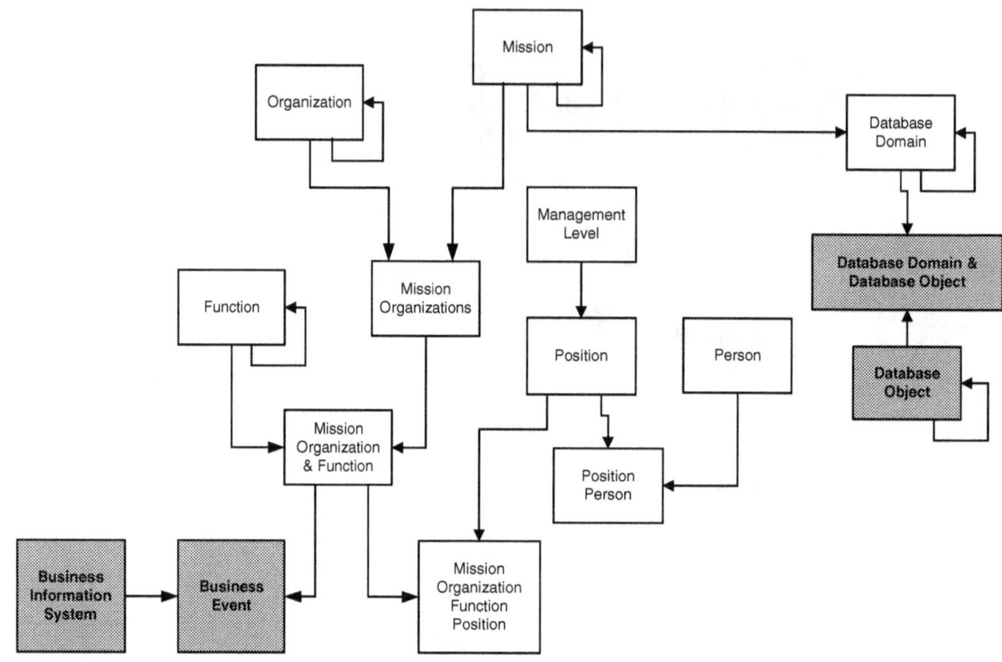

Figure 17. Mission, Organization, Function, Position data model.

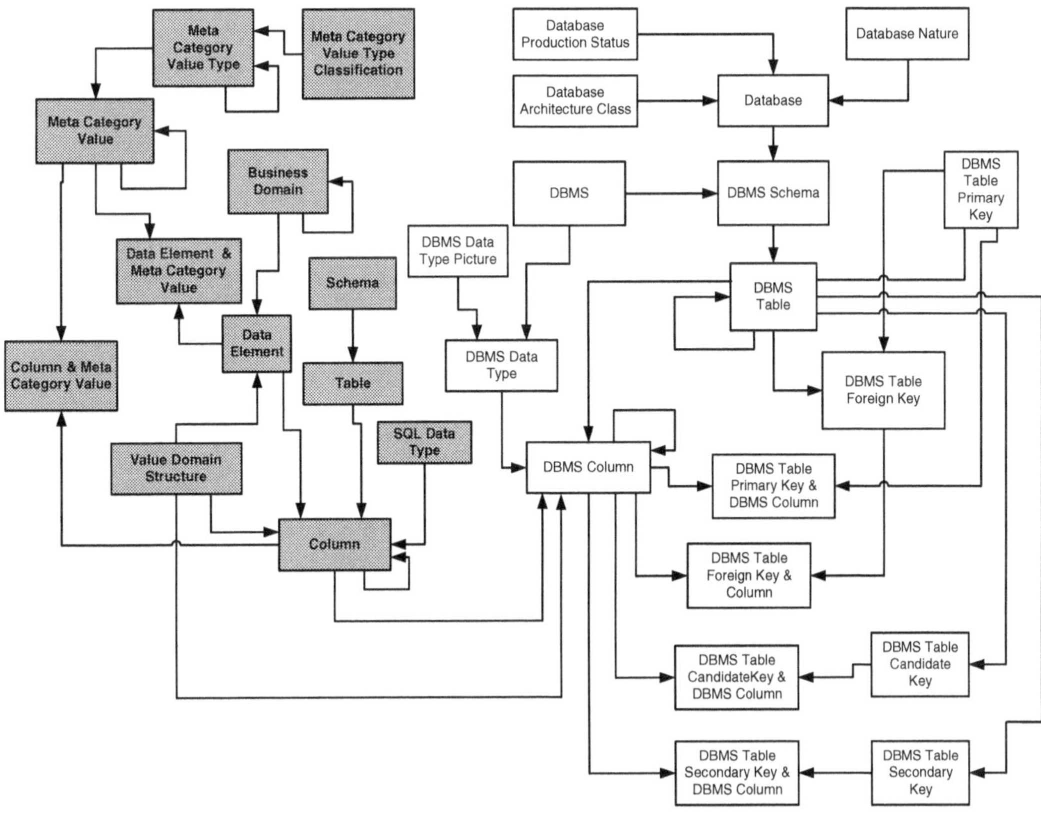

Figure 18. Operational Data Model data model.

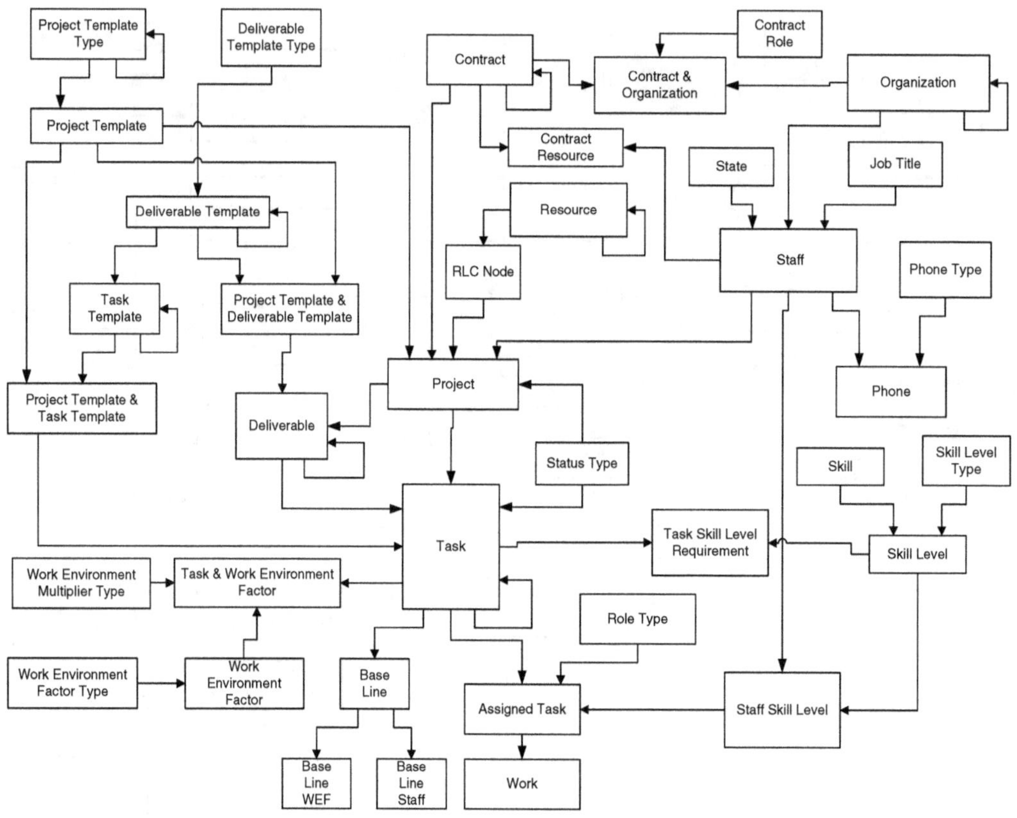

Figure 19. Project Management data model.

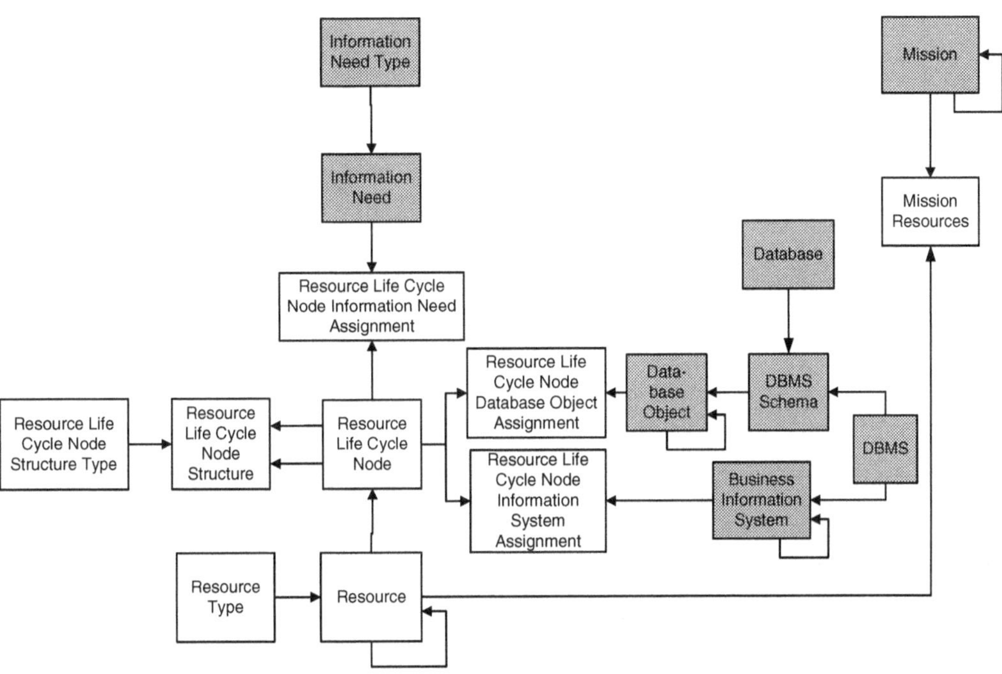

Figure 20. Resource Life Cycle Analysis data model.

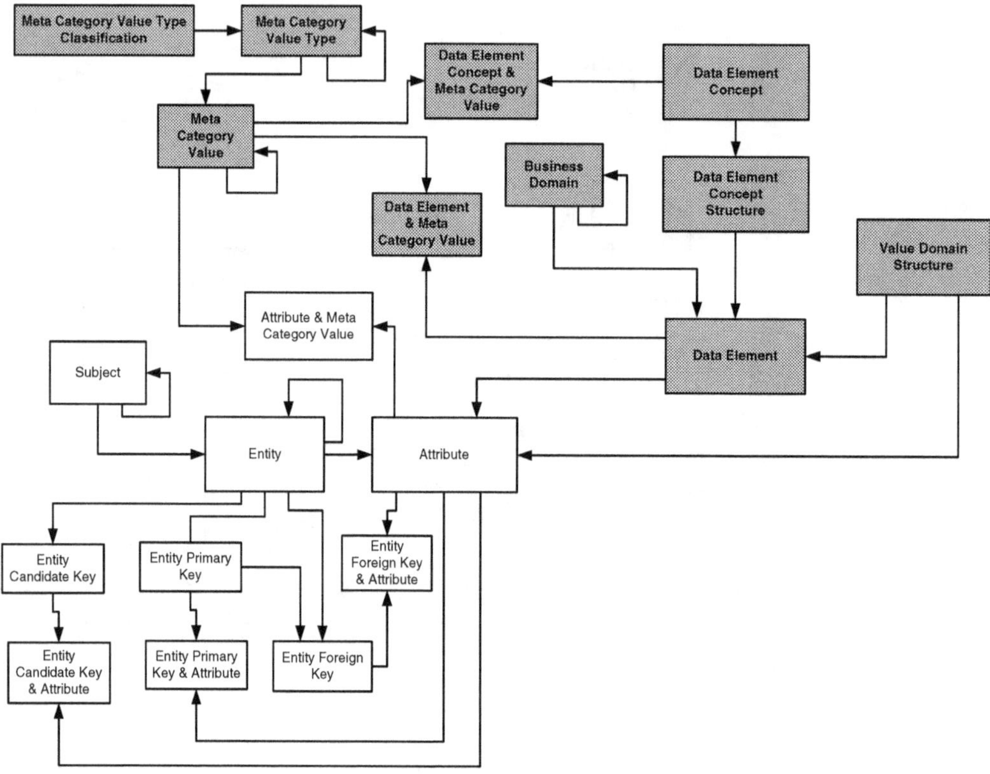

Figure 21. Specified Data Model data model.

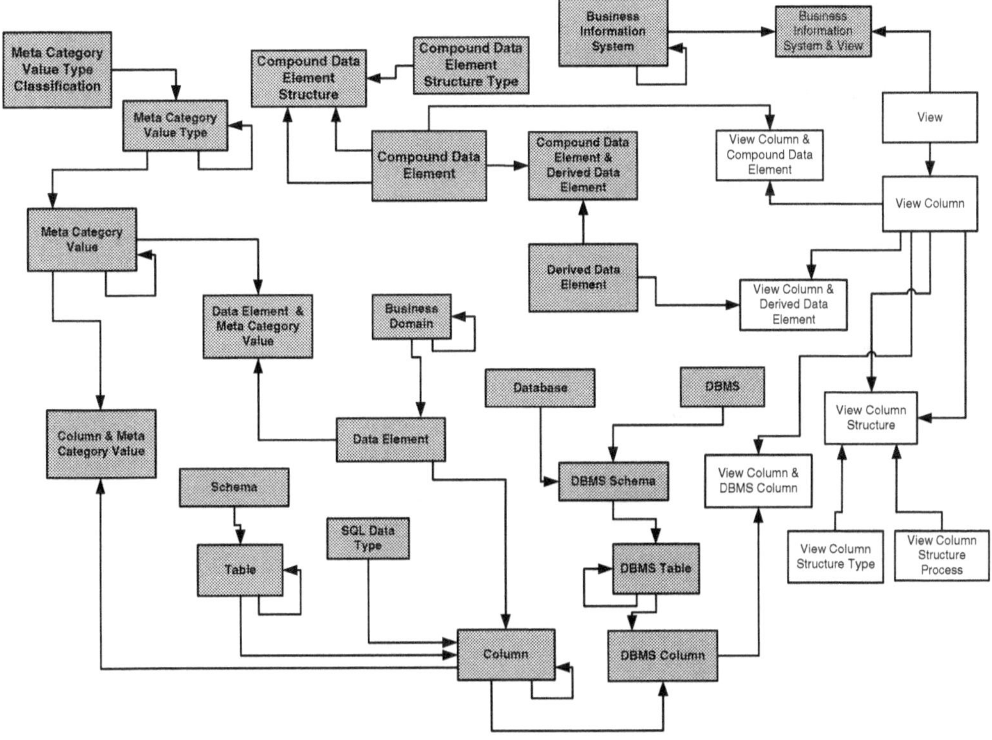

Figure 22. View Data Model data model.

5.3 Database Objects Summary

Database objects are the "what" that is collected in support of data interoperability specifications. Database object class specifications are not just simple database table specifications. Each database object class is a collection of tables that are interconnected by relationships, and are controlled by well defined processes that keep the database objects in a state of high-integrity.

Every database object class should be mapped to one or more missions. Further, once a data interoperability environment is established, these database object classes and their instantiated database objects should be the responsibility of one or more organizations as they perform their data interoperability functions through business information systems.

Database object classes are essentially the data-based policy specifications surrounding data interoperability. If interoperable data environments are to support audits, or to reflect history, then these requirements must be manifest in the specifications of the database object classes.

Figures 12 through 22 are third-normal form data model diagrams within which all the database object class data structures can be found. The actual database object tables processes are found in the next chapter and are all set within the context of business information systems.

6

Business Information Systems

6.1 Metadata Management Information Systems

In the broadest sense, a metadata management system is an application that captures, stores, reports and updates metadata in a business information system. Most likely its "data management engine" is a database management system (DBMS). Similar to all other management information systems, there is a database design (See Chapter 5), and then, a process design.

This chapter centers on the process design of the metadata management information system. Contained in this chapter are the functional specifications of the various metadata management systems that must exist to create the data interoperability database objects and to also interrelate, update, and report them. The sections are:

- Enterprise Architecture Metadata Management
- Information Systems Architecture Metadata Management
- Data Architecture Metadata Management
- Reverse Engineering Model Metadata Management
- Forward Engineering Model Metadata Management.

Each section has an overall general description, a set of subsections, and, then for each subsection, a table of the processes that need to exist to accomplish the collection, storage, reporting, and updating of the metadata. These processes are described generically so that they can be used to evaluate the functionality of any CASE/Repository system that would be employed by a Community of Interest as it develops and employs Data Interoperability products. The listing of the processes is provided in the following general order: create, assign, and reassign. How and when and what sequence these processes should be employed is explicitly stated in the Whitemarsh methodologies, and in the Whitemarsh metabase user guides.

6.2 Enterprise Architecture Metadata Management

Enterprise architecture metadata consists of the following classes:

- Missions.
- Organizations.
- Functions.
- Positions and Persons.
- Database Domains
- Database Object Classes
- Information Need Analyses

Collectively these metadata classes define the enterprise's architecture. It is within these metadata classes that all information systems and databases exist. It is critical that these metadata classes are very carefully accomplished. The time and effort it takes to create these metadata is quite small compared to the resources required for the creation and implementation of the databases and information systems represented by the metadata contained in these metadata classes. The value however is not only very great, but if done wrong or incompletely, the possibility of identifying the correct databases and information systems is tremendously lessened. In an analysis of 13 multi-hundred million dollar IT debacles that were analyzed by the United States Congress's Office of Accountability, it was shown that 95% of the errors that occur are outside the proper tasks of IT. That is, they occur almost totally with the proper collection and specification of enterprise architecture metadata.

6.2.1 Mission Models

The mission models, depicted in Figure 17, are the boundaries of the scope of the enterprise. It is within mission models that database domains that lead to database designs are created. Missions are also the scope boundaries for all enterprise organizations and functions.

Missions	
Process	**Description**
Create, modify or delete Missions	This process creates a mission and as appropriate a subordinate mission within an existing mission.
Create, modify or delete subordinate Mission.	This process creates subordinate missions within a mission hierarchy.
Reallocate Missions	This process reallocates a mission within a mission hierarchy to a different mission.

6.2.2 Organization Models

As a database project commences, an organization model, depicted in Figure 17, is built and then allocated to the various missions. This permits the easy identification of those components of the enterprise that are involved in any effort. Once organizations are created, they are allocated to missions such that every mission is addressed and every organization is responsible for one or more missions. Unallocated missions and/or missions that are allocated to every organization should be investigated.

Organizations	
Process	**Description**
Create, modify or delete Organizations	This process creates an organization and as appropriate a subordinate organization within an existing organization.
Create, modify or delete subordinate Organization.	This process creates subordinate organizations within an organization hierarchy.
Accomplish Mission and Organization Assignments	This process assigns one or more organizations to a mission.
Reallocate Organizations	This process reallocates an organization within an organization hierarchy to a different organization.

6.2.3 Function Models

As a database project continues, it is important to know just what functions, depicted in Figure 17, are accomplished by any organization within the scope of a mission. In the context of this book, all functions are manual processes. The hierarchical function models are created and interrelated with the various mission-organizations that perform them. Because functions are human activities, there may be multiples sets of functions that are generally equivalent but differ in style of knowledge worker processes. The differences are not critical because the relationship between a business information system and a business function is through the intermediary, business event.

Functions	
Process	**Description**
Create, modify or delete Functions	This process creates a function and as appropriate a subordinate function within an existing function.
Create, modify or delete subordinate Function.	This process creates subordinate functions within a function hierarchy.
Accomplish Mission-Organization and Function Assignments	This process assigns one or more functions to pairs of mission-organizations.
Reallocate Functions	This process reallocates a function within a function hierarchy to a different function.

6.2.4 Position and Person Models

The position, person and management levels, depicted in Figure 17, enable organizations to identify positions by management levels and the assignment of those to particular mission-organization-function combinations. This process also allows the inclusion of specific individuals and the association of those individuals to positions.

Position and Person	
Process	**Description**
Create, modify, or delete Management Level	This process creates a management level.
Create, modify or delete position	This process creates a position. This process also allows the allocation of a particular management level to that position.
Create, modify or delete person	This process creates a person.
Create, modify, or delete position-person association	This process creates an association between a person and a position.
Create Mission-Organization-Function and Position	This process creates one or more associations between a position and a set of mission-organization-functions.

6.2.5 Database Domain Models

Database domains, depicted in Figure 17, are "noun-intensive" descriptions of the data inferred by the lowest level of a mission hierarchy. Each database domain is thus restricted in scope to that mission leaf. Additionally, each database domain is represented by a simple entity-relationship diagram. When all the relevant database domains are completed, these entity-relationship diagrams are combined to ensure that the entities that are named the same are in fact the same and represent the same level of granularity. Similarity, all entities that are the same should have the same name and definition.

Database Domains	
Process	**Description**
Create, modify, or delete Database Domain	Select a particular mission leaf and then create a database domain corresponding to the "noun-story" that exists within the mission leaf.

Database Domains	
Process	**Description**
Create, modify, or delete database domain and database object association.	This process creates an association between a person and a position.
Reallocate Database Domains	This process reallocates a database domain within a database domain hierarchy to a different database domain.

6.2.6 Database Object Classes

Database object classes, depicted in Figure 13, are the encapsulated data structures, processes, and constraints necessary to transform a set of data from one value state to the next. Database object classes are essential to the integrity of databases. In this book, and throughout all Whitemarsh literature, the data structure of a database object class consists of an identified set of database tables within a single schema. A database table can be in only one database object class unless that database table is to represent the intersection between two or more database object classes. In such a case, only one of the database object classes can have cascade-delete behavior over that inter-database-object-table. The other database object classes can only have "set null" delete behavior.

In modern SQL DBMSs, there is no explicit notion of a database object class through explicit SQL syntax. Consequently, database object classes, while clearly and explicitly defined in the Implemented Data Model, have to be operationally realized in the Operational Data Model through existing SQL:2003 and earlier syntax. This can largely be done through the use of persistent SQL views that map to a collection of columns across a set of tables. While this is certainly far from ideal, it is the best that ANSI standard SQL has to offer.

The value state integrity of database objects within database object classes is governed by columns and table constraints. The value states are transformed through stored procedures within assertions and triggers. It is important to define database object classes within the domain of the DBMS to ensure that all external language agents such as 4GLs, query languages, and 3GLs are forced to proceed through these DBMS defined and encapsulated database object classes.

Database Objects	
Process	**Description**
Create, modify or delete Database Object Table Membership Rationale	This process creates a database object table membership process that is then employed to identify collections of database object tables within a database object according to their membership rationale.
Create, modify or delete Database Object	This process creates a database object within the scope of a schema.
Create, modify or delete Database Object Table Assignment	This process creates one or more database object tables, that is, one or more tables assigned to a database object. All the tables that are assigned to be in a database object must be within the same schema as the database object.
Create, modify or delete Database Object Information Systems	This process creates a database object information system within the scope of a database object.
Create, modify or delete Database Object State	This process creates a database object state within the scope of a database object.
Create, modify or delete Database Object Table Process	This process creates a database object table process within the scope of a database object table.
Accomplish Database Object Information Systems to Database Object Table Process Assignment	This process causes an assignment of one or more database object table processes to a database object information system.
Accomplish Database Object Information Systems to Database Object Table Process Reassignment	This process causes a change in the existing assignment of one or more database object table processes to a one database object information system.
Accomplish Database Object State to Database Object Information System Assignments	This process causes an assignment of one or more database object information systems to a database object state.

Database Objects	
Process	**Description**
Accomplish Database Object State to Database Object Information System Reassignment	This process causes a change in the existing assignment of one or more database object information systems to one database object state.
Accomplish Database Object Table Process to Column Assignment	This process causes an assignment of one or more database object table columns to one database object table process.
Accomplish Database Object Table Process to Column Reassignment	This process causes a change in the existing assignment of one or more database object table columns to one database object table process.
Accomplish Database Object to Database Domain Assignment	This process causes an assignment of one or more database objects to one database domain.
Accomplish Database Object to Database Domain Reassignment	This process causes a change in the existing assignment of one or more database objects to one database domain.
Accomplish Database Object to Schema Reassignment	This process causes a change in the existing assignment of one or more database objects to one schema.
Accomplish Database Object to Table Reassignments	This process causes a change in the existing assignment of one or more tables to one database object.

6.2.7 Information Needs Analysis Models

The purpose of Information Needs Analysis, depicted in Figure 16, is to answer the questions:

- Who needs what and in what organizational context?
- What function purpose does the information serve?
- What resource life cycle node does the information pertain to?
- What are the critical characteristics of the information?

- Through which databases and information needs is this information provided?

The information needs analysis permits recording of the characteristics of the information needs of the enterprise. Each information need can be described and the various characteristics and characteristic types can be allocated to each information need. Once information needs are characterized, they can be allocated to the various mission-organization-functions and then ranked. This permits enterprises to know the characteristics of what information is needed by whom within the different organizations in the performance enterprise missions.

Information needs analysis is essential for comprehensive database design. It is the necessary first step before beginning good database domain specification and Entity Relationship diagram building.

Information Needs Analysis	
Process	**Description**
Create, modify, or delete Ranking	This process creates an instance of ranking that can be used to classify collections of mission-organization-function information-needs.
Create, modify or delete Information Need Type	This process creates an instance of an information need type that can be used to classify collections information needs.
Create, modify or delete Characteristic Type	This process creates an instance of a Characteristic Type that can be used to classify collections of characteristics which, in turn, can be used to categorize information needs.
Create, modify or delete Information Need	This process creates an instance of an information need within a given information need type.
Create, modify or delete Characteristic	This process creates an instance of a characteristic within a given characteristic type.
Create, modify or delete association between Information Need and Characteristic	This process creates an association between an Information need and a particular Characteristic.

Information Needs Analysis	
Process	**Description**
Accomplish Mission Organization Functional Ranked Information Need Assignment	This process assigns one or more information needs to a mission organization function. The process then allows the assignment of a particular rank to the mission organization function information need.

6.2.8 Business Terms Models

The purpose of Business Terms is to act as a dictionary and/or glossary across the three classes of architecture: enterprise, information systems, and data. Business Terms answer the questions:

- What business terms, that is, words, specific terms, or whole phrases are important to the enterprise?
- How are business terms related one to the other?
- Where are business terms found in each of the architectures?

The business terms are not shown on any diagram because they are pervasive across all the models.

Business Terms	
Process	**Description**
Create, modify, or delete business term	This process creates an instance of a business term that can then be assigned to wherever it is used.
Discover business terms	This process "reads" definitions, descriptions, and names that have been constructed in the metadata across all the metadata models and offers candidates for business terms from an existing set of business terms.

Business Terms	
Process	**Description**
Create business term from a candidate business term	This process creates an instance of a business term from a candidate business term that is found by the discovery process.
Accomplish business term assignment	This process assigns a business term to one or more contexts.
Accomplish business term interrelationship	This process creates interrelationships among business terms.

6.2.9 Data Integrity Rule Models

The purpose of Data Integrity Rules, also sometimes called Data integrity rules is to represent and then enforce through implied and/or explicitly defined processes data constraints throughout the metadata management environment. Data Integrity Rules answer the questions:

- What relationships exist across the set of complete metadata and/or specifications implied by that metadata that are enforced in one-to-one, one-to-many, and many-to-many relationships?
- What metadata values are restricted across the set of complete metadata and/or specifications implied by that metadata and what are the domains of these values?
- What metadata values across the set of complete metadata and/or specifications implied by that metadata are contextually or hierarchically restricted across assignments of these metadata values?
- What metadata values across the set of complete metadata and/or specifications implied by that metadata are combined through processes ?

The data integrity rules are not shown on any diagram because they are pervasive across all the models.

Data Integrity Rule	
Process	**Description**
Create, modify, or delete data integrity rule	This process creates an instance of a data integrity that can then be assigned to wherever it is used.
Accomplish data integrity rule assignment	This process assigns a data integrity rule to one or more contexts.
Accomplish data integrity rule interrelationship	This process creates interrelationships among data integrity rules.

6.2.10 Data Interoperability Projects

The purpose of a Data Interoperability Project, depicted in Figure 19, is to accomplish some identified significant activity within the scope of accomplishing data interoperability across the enterprise. Data Interoperability Projects answer the questions:

- What activities are currently underway in the accomplishment of some significant aspect of achieving an interoperable data environment?
- What are the work plans, deliverables, organizations, time lines, costs, and current states of data interoperability projects?
- What are the interrelationships among data interoperability projects in regards to processes being performed, products built, and staff or organizations employed or affected?
- What data interoperability products are going to be completed on what time line and how will these completed products affect other products in other projects?

Data Interoperability Projects	
Process	**Description**
Create, modify, or delete data interoperability project	This process creates an instance of a data interoperability project.

Data Interoperability Projects	
Process	**Description**
Create work plans for each project	This process creates and/or assigns an existing work plan from the work plans templates to a data interoperability project.
Create deliverables for each project	This process creates and/or assigns an existing deliverable specification from the deliverables templates to a data interoperability project.
Create organization and staff assignments for each project	This process identifies, determines availability, and secures agreements for the assignment of organizations and staff to projects, tasks, and deliverables within projects.
Record the accomplishment of project work	This process records the work accomplished, milestones reached, and acceptable deliverables created from within projects.
Re-engineer projects as needed to achieve interoperable data environments	This process causes the re-engineering of projects as may be needed to reflect changes in priorities, time-lines, monies, and accomplishments by other projects.

6.3 Information Systems Architecture Metadata Management

Business Information Systems, depicted in Figure 12, Metadata enables the identification and interrelationship of various business information systems and their components to the application views that reference the databases upon which the business information systems act, and the business events that act as the triggers for the systems. Through these relationships the various business events along with their business cycles and calendars can be listed to then know of processing loads for each business information system.

6.3.1 Information Systems Models

A Business Information System, depicted in Figure 12, is a computer-based information system. It is known by its characteristics, its operation cycles (business event and calendar), subordinate business information systems, employed databases, views, and associated resource life cycle nodes.

Information Systems Models	
Process	**Description**
Create, modify or delete business information system levels.	This process creates a characteristic of an information system, Level, that can be used to classify collections of business information systems. Examples are control, management, and operational.
Create, modify or delete construction methods.	This process creates a characteristic of an information system, Construction Method, that can be used to classify collections of business information systems. Examples are custom, code generator, or COTS (commercial off the shelf).
Create, modify or delete status	This process creates a characteristic of an information system, Status, that can be used to classify collections of business information systems. Examples are development, maintenance, and production.
Create, modify or delete application types	This process creates a characteristic of an information system, Application Types, that can be used to classify collections of business information systems. Examples are management information systems, operational control systems, etc.
Create, modify or delete programming language	This process creates a characteristic of an information system, Programming Language, that can be used to classify collections of business information systems. Examples are COBOL, Fortran, 4GL, or some other programming language environment.

Information Systems Models	
Process	**Description**
Create, modify or delete environment type	This process creates a characteristic of an information system, Environment Type, that can be used to classify collections of business information systems. Examples are mainframe, server, or desktop.
Create, modify or delete predominant user class	This process creates a characteristic of an information system, Predominant User Class, that can be used to classify collections of business information systems. Examples are Executive, middle management, and line management.
Create, modify or delete DBMS environment	This process creates a characteristic of an information system, DBMS Environment, that can be used to classify collections of business information systems. Examples are Single brand, Multi-brand.
Create, modify or delete business information system	This process creates a business information system.
Accomplish association between business information system and resource life cycle node.	This process creates an association between an information system and a resource life cycle node.
Accomplish association between business information system and business event.	This process creates an association between an information system and a business event.
Accomplish association between business information system and view.	This process creates an association between an information system and a view.
Accomplish association between business information system and database object information system.	This process creates an association between an information system and a database object information system.

6.3.2 Resource Life Cycle Models

Resources and Life Cycles, depicted in Figure 20, metadata enable the identification of the various resources within the enterprise that collectively represent either the infrastructure or an external product set of the enterprise. Infrastructure resources include for example, staff, facilities, contracts, finance, and the like. External products include manufactured products, services to customers, and the like. Each resource is then defined in terms of its life cycle. Resource life cycle nodes from different life cycles are interrelated to show enterprise-based interdependencies. Databases and Business information systems, and information needs are then interrelated to each life cycle node. Collectively the fully attributed resource life cycles enable the enterprise to view its complete operation in terms of its essential resources that define its very existence.

Resource Live Cycles	
Process	**Description**
Create, modify or delete Resource Type	This process creates a resource type that, in turn, is used to classify collections of resources.
Create, modify or delete Resource	This process creates a resource within the context of a resource type. Resources may be hierarchical.
Create, modify or delete Resource Life Cycle Node Structure Type	This process creates various classifications of resource life cycle structures that are then used to identify specific collections of records in resource life cycle structures.
Create, modify or delete Resource Life Cycle Node Structure	This process creates a relationship between two resource life cycle nodes from two different resources.
Create, modify or delete Resource Life Cycle Node	This process creates a resource life cycle node within the context of a resource.
Accomplish Resource Life Cycle Node Business Information Systems Assignments	This process assigns one or more business information systems to a resource life cycle node.

Resource Live Cycles	
Process	**Description**
Accomplish Resource Life Cycle Node Database Object Assignments	This process assigns one or more database objects to a resource life cycle node.
Accomplish Resource Life Cycle Node Information Need Assignments	This process assigns one or more information needs to a resource life cycle node.
Accomplish Resource Life Cycle Node Mission Assignments	This process assigns one or more missions to a resource life cycle node.

6.3.3 Business Event Models

Business Events metadata, depicted in Figure 12, enables the identification and interrelationship of the various business events that occur within the accomplishment of functions and then for each business event the various collections of business information systems that are executed in support of that particular business event.

Business event calendars and business cycle components enable the creation and interrelationship of the various business calendars and business cycles that govern the accomplishment of business information systems.

Business Events	
Process	**Description**
Create, modify or delete Business Event Cycle	This process creates specific instances of business event cycles that are then gathered into assemblies for use in properly representing business events. Examples include: End of School cycle, Back to School Cycle, Vacation Cycle, and a Holiday Cycle

Business Events	
Process	**Description**
Create, modify or delete Business Events	This process creates specific business events and represents their associated business functions and business information systems as well as associating business events within proper business event cycles and business event calendars.
Create, modify or delete Calendar Cycle	This process creates specific instances of business event calendar cycles that are gathered into assemblies for use in properly representing business events.
Create, modify or delete Business Event Cycle Structures	This process creates specific instances of assemblies of business event cycles.
Create, modify or delete Business Event Cycle Structure Types	This process creates various classifications of business event cycles that are used to identify specific collections of records in Business Event Cycle Structures
Create, modify or delete Business Information System Level	This process creates a level-based classification schema for categorizing business information systems. This level is assigned to each business information system.
Create, modify or delete Business Information System View Role	This process causes the creation, modification, and/or deletion of a particular input or output role to a business information system view role.
Create, modify or delete Calendar Cycle Structures	This process creates specific instances of assemblies of business event calendar cycles.
Create, modify or delete Calendar Cycle Structure Types	This process creates various classifications of business event cycles that are used to identify specific collections of records in Business Event Calendar Cycle Structures
Create, modify or delete Application Types	This process creates an application type that is employed to distinguish different business information systems.

Business Events	
Process	**Description**
Create, modify or delete Business Information System	This process creates the name and specification of a business information system. Business information systems may be hierarchically organized.
Create, modify or delete DBMS Environment Types	This process creates a DBMS Environment type that is employed to distinguish different business information systems.
Create, modify or delete Predominant User Type	This process creates a predominant user type that is employed to distinguish different business information systems.
Create, modify or delete [Application] Environment Types	This process creates an application environment type that is employed to distinguish different business information systems.
Accomplish Business Information System Database Object Assignments	This process assigns various business information systems to database objects.
Accomplish Business Information System View Assignment	This process assigns various views to business information systems and categorizes each view as either an input view or an output view.

6.4 Data Architecture Metadata Management

The data element and semantics, depicted in Figure 14, component is engineered to capture data element specifications. That is, context independent business fact semantic templates. Fully supporting data elements are semantic hierarchies, conceptual value domains, value domains, data element classifications, data element concepts, compound data elements, and derived data elements.

Collectively, these data element semantics support the complete understanding of these context independent business fact templates so that they can be efficiently and effectively employed as attributes within entities of specified data models and as columns within tables of implemented data models.

6.4.1 Meta Category Models

Meta Category Value models , depicted in Figure 14, support the creation of the semantics of data items, that is, data element concepts, data elements, attributes, and columns are both inherited and assigned. For example, a data element concept inherits its semantics from Concepts and Conceptual Value Domain; a data element inherits its semantics from a data element concept, its business domain and a value domain; and attributes inherit their semantics from their host entities and data elements.

In addition to this method of semantic inheritance, meta category values, for example geography, and precision serve to additionally modify the semantics of data element concepts, data elements, attributes or columns. Meta category values are either prefix semantics or suffix semantics. Prefix meta category values appear prior to the data item's common business name. Suffix meta category values appear at after the data item's common business name. The order of appearance is not arbitrary or able to be change by an end-user. The order is specified by the metadata administrator within the table and meta category type. If the geographic meta category value type's sequence number is 2 and the temporal meta category value type's is 3, then regardless of the sequence of tagging, geographic meta category values will always be prefixed into the data item's constructed name before those for the temporal meta category value type.

Once the meta category values are assigned, for example, to the data element concept, or the data element, etc., the process automatically constructs the data item's name.

Meta Category Values	
Process	**Description**
Create, modify or delete Data Element Concept Meta Category Values	This process enables the allocation of meta category values to a data element concept. Only one meta category value from each meta category value type is allowed to be assigned. As a meta category value is assigned, if there are any meta category values already assigned to a descendant data element, attribute, or column, then the assigned meta category values are evaluated to ensure that there are no semantic conflicts.
Create, modify or delete Data	This process enables the allocation of meta category

Meta Category Values	
Process	**Description**
Element Meta Category Values	values to a data element. Only one meta category value from each meta category value type is allowed to be assigned. As a meta category value is assigned, if there are any meta category values already assigned either to a parent data element concept, or to a descendant attribute or column, then the assigned meta category values are evaluated to ensure that there are no semantic conflicts.
Create, modify or delete Meta Category Value	This process creates a meta category value.
Create, modify or delete Meta Category Value Type	This process creates a meta category value type.
Create, modify or delete Meta Category Value Type Class	This process creates a meta category value type class
Reallocate Meta Category Value Types	This process causes a change in the existing allocation of one or more meta category value types to a different meta category value type.
Reallocate Meta Category Values	This process causes a change in the existing allocation of one or more meta category values to a different meta category value.
Remove Data Element Concept Meta Category Value Assignments	This process removes the meta category value assignments from a data element concept.
Remove Data Element Meta Category Value Assignments	This process removes the meta category value assignments from a data element.

6.4.2 Concept Models

Concepts , depicted in Figure 14, represent the sets of ideas, abstractions, or even things in the real world that are identified with explicit boundaries and meaning and whose properties and behavior follow the same rules. Concepts are used as a basis for specifying the concepts of data elements, that is, data element concepts.

Concepts	
Process	**Description**
Create, modify or delete Concept Structure Types	This process creates various classifications of concepts that are used to identify specific collections of records in concept structures
Create, modify or delete Concept Structures	This process creates specific instances of assemblies of concepts.
Create, modify or delete Concepts	This process creates an instance of concept
Accomplish Data Element Concepts to Concept Reassignments	This process causes a change in the existing assignment of one or more data element concepts to one concept.
Accomplish Data Elements to a Compound Data Element Assignments	This process assigns one or more data elements to a compound data element.
Promote Data Element Concept to Concept	This process promotes a data element concept to be a concept. The existing data element concept is related to the newly created concept.

6.4.3 Conceptual Value Domain Models

Conceptual Value Domains, depicted in Figure 14, are collections of meanings that apply to both value domains and also data element concepts. A data element concept can have only one conceptual value domain. A conceptual value domain may be composed of other conceptual value domains or may be a member (component) of a larger conceptual value domain. Conceptual value domains may also be interrelated in a bill-of-materials network fashion to fully support the underlying concepts of data element domains and value domains.

Conceptual value domains also encompass value domains. If, for example, the conceptual value domain relates to the notion of countries, then the corresponding value domain for countries would relate to the enumerated set of countries that might be specified in ISO standard 3166, Codes for the representation of names of countries.

Conceptual Value Domain	
Process	**Description**
Create, modify or delete Conceptual Value Domain Structure Types	This process creates various classifications of conceptual value domains that are used to identify specific collections of records in conceptual value domain structures
Create, modify or delete Conceptual Value Domain Structures	This process creates specific instances of assemblies of conceptual value domains.
Create, modify or delete Conceptual Value Domains	This process creates a conceptual value domain.
Accomplish Data Element Concepts to Conceptual Value Domain Reassignments	This process causes a change in the existing assignment of one or more data element concepts to one conceptual value domain.
Accomplish Value Domain to Conceptual Value Domain Reassignments	This process enables the reassignment of value domains to a conceptual value domain. Only one value domain is allowed to be assigned. As a value domain is assigned if there are any value domains already assigned to a descendant data element concept, data element, attribute, column, or DBMS column, then the assigned value domains are evaluated to ensure that there are no conflicts.

6.4.4 Data Element Concept Models

Data element concepts, depicted in Figure 14, represent the joining of concepts and conceptual value domains. Data element concepts are a key component for the development of data elements. The components of the meta entities that comprise data element concepts focus on semantics rather than on any internal or external physical representation.

Data element concepts also allow for a full bill-of-materials structure supporting both network and hierarchical data element concepts in support of data element specifications.

Data Element Concepts	
Process	**Description**
Create, modify or delete Data Element Concept	This process creates a specific instance of a data element concept
Create, modify or delete Data Element Concept Structure Types	This process creates various classifications of data element concepts that are used to identify specific collections of records in data element concept structures
Create, modify or delete Data Element Concept Structures	This process creates specific instances of assemblies of data element concepts.
Accomplish Data Element Concepts to Concept Reassignments	This process causes a change in the existing assignment of one or more data element concepts to one concept.
Accomplish Data Element Concepts to Conceptual Value Domain Reassignments	This process causes a change in the existing assignment of one or more data element concepts to one conceptual value domain.
Accomplish Data Elements to Data Element Concept Reassignments	This process causes a change in the existing assignment of one or more data elements to one data element concept.
Promote Data Element Concept to Concept	This process promotes a data element concept to be a concept. The existing data element concept is related to the newly created concept.
Promote Data Elements to Data Element Concept	This process promotes a data element to be a data element concept. The meta category values and value domains are removed from the data element and allocated to the newly created data element concept. The data element concept is assigned to the "unknown" conceptual value domain and the "unknown" concept.
Remove Data Element Concept	This process removes the meta category value

Data Element Concepts	
Process	**Description**
Meta Category Value Assignments	assignments from a data element concept.

6.4.5 Value Domain Models

Value Domains, depicted in Figure 14, are to provide specific descriptions about the allowed values associated with one or more value domains. Value domains that are assignable to a data element must be in the same conceptual domain family as is the data element's data element concept. Value domains assigned to an attribute of an entity within the specified data model, or column within a table of the implemented data model or a DBMS column within a DBMS table of the operational data model must all be hierarchically related

Value Domains	
Process	**Description**
Create, modify or delete Value Domain Structure Types	This process creates various classifications of value domain structures that are used to identify specific collections of records in value domain structures
Create, modify or delete Value Domain Structures	This process creates specific instances of assemblies of value domain structures.
Create, modify or delete Value Domain Value Data Types	This process creates data types that control value domain values. Value domain data types have descendent SQL data types and DBMS data types.
Create, modify or delete Value Domain Value Structure Types	This process creates various classifications of value domain value structures that are used to identify specific collections of records in value domain value structures
Create, modify or delete Value Domain Value Structures	This process creates specific instances of assemblies of value domain value structures.
Create, modify or delete Value	This process creates one or more value domain

Value Domains	
Process	**Description**
Domain Values	values for any given value domain.
Create, modify or delete Value Domains	This process creates one or more value domains for a particular conceptual value domain.
Accomplish Data Elements to Value Domains Reassignments	This process enables the reassignment of value domains to a data element. Only one value domain is allowed to be assigned. As a value domain is assigned if there are any value domains already assigned to a parent data element concept, or a descendant, attribute, column, or DBMS column, then the assigned value domains are evaluated to ensure that there are no conflicts.
Accomplish Value Domain to Conceptual Value Domain Reassignments	This process enables the reassignment of value domains to a conceptual value domain. Only one value domain is allowed to be assigned. As a value domain is assigned if there are any value domains already assigned to a descendant data element concept, data element, attribute, column, or DBMS column, then the assigned value domains are evaluated to ensure that there are no conflicts.
Accomplish Value Domain Value to Value Domain Reassignments	This process causes a change in the existing assignment of one or more value domain values to one value domain.

6.4.6 Data Element Models

Data Elements, depicted in Figure 14, represent the inheritable semantics for attributes of entities, and columns of tables. A data element is a context independent (i.e., entity and/or table independent) business fact semantic template. It is well-accepted practice that the quantity of data elements is a small fraction of the quantity of attributes and/or columns. For example, if an enterprise has 100 databases and each has 200 tables, and each table has 10 columns then there are 200,000 columns. In this example, if, as is commonly true, a data element's semantics is reused 50 or more times over all the database tables then there are only 4,000 data elements. Supporting data elements are multiple higher levels of data element metadata including concepts, conceptual value domains, data element concepts, value domains and sets of value domain values. The value sets can be directly allocated to DBMS schema columns as constraints. Often, they might form the rows of data within the reference data database.

The data element model also contains compound and derived data elements. A compound data element is a special data element that contains multiple data elements that ultimately represent a value might be for example, a Telephone Number with the contained data elements of Country Code, Area Code, Exchange, Number, and possibly extension. A derived data element is another specialized data element where its value is calculated or derived through some process. An example is age. The value, in years, would be ("Today" minus Birthdate)/365.5, or Total Department Salary where the value is calculated by summing the values from all employee salaries.

Data Elements	
Process	**Description**
Create, modify or delete Compound Data Element Structure Types	This process creates various classifications of compound data elements that are used to identify specific collections of records in compound data element structures
Create, modify or delete Compound Data Element Structures	This process creates specific instances of assemblies of compound data elements.
Create, modify or delete Compound Data Elements	This process creates a compound data element that serves as the collective for the assigned data elements.
Create, modify or delete Data Element Classification	This process creates a data element classification.
Create, modify or delete Data Element Classification Structure Types	This process creates various classifications of data element classifications that are used to identify specific collections of records in data element classification structures
Create, modify or delete Data Element Classification	This process creates specific instances of assemblies of data element classifications.

Data Elements	
Process	**Description**
Structures	
Create, modify or delete Data Elements	This process creates a data element.
Create, modify or delete Derived Data Elements	This process creates a derived data element.
Accomplish Data Element Classifications to Data Element Assignments	This process assigns one or more data element classifications to a data element.
Accomplish Data Elements to a Compound Data Element Assignments	This process assigns one or more data elements to a compound data element.
Accomplish Data Elements to Business Domain Reassignments	This process causes a change in the existing assignment of one or more data elements to one business domain.
Accomplish Data Elements to Data Element Concept Reassignments	This process causes a change in the existing assignment of one or more data elements to one data element concept.
Accomplish Data Elements to Value Domains Reassignments	This process enables the reassignment of value domains to a data element. Only one value domain is allowed to be assigned. As a value domain is assigned if there are any value domains already assigned to a parent data element concept, or a descendant, attribute, column, or DBMS column, then the assigned value domains are evaluated to ensure that there are no conflicts.
Accomplish Derived Data Elements to Compound Data Element Assignments	This process assigns one or more derived data elements to a compound data element.
Accomplish Derived Data Elements to Data Element Assignments	This process assigns one or more data elements to a derived data element.

Data Elements	
Process	**Description**
Promote Data Elements to Data Element Concept	This process promotes a data element to be a data element concept. The meta category values and value domains are removed from the data element and allocated to the newly created data element concept. The data element concept is assigned to the "unknown" conceptual value domain and the "unknown" concept.
Reallocate Business Domains	This process causes a change in the existing allocation of one or more business domains to a different business domain.

6.4.7 Data Element Classification Models

Data element classifications, depicted in Figure 14, are used to manage classification schemes and the classification scheme items that are in the classification schemes. A classification scheme may be a taxonomy, a network, an ontology, or any other system for systematizing where the categories are mutually exclusive. The classification may also be just a list of controlled vocabulary of property words (or terms). The list might be taken from the "leaf level" of taxonomy.

The classification scheme allows for a full bill-of-materials structure supporting both network and hierarchical classification schemes in support of an administered item. Administered items relate to one or more data elements.

Data Element Classifications	
Process	**Description**
Create, modify or delete Data Element Classification	This process creates a data element classification.
Create, modify or delete Data Element Classification Structure Types	This process creates various classifications of data element classifications that are used to identify specific collections of records in data element classification structures

Data Element Classifications	
Process	**Description**
Create, modify or delete Data Element Classification Structures	This process creates specific instances of assemblies of data element classifications.
Accomplish Data Element Classifications to Data Element Assignments	This process assigns one or more data element classifications to a data element.

6.5 Reverse Engineering Model Metadata Management

The overall process of reverse engineering consists of starting with existing database schemas and performing the following processes:

- Importing and processing operational data models.
- Promoting one operational data model to be an implemented data model and reconciling all the operational data models to the created implemented data model.
- Promoting implemented data model clusters to make sets of specified data models of a single subject area each, and reconciling the implemented data model to the created specified data models.
- Promoting either from the implemented data model or the specified data model columns or attributes to create data elements.

6.5.1 Operational Data Models.

The operational data model , depicted in Figure 18, is the representation of an implemented database that may have been subsetted and/or transformed to serve the particular needs of a DBMS, or performance requirement. Operational databases are mapped back to their "parent" implemented models through a column (Implemented Data Model) to DBMS column (Operational Data Model) mapping. Operational Data Models are "hosts" to the various SQL views that in turn act as intermediaries to the business information systems that access the databases. There may be multiple transformations of a particular implemented database, and each exists and is mapped back to its "parent" implemented database.

The process of discovering the legacy metadata involves identifying and cataloguing all the existing database schemas within running applications. Database schemas should be used in preference to ER modeler data models as they seldom match the actual running database schemas. For the same reason, COBOL based file structures, or where enforced, COPYLIBS, are employed for non-database file structures.

The discovered metadata is transformed to SQL DDL. Metadata scrapers are employed to capture non data model based metadata such as definitions. These are all imported. To start, the first applications that should be discovered and imported are those that represent the backbone and rib-cage (HR, Finance, Inventory Customer Management, Sales) applications. Within these, pick the most commonly used schemas across the enterprise that support the backbone and rib-cage applications. Then finally, pick the subset of schemas that have the most commonly used tables (note commonly used is different from exactly the same as). Once a set of where-used and frequency-used matrices are employed to identify the most commonly used schemas and tables. The vast majority of enterprise data can be imported into the Operational Data Model layer.

Operational Data Model	
Process	**Description**
Create DBMS Columns	This process creates a DBMS column.
Create, modify or delete Candidate Key Definition	This process creates a candidate key.
Create, modify or delete DBMS schema	This process creates a candidate key.
Create, modify or delete DBMS tables	This process creates a candidate key.
Create, modify or delete Foreign Keys	This process creates a foreign key. The target DBMS table is identified and then the source primary key is identified. Then, the referential actions and other

Operational Data Model	
Process	**Description**
	SQL necessary information are entered. The foreign key name is automatically created and consists of the parent DBMS table name, must/may depending on chosen referential actions, an action word, and the child DBMS table name.
Create, modify or delete Primary Key Definition	This process creates a primary key.
Create, modify or delete Secondary Key Definition	This process creates a secondary key.
Accomplish DBMS Column to DBMS Table Reassignment	This process reassigns a DBMS column from one DBMS table to another.
Accomplish DBMS Columns to Column Reassignment	This process causes a change in the existing assignment of one or more DBMS columns to one DBMS column.
Accomplish DBMS Columns to DBMS Data Type Reassignment	This process causes a change in the existing assignment of a DBMS column's data type to a different DBMS data type.
Accomplish DBMS Tables to DBMS Schema Reassignment	This process causes a change in the existing assignment of a DBMS table from one DBMS schema to another DBMS Schema.
Accomplish DBMS Tables to DBMS Table Reassignment	This process causes a change in the sub/super type relationship among DBMS tables within a given DBMS schema. If a DBMS table's primary key is a foreign key in another table, then the DBMS table cannot be reassigned.
Allocate DBMS columns to the Candidate Key	This process assigns one or more columns to a candidate key.
Allocate DBMS columns to the Primary Key	This process assigns one or more columns to a primary key.
Allocate DBMS columns to the Secondary Key	This process assigns one or more columns to a secondary key.

Operational Data Model	
Process	**Description**
Export SQL DDL	This process traverses the complete set of DBMS tables, DBMS columns, and keys for a given DBMS schema and formulates a set of SQL DDL that completely represents the DBMS schema-based data model.
Import Column from Implemented Data Model	This process causes the importation of a single column of a table from a schema in the implemented data model to be imported into a DBMS table of a DBMS schema of the operational data model.
Import SQL DDL	This process imports a full stream of SQL DDL and creates a full set of DBMS tables, DBMS columns, and keys for the selected DBMS schema.
Import Table Set from Implemented Data Model	This process imports a set of tables from the implemented data model that are all associated with one schema. All associated keys and DBMS columns are made. Relationships from the newly created DBMS table to the implemented data model tables are also created.
Import Table Tree from Implemented Data Model	This process imports a set of interrelated tables from the implemented data model. All associated keys and DBMS columns are made. Relationships from the newly created DBMS tables to the implemented data model tables are also created.
Maintain DBMS Column Value Domains	This process enables the allocation of a value domain to a DBMS column. Only one value domain is allowed to be assigned. As a value domain is assigned, if there are any value domains already assigned either to a parent column, data element, data element parent data element concept, then the assigned value domains are evaluated to ensure that there are no value domain hierarchy conflicts.
Promote DBMS Table to Implemented Data Model	This process promotes an attribute to be a data element. The meta category values and value domains are removed from the attribute and

Operational Data Model	
Process	**Description**
	allocated to the newly created data element. The data element is assigned to the "unknown" conceptual value domain and the "unknown" data element concept.
Promote Operational Data Model to Implemented Data Model	This process promotes an entire operational data model to be an implemented data model. Created is the schema (from the DBMS schema), all tables, columns and all keys. Relationships between the newly create implemented data model table columns and the operational data model table columns are automatically created.
Remove DBMS Table Column to Column Assignments	This process removes the relationships between a complete set of DBMS columns of a DBMS table and their corresponding columns.
Report DBMS Column Data Hierarchies	This process presents a DBMS column, its associated column, attributes, data elements, data element concepts and concepts. For each the appropriate subject, entity, schema, table, DBMS schema, and DBMS table are also shown.

6.5.2 Implemented Data Models

An Implemented Data Model, depicted in Figure 15, is a collection of tables, columns, and relationships bounded by a schema. Implemented Data Models are built as a precursor to the design of the database object classes that operate to maintain data integrity and value transformations. It is common to build an implemented database within the scope of a reasonably large mission hierarchy such as human resources, finance, facilities, customers, sales management, distribution, or inventory. Database object classes are transformed through business information systems.

Implemented databases commonly conform to particular database architecture classes such as original data collection, information exchange data model, data warehouses, data marts, and reference data databases. Implemented database table columns should all be derived from attributes of entities from one or more Specified Data Models. Implemented Data Models also act as the "parent" of one or more Operational Data Models. Implemented Data Models can be created inductively through Operational Data Model imports that exist within a certain scope, and then, through the promotion of a single Operational Data Model, to the Implemented Data Model level. Then, data modeling activities would occur to expand the scope of the Implemented Data Model to be that of the union of all the Operational Data Models.

Operational databases commonly represent the database required to fit an operational performance demand. Additionally, if there are multiple operational databases in the same functional area there will be some common entities. The design goal of the implemented database is to have the union of all Operational Data Model databases. The overall process to achieve this is to:

- Promote to the most comprehensive Operational Data Model to the Implemented data Model layer

- Re-engineer the Implemented Data Model layer
  - Promote other Operational Data Model tables to the Implemented Data Model to complete the union Implemented Data Model
  - Reassign tables within tables (sub-typing)
  - Reassign column semantics
  - Conform column names to table scope
  - Reassign columns to different tables
  - Reassign columns to different data elements

When this is accomplished, there will likely be a different data model at the Implemented Data Model level than exists at the Operational Data Model level. That is quite acceptable as the Implemented Data Model is to both be completely "logical" and also the union of all related Operational Data Models. In the case of an Information Exchange Data Model implemented data model, it may only be the intersection of all shared data. It is however critical that every difference be reconcilable in either of the following two ways. First, the Operational Data Model is a proper subset of the Implemented Data Model, or second, that the difference between an implemented and Operational Data Model can be represented by one or more nested SQL select statements. In short, the differences must all be semantically coherent.

Implemented Data Model	
Process	**Description**
Create Many Columns	This process causes the creation of many columns by tagging one data element and a set of tables. As each column is created, it is assigned to the table and also to the data element upon which its semantics are based. The column is also assigned to the "unknown" attribute.
Create, modify or delete Allocation of Columns to the Candidate Key	This process allocates one or more columns to a candidate key.
Create, modify or delete Allocation of Columns to the Primary Key	This process allocates one or more columns to a primary key.
Create, modify or delete Candidate Key	This process creates a candidate key within a specific table. A sub-table cannot have a candidate key.
Create, modify or delete Foreign Keys	This process creates a foreign key. The target table is identified, then the source primary key is identified. Then the referential actions and other SQL necessary information are entered. The foreign key name is automatically created and consists of the parent table name, must/may depending on chosen referential actions, an action word, and the child table name.
Create, modify or delete Primary Key	This process creates a primary key within a specific table. A sub-table cannot have a primary key.
Create, modify or delete Schema	This process creates a schema.
Create, modify or delete Tables	This process creates a table
Create One Column	This process causes the creation of one column by tagging one data element and one table. As the column is created, it is assigned to the table and also to the data element upon which its semantics is based.

Implemented Data Model	
Process	**Description**
Create SQL Data Types	This process creates an SQL data type and enables it to be related to a value domain data type.
Accomplish Assign Columns to Attribute Reassignments	This process causes a change in the existing assignment of one or more columns to one attribute. If there is a conflict between the data element that is already assigned to the column and the data element assigned to the attribute, then the column is assigned to the unknown data element.
Accomplish Assign Columns to Column Reassignments	This process causes a change in the existing assignment of one or more columns to one column.
Accomplish Assign Columns to Data Elements Reassignments	This process causes a change in the existing assignment of one or more columns to one data element.
Accomplish Assign Columns to SQL Data Types Reassignments	This process causes a change in the existing assignment of one or more column SQL data type to a different SQL data type.
Accomplish Columns to Table Reassignments	This process causes a change in the existing assignment of one or more columns to a different table. If the column is part of any type of key, the reassignment is rejected.
Accomplish Tables to Schema Reassignments	This process causes a change in the existing assignment of one or more tables to one Schema.
Accomplish Tables to Tables Reassignments	This process causes a change in the sub/super type relationship among tables within a given schema.
Export SQL DDL	This process traverses the complete set of tables, columns, and keys for a given schema and formulates a set of SQL DDL that completely represents the schema-based data model.

Implemented Data Model	
Process	**Description**
Import Attribute from Specified Data Model	This process causes the importation of a single attribute of an entity from a subject in the specified data model to be imported into a table of a schema of the implemented data model.
Import Entity Set from Specified Data Model	This process imports a set of entities from the specified data model that are all associated with one subject. All associated keys and columns are made. Relationships from the newly created table to the specified data model entities are also created.
Import Entity Tree from Specified Data Model	This process imports a set of interrelated entities from the specified data model. All associated keys and columns are made. Relationships from the newly created table to the specified data model entities are also created.
Import SQL DDL	This process imports a full stream of SQL DDL and creates a full set of tables, columns, and keys for the selected schema.
Maintain Column Meta Category Values	This process enables the allocation of meta category values to a column. Only one meta category value from each meta category value type is allowed to be assigned. As a meta category value is assigned, if there are any meta category values already assigned either to a parent data element, attribute, or data element concept, then the assigned meta category values are evaluated to ensure that there are no semantic conflicts.
Maintain Column Value Domains	This process enables the allocation of value domains to a column. Only one value domain is allowed to be assigned. As a value domain is assigned if there are any value domains already assigned either to a parent data element, data element parent data element concept, or to a descendant DBMS column, the assigned attribute value domains are evaluated to ensure that there are no value domain hierarchy

Implemented Data Model	
Process	**Description**
	conflicts.
Maintain Columns	This process provides update support for a column.
Promote Column to Data Element	This process promotes a column to be a data element. The meta category values and value domains are removed from the column and are allocated to the newly created data element. The data element is assigned to the "unknown" conceptual value domain and the "unknown" data element concept.
Promote Implemented Data Model Table to Specified Data Model Entity	This process promotes an implemented data model table to be a specified data model entity within an existing subject. Created are all the associated attributes and as appropriate primary keys, and candidate keys. Relationships between the newly create specified data model entity attributes and the implemented data model table columns are automatically created.
Promote Implemented Data Model to Specified Data Model	This process promotes an entire implemented data model to be a specified data model. Created is the subject (from the schema), all entities, attributes and all keys. Relationships between the newly create specified data model entity attributes and the implemented data model table columns are automatically created.
Remove Column Attribute Assignments	This process removes the relationships between a complete set of columns of a table and their corresponding attributes.
Remove Column Meta Category Values	This process removes meta category value assignments from a column.

Implemented Data Model	
Process	**Description**
Report Column Data Hierarchies	This process presents a column, its associated data element, data element concept, conceptual value domain and concept, as well as its associated DBMS columns. For each appropriate subject, entity, schema, table, DBMS schema, and DBMS table are also shown.

6.5.3 Data Element Model

It has been clearly shown that across a wide spectrum of databases within an enterprise that data elements, depicted in Figure 14, are used over and over. Thus, a data element is actually the semantic template for attributes of entities or columns of tables. During the process of Implemented Data Model development and/or Specified Data Model development data elements are often discovered. When discovered they are created through a promotion process. Once promoted, the upper levels of data element metadata should be created.

Data Elements	
Process	**Description**
Create, modify or delete Compound Data Element Structure Types	This process creates various classifications of compound data elements that are used to identify specific collections of records in compound data element structures
Create, modify or delete Compound Data Element Structures	This process creates specific instances of assemblies of compound data elements.
Create, modify or delete Compound Data Elements	This process creates a compound data element that services as the collective for the assigned data elements.
Create, modify or delete Data Element Classification	This process creates a data element classification.

Data Elements	
Process	**Description**
Create, modify or delete Data Element Classification Structure Types	This process creates various classifications of data element classifications that are used to identify specific collections of records in data element classification structures
Create, modify or delete Data Element Classification Structures	This process creates specific instances of assemblies of data element classifications.
Create, modify or delete Data Elements	This process creates a data element.
Create, modify or delete Derived Data Elements	This process creates a derived data element.
Accomplish Data Element Classifications to Data Element Assignments	This process assigns one or more data element classifications to a data element.
Accomplish Data Elements to a Compound Data Element Assignments	This process assigns one or more data elements to a compound data element.
Accomplish Data Elements to Business Domain Reassignments	This process causes a change in the existing assignment of one or more data elements to one business domain.
Accomplish Data Elements to Data Element Concept Reassignments	This process causes a change in the existing assignment of one or more data elements to one data element concept.
Accomplish Data Elements to Value Domains Reassignments	This process enables the reassignment of value domains to a data element. Only one value domain is allowed to be assigned. As a value domain is assigned if there are any value domains already assigned to a parent data element concept, or a descendant, attribute, column, or DBMS column, then the assigned value domains are evaluated to ensure that there are no conflicts.

Data Elements	
Process	**Description**
Accomplish Derived Data Elements to Compound Data Element Assignments	This process assigns one or more derived data elements to a compound data element.
Accomplish Derived Data Elements to Data Element Assignments	This process assigns one or more data elements to a derived data element.
Promote Data Elements to Data Element Concept	This process promotes a data element to be a data element concept. The meta category values and value domains are removed from the data element and allocated to the newly created data element concept. The data element concept is assigned to the "unknown" conceptual value domain and the "unknown" concept.
Reallocate Business Domains	This process causes a change in the existing allocation of one or more business domains to a different business domain.

6.5.4 Specified Data Models

Specified Data Models, depicted in Figure 21, are collections of entities, attributes and relationships that can be used as data model templates for implemented databases. Each entity within a specified model should be the data specification of a well-defined policy within the enterprise. A collection of entities within a particular subject should conform to a larger and more complex policy.

An implemented database is bounded by schema and is intended to be implemented by a particular DBMS that arises from an operational database that collects, stores, and maintains actual business data. In contrast, the specified database's entities are bounded only by the subject within which it is defined. In the construction of an Implemented Data Model, one or more entities may contribute attributes to form the column of the Implemented Data Model's tables.

Specified Data Models enable the creation of standard data structures that when employed in an Implemented Data Model ensure completeness, rigor, and the data standardization essential for data sharing. The semantics of attributes of a Specified Data Model entity are derived from ISO 11179 data elements. Specified Data Models can be created inductively through the promotion of a single Implemented Data Model to the Specified Data Model level. Then, data modeling activities would occur to break apart the Specified Data Model into individual subjects and collections of entities within those subjects. Entities can be interrelated across subject areas to represent Specified Data Model factoring.

The implemented data model should represent a completely third normal form database if its database architecture class is original data capture, reference data, or subject area databases. If the database architecture class is an Information Exchange Data Model or a data warehouse, the design may not be in third normal form. Regardless, the goal of this effort is to discover entity collections within narrow subject areas. These are most often related to a functionally cohesive community of interest. This goal stands in stark contrast to the goal of the Implemented Data Model that is, that it is the union of all related Operational Data Models or the data interoperability intersection of operational data models with an Implemented Exchange Data Model. It is likely that functional community of interest data models exist at the Specified Data Model level while the cross-functional data models exist at the Implemented and Operational Data Model levels. The overall process to achieve a Specified Data Model is to:

- Promote the most multi-subject area Implemented Data Model to Specified Data Model layer
- Re-engineer the Specified Data Model layer
    - Create new subjects as needed
    - Assign entities to different subjects
    - Reassign entities to within entities (sub-typing)
    - Reassign attributes' semantics
    - Conform attribute names to subject area scope
    - Reassign attributes to different entities
    - Reassign attributes to different data elements
    - Reallocate foreign keys to encapsulate subjects' foreign keys
        - Make a list of entities
        - Make a subject area based e-r model diagram
        - Delete unnecessary foreign keys from existing entities
        - Make new foreign keys where needed
        - Export to E-R diagramer to verify result
        - Recycle as necessary

When this is accomplished, there will likely be more Specified Data Models than Implemented Data Models. That is because an Implemented Data Model may consist of some tables that are in a one-to-one relationship with a Specified Data Model entity. Or multiple implemented model tables may represent a single entity where the attributes are essentially the same only named differently. For example, customer address, employee address, shipping address, or billing address. Finally, a given Implemented Data Model tables may contain attributes from an entity multiple times. For example in the customer entity there may be a person name attribute set for the customer key contact, billing contact, shipping contact, etc. This is not only acceptable but desired as the goal of the Specified Data Model effort is to create narrowly focused subject of highly third-normal form entity collections.

The collection of all entities across all the subjects represent the complete data requirements for the enterprise. Each set of subject area entities acts as a data model template for one or more Implemented Data Models. This enables (and requires) all the columns in all the tables of all Implemented Data Models to be mapped to Specified Data Model attributes.

Specified Data Model	
Process	**Description**
Create Many Attributes	This process causes the creation of many attributes by tagging one data element and a set of entities. As each attribute is created, it is assigned to the entity and also to the data element upon which its semantics is based.
Create modify or delete Candidate Key Definition	This process creates a candidate key within a specific entity. A sub-entity cannot have a candidate key.
Create, modify or delete Entities	This process creates an entity. When the entity is a sub-entity, then the parent entity is identified.
Create modify or delete Foreign Keys	This process creates a foreign key. The target entity is identified and the source primary key is identified. Then the referential actions and other SQL necessary information is entered. The foreign key name is automatically created and consists of the parent entity name, must/may depending on chosen referential actions, an action word, and the child

Specified Data Model	
Process	**Description**
	entity name.
Create modify or delete Primary Key Definition	This process creates a primary key within a specific entity. A sub-entity cannot have a primary key.
Create, modify or delete Subjects	This process creates a subject. When the subject is a sub-entity, then the parent subject is identified.
Create One Attribute	This process causes the creation of one attribute by tagging one data element and one entity. As the attribute is created, it is assigned to the entity and also to the data element upon which its semantics is based.
Accomplish Attributes to Data Element Reassignments	This process causes a change in the existing assignment of one or more entity attributes to a data element.
Accomplish Attributes to Entity Reassignments	This process causes a change in the existing assignment of one or more entity attributes to a different entity.
Accomplish Entities to Entity Reassignments	This process causes a change in the sub/super type relationship among entities within a given subject.
Accomplish Entity to Subject Reassignments	This process causes a change in the existing assignment of an entity to a given subject.
Accomplish Subject to Subject Reassignments	This process causes a change in the hierarchical relationship among subjects.
Allocate Attributes to the Candidate Key	This process causes the allocation of one or more attributes to a candidate key. No primary key attribute can be assigned to a candidate key.
Allocate Attributes to the Primary Key	This process causes the allocation of one or more attributes to a primary key. No candidate key attribute can be assigned to a primary key. A sub-entity cannot have a primary key.
Export SQL DDL	This process traverses the complete set of entities,

Specified Data Model	
Process	**Description**
	attributes, and keys for a given subject and formulates a set of SQL DDL that completely represents the subject-based data model. Since there are no data types in the specified data model CHAR 1 data types are created by default.
Import SQL DDL	This process imports a full stream of SQL DDL and creates a full set of entities, attributes, and keys for the selected subject.
Maintain Attribute Meta Category Values	This process enables the allocation of meta category values to an attribute. Only one meta category value from each meta category value type is allowed to be assigned. As a meta category value is assigned, if there are any meta category values already assigned either to a parent data element, data element parent data element concept, or to a descendant column, then the assigned meta category values are evaluated to ensure that there are no semantic conflicts.
Maintain Value domains	This process enables the creation of value domains that are assigned to data element concepts, data elements, attributes, columns, and DBMS columns.
Maintain Attributes	This process enables an update to all the attributes of an entity attribute.
Promote Attribute to Data Element	This process promotes an attribute to be a data element. The meta category values and value domains are removed from the attribute and allocated to the newly created data element. The data element is assigned to the "unknown" conceptual value domain and the "unknown" data element concept.
Remove Attribute Meta Category Value Assignments	This process removes the meta category values that are currently assigned to attributes.
Report Data Hierarchies	This process displays the completely interlinked set

Specified Data Model	
Process	**Description**
	of attributes within entities their assigned columns in tables, DBMS columns within DBMS tables, and their parent data element and data element concept.

6.5.5 Reverse Engineering Summary

In total, the ISO 11179 data elements, Specified Data Models, Implemented Data Models, and Operational Data Models all form a general hierarchy of business facts within the enterprise that enable a clear picture of where and how all business facts are defined and deployed.

6.6 Forward Engineering Model Metadata Management

The overall process of reverse engineering consists of starting with existing data elements and specified data models and performing the following processes:

- Importing collections of entities and/or partial entities and processing specified data models into implemented data models.
- Importing collections of tables from one or more schemas and/or partial tables and processing specified data models into operational implemented data models.
- Creating view data models for use by business information systems.

6.6.1 Implemented Data Model

Once the implemented data model, depicted in Figure 15, along with the specified, and data element models are built the process of forward engineering can begin for any derivative data model and/or any re-engineered data model. The process of creating a data model at the implemented level and the operational level is quite simple. It is simple because all the hard work has been previously accomplished.

Once an Operational Data Model is created, it can be immediately used in two different ways. First it can be exported to SQL DDL, and then, given to an SQL-BASED DBMS for schema development.

Implemented Data Model	
Process	**Description**
Create Many Columns	This process causes the creation of many columns by tagging one data element and a set of tables. As each column is created, it is assigned to the table and also to the data element upon which its semantics is based. The column is also assigned to the "unknown" attribute.
Create, modify or delete Allocation of Columns to the Candidate Key	This process allocates one or more columns to a candidate key.
Create, modify or delete Allocation of Columns to the Primary Key	This process allocates one or more columns to a primary key.
Create, modify or delete Candidate Key	This process creates a candidate key within a specific table. A sub-table cannot have a candidate key.
Create, modify or delete Foreign Keys	This process creates a foreign key. The target table is identified and the source primary key is identified. Then the referential actions and other SQL necessary information is entered. The foreign key name is automatically created and consists of the parent table name, must/may depending on chosen referential actions, an action word, and the child table name.
Create, modify or delete Primary Key	This process creates a primary key within a specific table. A sub-table cannot have a primary key.
Create, modify or delete Schema	This process creates a schema.
Create, modify or delete Tables	This process creates a table

Implemented Data Model	
Process	**Description**
Create One Column	This process causes the creation of one column by tagging one data element and one table. As the column is created, it is assigned to the table and also to the data element upon which its semantics is based.
Create SQL Data Types	This process creates an SQL data type and enables it to be related to a value domain data type.
Accomplish Assign Columns to Attribute Reassignments	This process causes a change in the existing assignment of one or more columns to one attribute. If there is a conflict between the data element that is already assigned to the column and the data element assigned to the attribute, then the column is assigned to the unknown data element.
Accomplish Assign Columns to Column Reassignments	This process causes a change in the existing assignment of one or more columns to one column.
Accomplish Assign Columns to Data Elements Reassignments	This process causes a change in the existing assignment of one or more columns to one data element.
Accomplish Assign Columns to SQL Data Types Reassignments	This process causes a change in the existing assignment of one or more column SQL data type to a different SQL data type.
Accomplish Columns to Table Reassignments	This process causes a change in the existing assignment of one or more columns to a different table. If the column is part of any type of key, the reassignment is rejected.
Accomplish Tables to Schema Reassignments	This process causes a change in the existing assignment of one or more tables to one Schema.
Accomplish Tables to Tables Reassignments	This process causes a change in the sub/super type relationship among tables within a given schema.

Implemented Data Model	
Process	**Description**
Export SQL DDL	This process traverses the complete set of tables, columns, and keys for a given schema and formulates a set of SQL DDL that completely represents the schema-based data model.
Import Attribute from Specified Data Model	This process causes the importation of a single attribute of an entity from a subject in the specified data model to be imported into a table of a schema of the implemented data model.
Import Entity Set from Specified Data Model	This process imports a set of entities from the specified data model that are all associated with one subject. All associated keys and columns are made. Relationships from the newly created table to the specified data model entities are also created.
Import Entity Tree from Specified Data Model	This process imports a set of interrelated entities from the specified data model. All associated keys and columns are made. Relationships from the newly created table to the specified data model entities are also created.
Import SQL DDL	This process imports a full stream of SQL DDL and creates a full set of tables, columns, and keys for the selected schema.
Maintain Column Meta Category Values	This process enables the allocation of meta category values to a column. Only one meta category value from each meta category value type is allowed to be assigned. As a meta category value is assigned, if there are any meta category values already assigned either to a parent data element, attribute, data element concept, then the assigned meta category values are evaluated to ensure that there are no semantic conflicts.

Implemented Data Model	
Process	**Description**
Maintain Column Value Domains	This process enables the allocation of value domains to a column. Only one value domain is allowed to be assigned. As a value domain is assigned, if there are any value domains already assigned either to a parent data element, data element parent data element concept, or to a descendant DBMS column, then the assigned attribute value domains are evaluated to ensure that there are no value domain hierarchy conflicts.
Maintain Columns	This process provides update support for a column.
Promote Column to Data Element	This process promotes a column to be a data element. The meta category values and value domains are removed from the column, and then allocated to the newly created data element. The data element is assigned to the "unknown" conceptual value domain and the "unknown" data element concept.
Promote Implemented Data Model Table to Specified Data Model Entity	This process promotes an implemented data model table to be a specified data model entity within an existing subject. Created are all the associated attributes and as appropriate primary keys, and candidate keys. Relationships between the newly create specified data model entity attributes and the implemented data model table columns are automatically created.
Promote Implemented Data Model to Specified Data Model	This process promotes an entire implemented data model to be a specified data model. Created is the subject (from the schema), all entities, attributes and all keys. Relationships between the newly create specified data model entity attributes and the implemented data model table columns are automatically created.

Implemented Data Model	
Process	**Description**
Remove Column Attribute Assignments	This process removes the relationships between a complete set of columns of a table and their corresponding attributes.
Remove Column Meta Category Values	This process removes meta category value assignments from a column.
Report Column Data Hierarchies	This process presents a column, its associated data element, data element concept, conceptual value domain and concept, as well as its associated DBMS columns. For each, the appropriate subject, entity, schema, table, DBMS schema, and DBMS table are also shown.

6.6.2 Operational Data Model

The operational data model , depicted in Figure 18, is a representation of an implemented database that may have been subsetted and/or transformed to serve the particular needs of a DBMS, or performance requirement. Operational databases are created through importing and building processes. Thereafter the operational database is employed to build view data models for use by business information systems.

Operational Data Model	
Process	**Description**
Create DBMS Columns	This process creates a DBMS column.
Create, modify or delete Candidate Key Definition	This process creates a candidate key.
Create, modify or delete DBMS schema	This process creates a candidate key.
Create, modify or delete DBMS tables	This process creates a candidate key.

Operational Data Model	
Process	**Description**
Create, modify or delete Foreign Keys	This process creates a foreign key. The target DBMS table is identified and the source primary key is identified. Then the referential actions and other SQL necessary information are entered. The foreign key name is automatically created and consists of the parent DBMS table name, must/may depending on chosen referential actions, an action word, and the child DBMS table name.
Create, modify or delete Primary Key Definition	This process creates a primary key.
Create, modify or delete Secondary Key Definition	This process creates a secondary key.
Accomplish DBMS Column to DBMS Table Reassignment	This process reassigns a DBMS column from one DBMS table to another.
Accomplish DBMS Columns to Column Reassignment	This process causes a change in the existing assignment of one or more DBMS columns to one DBMS column.
Accomplish DBMS Columns to DBMS Data Type Reassignment	This process causes a change in the existing assignment of a DBMS column's data type to a different DBMS data type.
Accomplish DBMS Tables to DBMS Schema Reassignment	This process causes a change in the existing assignment of a DBMS table from one DBMS schema to another DBMS Schema.
Accomplish DBMS Tables to DBMS Table Reassignment	This process causes a change in the sub/super type relationship among DBMS tables within a given DBMS schema. If a DBMS table's primary key is a foreign key in another table, then the DBMS table cannot be reassigned.
Allocate DBMS columns to the Candidate Key	This process assigns one or more columns to a candidate key.
Allocate DBMS columns to the	This process assigns one or more columns to a

Operational Data Model	
Process	**Description**
Primary Key	primary key.
Allocate DBMS columns to the Secondary Key	This process assigns one or more columns to a secondary key.
Export SQL DDL	This process traverses the complete set of DBMS tables, DBMS columns, and keys for a given DBMS schema and formulates a set of SQL DDL that completely represents the DBMS schema-based data model.
Import Column from Implemented Data Model	This process causes the importation of a single column of a table from a schema in the implemented data model to be imported into a DBMS table of a DBMS schema of the operational data model.
Import SQL DDL	This process imports a full stream of SQL DDL and creates a full set of DBMS tables, DBMS columns, and keys for the selected DBMS schema.
Import Table Set from Implemented Data Model	This process imports a set of tables from the implemented data model that are all associated with one schema. All associated keys and DBMS columns are made. Relationships from the newly created DBMS table to the implemented data model tables are also created.
Import Table Tree from Implemented Data Model	This process imports a set of interrelated tables from the implemented data model. All associated keys and DBMS columns are made. Relationships from the newly created DBMS tables to the implemented data model tables are also created.
Maintain DBMS Column Value Domains	This process enables the allocation of a value domain to a DBMS column. Only one value domain is allowed to be assigned. As a value domain is assigned, if there are any value domains already assigned either to a parent column, data element, data element parent data element concept, then the assigned value domains are evaluated to ensure that

Operational Data Model	
Process	**Description**
	there are no value domain hierarchy conflicts.
Remove DBMS Table Column to Column Assignments	This process removes the relationships between a complete set of DBMS columns of a DBMS table and their corresponding columns.

6.6.3 View Data Model

The view data model, depicted in Figure 22, is designed to capture specifications of models of data that represent the interface between a DBMS's database schema as expressed in the Operational Data Model, and the Business Information Systems' need for data.

View Data Model	
Process	**Description**
Create, modify or delete View Column Structure	This process creates a relationship between two view columns in different views for the purpose of an ETL class of process.
Create, modify or delete View Column Structure Process	This process provides the ability to describe the process in a sort of pseudo code in support of the transformation process between one or more view columns of one view transformed to one or more view columns in another view.
Create, modify or delete View Column Structure Type	This process creates various classifications of view column structures that are used to identify specific collections of records in view column structures.
Create, modify or delete View Columns	This process creates view columns within a view.
Create, modify or delete Views	This process creates a view.
Accomplish DBMS Columns to	This process assigns one or more DBMS columns to

View Data Model	
Process	**Description**
View Column Assignments	a view column.
Accomplish View Column to Compound Data Element Assignments	This process assigns one or more view columns to a compound data element.
Accomplish View Column to Derived Data Element Assignments	This process assigns one or more business information systems to a resource life cycle node.
Generate View Columns	This process creates view columns for an entire table.
Generate Views	This process creates views for every table in a DBMS Schema.

6.7 Business Information System Summary

This chapter serves several purposes. First it sets out the overall architectural context of the business information systems, that is: Enterprise Architecture, Information Systems Architecture, and Data Architecture. Within each of these, this chapter sets out the various metadata-base business information systems that need to exist to capture the metadata sufficient for interoperable environments. And, within each of these business information systems, this chapter sets out the database object table processes that need to exist to accomplish the work of the metadata-based business information systems.

Second, this chapter sets down two strategies for capturing metadata: Reverse, and Forward Engineering. Reverse engineering is far and away the most common as almost all enterprise have large collections of un-integrated databases and information systems. Once the reverse engineering is accomplished, then Forward Engineering can occur in support of manufacturing databases and information systems. Once the change over occurs, what used to take years and months will now take months and weeks.

Experience has shown that the payoff from these efforts is almost immediate and sometimes occurs within the first project.

7

Business Events

There are four classes of business events within the data interoperability program. These are:

- General business events.
- Subgroup establishment events.
- Officer appointment events.
- Data Interoperability Program events.
- Community of Interest events.

7.1 General Business Events

7.1.1 Meeting Calender Establishment

Subgroups within the Data Interoperability Program create a meeting calendar of all meetings and publish it to all committees within the Data Interoperability Program. Meeting calendars will project out at least one year. Meeting schedules of technical committees within Communities of Interest are subject to review by the Community of Interest. Similarly, meeting schedules of Communities of Interest are subject to review by the Data Interoperability Projects committee. And finally, all Data Interoperability Program contained committee meetings are subject to review by the Data Interoperability Program Committee.

7.1.2 Meetings

All meeting agendas, and thus all minutes should have a similar format which is suggested to be:

Doc. No.: <document number>
Date: <document last update date>
Project: <specific project> or "N/A"
Ref. Doc: <reference to main document> or "NA"
Status: <draft | final>
Reply to: <subgroup secretary name>
: <subgroup secretary organization name>
: <subgroup secretary address line 1>
: <subgroup secretary city, state zip>
: <subgroup secretary telephone number>
: Internet: <subgroup secretary email address>

SUBGROUP: <Subgroup Official Name>
SUBJECT: <Title of this document> Note: usually Minutes of Meeting ###
Date: <Start date of the meeting>
Location: <Actual location of the meeting> or Electronic

The <English words for the meeting number> meeting of <Subgroup Official Name> was called to order by <Chair Name> | <designated chair name> at <Time and Time zone> on <start date of meeting>

AGENDA

1 Preliminary and Administrative Matters
1.1 Attendance and Membership Status
1.1.1 Introduce participants
1.1.1.1 <Standing Document Number>:Participants List
1.1.2 Membership status
1.1.2.1 <Standing Document Number>: Attendance Rules
1.1.2.2 Membership Jeopardy notices (<Document Number> - Author)
1.2 Agenda
1.2.1 Document distribution
1.2.1.1 Agenda for Meeting <Meeting Number> <Meeting Date> (<Document Number> - Author)
1.2.2 Agenda revision and approval
1.3 Review of the INCITS Antitrust Guidelines
1.3.1 H2-SD-016_2006-01-09

1.4 Minutes
1.4.1 Approval of minutes
1.4.1.1 Minutes for Meeting <Meeting Number> <Meeting Date> (<Document Number> - Author)
1.4.2 Action item review
1.5 Liaison Reports
1.5.1 Domestic Liaison
1.5.1.1 <document within this category that is to be presented and/or requires subgroup action> (<Document Number> - Author)
1.5.2 International liaison
1.5.3 Other liaison
1.5.3.1 <Standing Document Number>: Liaisons List
1.6 Administration
1.6.1 Treasurer's report
1.6.1.1 Treasurer's Report (<Document Number> - Author)
1.6.2 Future meetings
1.6.2.1 <Standing Document Number>: Meeting Schedule
1.6.3 Other administrative matters
1.6.3.1 <Standing Document Number>: Standing Documents

2 Unfinished Business from Previous Meetings

3 <First Main Standard Title> <Standard Project Identifier>

3.1 <Maintenance project for existing standard within overall main project> [<Project Identifier>]
3.1.1 <document within this category that is to be presented and/or requires subgroup action> (<Document Number> - Author)

3.2 <First subproject within main project for development of new standard version> [<Project Identifier>]
3.2.1 <First formal document within standard for Framework [<Project Identifier><.><Document Sequence Number>]
3.2.1.1 <document within this category that is to be presented and/or requires subgroup action> (<Document Number> - Author)
3.2.2 <Second formal document within standard for Framework [<Project Identifier><.><Document Sequence Number>]
3.2.2.1 <document within this category that is to be presented and/or requires subgroup action> (<Document Number> - Author)

4 <Second Standard Title><Standard Project Identifier>

5 Other Projects

6 New Business

7 Late Papers

8 Adjourn

9 Action Items

10 Carry Forward Papers

11 Meeting Document Log

<Document Number> <Agenda number> <Document Title> (<Author>)

An actual set of minutes from the ANSI INCITS H2 Technical Committee on Database are included as Appendix 1.

7.2 Subgroup Establishment

Within the data interoperability program the key subgroups are:

- Data Interoperability Program Committee
- Subsidiary Boards
- Communities of Interest
- Community of Interest Technical Committees

The subgroups are described in Chapter 9 of this book. To stand up the Data Interoperability Program committee the following needs to be adopted or revised from the materials in this book:

- Mission
- Organization

- Function
- Product
- Documents
- Positions
- Rules

Once these seven materials are created for the Data Interoperability Program Committee and it is approved by the parent organization then that committee can set about standing up the contained subsidiary boards. That is, the Finance, Procedures, Standards Policy and Standards Development boards. Each subsidiary board would also have these same seven items adopted or modified from this book.

The Standards Development Board of the Data Interoperability Program identifies the data interoperability standards that need to be created. Once the standards are identified, and a project proposal (see Section 11.1) is created then the various Communities of Interest can start. The first task of every Community of Interest is to either adopt or adapt the seven materials that would be appropriate for that Community of Interest. A second task of the Community of Interest would be to establish their Technical Committees by creating for each an appropriate set of the seven materials.

Throughout the life of every subgroup that is established these seven materials can be modified to fit the needs of the subgroup, subject, of course to the oversight of the subgroup's parent subgroup.

7.3 Officer Appointment

Three officers will make or break any subgroup. These are:

- Chair
- Editor
- Secretary

All three offices must be faceless. That is, the officer must not have any particular agenda save moving the scope and program of work forward. If an officer is appointed that has a set of personal goals such as peer recognition, professional advancement, business development, or such, then the first organization to suffer will be the subgroup. Members of the subgroup will almost instantly recognize that there are ulterior motives behind actions of the officer. This will cause "games" to be played. Work will suffer both in terms of quantity and quality. The value of these three offices cannot be overestimated.

Because the offices of Chair and Editor are so important, an analysis was made of the top five reasons that make a great chair and the five reasons why a chair will likely cause the work of the committee to fail. The top five characteristics of a great chair of a community of interest are:

- Impartial - treats all participants equally (no personal agenda or ax to grind).
- Single focus on carrying out work of group (e.g., producing the standard).
- Ability to keep participants on track and working constructively toward group objective.
- Pleasant/welcoming demeanor conducive to leading collegial cooperative effort.
- Knowledgeable about the subgroup's procedures and Robert's (and/or other applicable) Rules.

The 5 or so worst characteristics of a Chair of a Community of Interest are:

- Bias toward one person, group or agenda.
- Lack of understanding of and focus on the subgroup's objective.
- Weak leadership not resulting in convergence on the group's objective.
- Attempt to mandate (in drill sergeant fashion) work by reluctant subgroup of volunteers.
- Ignorance of subgroup's procedures and relevant rules.

Similarly, the top five characteristics of a great editor of a community of interest are:

- Ability to build trust, ensuring that all participants feel comfortable that their proposals will be properly handled.

- Commitment to do the work in a timely fashion, in spite of conflicts.

- Well-organized, with attention to detail; ability to do the work in face of incomplete or inadequate proposals.

- Good-natured and self-effacing -- ability to accept criticism and continue to the job.

- Technical competence in field of discourse of the community.

The 5 or so worst characteristics of a Editor of a Community of Interest are:

- Exaggerated sense of self-important ("I know better, so I'll do it the 'right' way, regardless of community decisions").

- Inattention to intent of decisions, inability (or unwillingness) to ask for clarification when needed.

- Rigidity, low tolerance for ambiguity, significantly impatient.

- Inability to distinguish own roles (allow partisan opinions to affect editorial work).

- Absence of commitment to deliver work on communities schedule.

The business events associated with an officer appointment are:

- Officer vacancy announcement
- Officer candidate review
- Officer appointment
- Officer training
- Officer performance review
- Officer recall

An officer vacancy announcement should go to all organizations that are currently participating in the affected subgroup. If there are no acceptable candidates within the subgroup, then the vacancy announcement should go to other subgroups within the Data Interoperability Program. Only thereafter should an officer vacancy notice go to outside organizations. Those applying for a vacancy should communicate that desire to the immediate parent subgroup and/or one subgroup higher and the names of the candidates should be held confidential.

Officer candidate review is critical to determine the best candidate for the office. For the chair, editor and secretary, these offices are the most critical because they ultimately determine the quality and velocity of the standards being produced. Officer candidate review should be accomplished by the immediate parent subgroup and/or one subgroup higher so that there can be a fair evaluation of all candidates. All evaluations should be held confidential.

Officer appointment from among the candidates should merely be announced. No grades should be given and no evaluation materials should be made public. This is especially important since it is likely that all the candidates are already members of the subgroup.

Officer training is very important since over time, and regardless of the officer, the committee documents and products of a given class should have the same format and level of quality. Chair training is especially important because a well organized and operating committee is essential to the timely production and/or maintenance of a standard.

Every year the performance of officers should be reviewed by the immediate parent subgroup and/or one subgroup higher to ensure that productivity of all subgroups are maintained at a high level and at a high quality.

If officers are not able to perform on par with the rest of the officers of that class across the other subgroups then that officer should be evaluated and remedied if at all possible. If remediation is not possible then the officer should be encouraged to resign. Failing that, the officer should be removed by recommendation of the immediate parent subgroup and confirmed by one subgroup higher.

7.4 Data Interoperability Program Business Events

The key business events for the Data Interoperability Program committee are:

- Data Interoperability Program Management Plan Development
- Data Interoperability Program Integrated Schedule Development

The overall data interoperability program management plan includes the overall architecture and operations strategy for an entire data interoperability program. This book is largely that document. It defines scope, mission, functions, roles, offices and the like. The Data Interoperability Program project committee should review this book and propose changes to it to the Data Interoperability Program committee to ensure that the material fits the needs of all the data interoperability projects.

The Data Interoperability Program Integrated Schedule is a document that results from the input from all the different Communities of Interest for all the different standards that are under development. This schedule also includes standards review activities, officer training, and the various meetings and product development schedules of all the subsidiary Data Interoperability Program committee boards.

7.5 Community of Interest Business Events

Communities of Interest business events are generally centered around the milestones that should be reached to mark the progress of developing a data interoperability standard. These mile stones are:

- Milestone 1 - Approval of the Project Proposal
- Milestone 2 - Notification to the Public
- Milestone 3 - Technical Development
- Milestone 4 - Initial Public Review
- Milestone 5 - Management Review
- Milestone 6 - Data Interoperability Program Committee Approval
- Milestone 7 - Community of Interest Approval
- Milestone 8 - Publication.

7.5.1 Milestone 1 -Approval of the Project Proposal

A Project Proposal may be developed by any individual or organization whether or not affiliated with the Data Interoperability Program. Project proposals should be developed in accordance with the format of the Data Interoperability Program Project Proposal Guide.

No technical work may be done in developing or revising a standard without an authorizing Project Proposal. Each standard requires its own authorizing Project Proposal.

If the Project Proposal originates within a Community of Interest, voting on the submission of the Project Proposal is conducted by the Community of Interest; the vote must be included with submission of the Project Proposal.

The Project Proposal must meet the two-week rule for the meeting at which action is expected. If the Project Proposal is approved, work on the project may begin immediately on the project.

Within fourteen calendar-days, the Chair of the originating Community of Interest will forward to the Data Interoperability Program Committee the following information:

- The approved Project Proposal.
- The next Community of Interest meeting information.
- Any other supplemental information the Community of Interest may wish to provide (i.e., draft press release) for registration of the Community of Interest project number and web announcement.

Upon receipt of the information package from the Chair of the originating Community of Interest, the Data Interoperability Program Committee chair will electronically notify the Data Interoperability Program Committee members of the approved Project Proposal.

Any Data Interoperability Program Committee member may request an appeal of the approved Project Proposal within seven calendar-days.

If there is no appeal of the approved Project Proposal, a project number is assigned and announced by the Data Interoperability Program Committee.

If an appeal is made of the approved Project Proposal, the Chair of the originating Community of Interest is notified and Data Interoperability Program Committee voting is conducted.

If the Project Proposal is not approved, the Data Interoperability Program Committee so notifies the proposer.

7.5.2 Milestone 2 - Notification to the Public

If the project is approved, the Data Interoperability Program Committee announces the assignment of the project. The project number assigned by the Data Interoperability Program Committee is entered into the Community of Interest Projects database.

The Data Interoperability Program Committee will issue a press release announcing the establishment of the project and solicit technical contributions and membership. The press release will include a notification to the public of the Data Interoperability Program patent policies, and a call for information on potentially pertinent patents will be made. The call will also encourage disclosure, where possible, of the existence of pending U.S. patent applications relating to the standard under development, and of any relevant unexpired foreign patents.

7.5.3 Milestone 3 - Technical Development

The Community of Interest will prepare a detailed work plan for completion of the project. The Community of Interest will review and/or revise the work plan as part of its annual report presented to Standards Development Board.

Contributions may include collections of basic data, suggested drafts of text, candidate standards, etc. Contributions from any source will be accepted and considered. Use of trademarks, copyrighted, or patented material will be in accordance with the Data Interoperability Program approved policy.

7.5.4 Milestone 4 - Initial Public Review

When the Community of Interest determines that the development process has reached the step where the initial 45-day public review is warranted, the vote to initiate the initial public review will be conducted. For a draft standard that has reached Committee Draft stage, the initial public review is initiated by the Community of Interest upon receipt of the Committee Draft ballot.

The Community of Interest Chair will forward the draft to any close liaisons, and will simultaneously forward to the Data Interoperability Program Committee a submittal package that includes, but is not limited to:

- The draft standard.
- The expository remarks, i.e., the background or history of the project development.
- A copy of the authorizing Project Proposal.

- The tally of the ballot by the Community of Interest developing the draft standard.

- The name, address and telephone number of the project editor.

Liaisons identified in the project proposal are expected to review the draft in accordance with the voting requirements. Liaisons must inform the Data Interoperability Program Committee and the Chair of the Community of Interest developing the draft standard by correspondence prior to the close of the initial public review period if the draft standard appears to raise questions or conflicts with the work of the liaison Committee. Lack of comment will be considered as an indication that no problems were identified.

The Data Interoperability Program Committee will initiate several simultaneous activities for draft Standards:

- Assignment of a Standards number to the draft standard because the draft has now reached the status of draft standard.

- An announcement in the Data Interoperability Program Standards Action of a 45-day public review through the submittal of a draft standard's review package.

- A compliance review. The Data Interoperability Program Committee will conduct a review of the draft standard for compliance with its authorizing Project Proposal.

When the Data Interoperability Program Committee review indicates that the draft standard is in compliance with the scope and program of work of the authorizing Project Proposal, the Community of Interest is so notified. When the compliance review indicates that the proposed draft standard is not in compliance, the Data Interoperability Program Committee will so advise the Community of Interest. The Data Interoperability Program Committee concerns must be resolved prior to the initiation of the second public review. The Data Interoperability Program Committee is notified of the review result via:

- A call for information on potentially pertinent patents will be made to the Data Interoperability Program members and the Community of Interest simultaneously. The call will also encourage disclosure, where possible, of the existence of pending U.S. patent applications relating to the standard under development, and of any relevant unexpired foreign patents.

- Notification to the Community of Interest of the responses received by the Data Interoperability Program Committee resulting from previous calls for patents.

- Issuance of a press release describing the draft standard, and announcing the availability of the document for a 45-day technical review and comment period.

- The Community of Interest preliminary edit of the draft standard.

All comments received during the initial public review are distributed to the Community of Interest developing the standard. A formal response must be developed for each comment and approved by the Community of Interest. The standard submitted for public review will contain a notice that any comments should to be sent to the Data Interoperability Program Committee with a copy to the Community of Interest. The Data Interoperability Program Committee will register every public review comment.

Each comment will be sent immediately to the originating Community of Interest for consideration and to the Data Interoperability Program Committee for information. Formal responses generated for each comment is subject to approval by a Community of Interest vote. Responses to registered comments will include the provision that the commenter has twenty working days from the postmark to reply and indicate if the comment(s) has not been satisfactorily resolved. If no response from the commented is received, the comment will be considered as satisfactorily resolved.

The response may be either a modification to the draft standard, or a statement of the rationale for not making a change. Serious effort should be made to accommodate the comment by correspondence or discussion with the author.

Editorial recommendations from the Community of Interest will be considered and incorporated if practicable.

7.5.5 Milestone 5 - Management Review

For a standard that has reached draft standard stage, Milestone 5 consists of the second public review that is initiated by the Community of Interest upon receipt of the draft standard ballot.

For other projects, the second public review may begin after the Community of Interest approval ballot and the Data Interoperability Program Committee review.

After consideration of all comments and resolution of as many comments as possible, the Community of Interest approves the text as suitable for adoption as a standard. The Community of Interest approval vote will be conducted.

The Community of Interest forwards the proposed final text of the standard to the Data Interoperability Program Committee. The submittal package includes, but is not limited to:

- The draft standard.
- The expository remarks, i.e., the background or history of the project development, the final tally of the ballot, and any unresolved comments by the Community of Interest developing the draft standard.
- Any comments from other Communities of Interest reviewing the draft standard.
- The response to Data Interoperability Program Committee concerns that were communicated to the Community of Interest with the results of the compliance review.
- All public review comments and the Community of Interest response to each (identifying any unresolved comments).
- A record of attempts to resolve comments on negative votes during the Community of Interest vote to forward the document.
- The name, address and telephone number of the project editor.
- The list of Community of Interest participants.

The Standards Development Board will conduct a review of the submittal package to ensure that the Data Interoperability Program procedural requirements have been met. This review may be initiated at the commencement of the initial public review. An indication that the Data Interoperability Program procedures have been violated will result in the submittal package being returned to the Community of Interest without action.

When the management review indicates a second or subsequent public review is not warranted, the Data Interoperability Program Committee will provide the Community of Interest with the results of the public review. If public review comments are not received, the Data Interoperability Program Committee will initiate the Data Interoperability Program Committee Letter Ballot. If public review comments are received, the management review will be extended to consider the Community of Interest disposition of those comments.

When the Standards Development Board management review indicates processing should continue, the Data Interoperability Program Committee will initiate several simultaneous activities:

- An announcement in the Data Interoperability Program's Standards Action publication of a 45-day public review.

- A call for information on potentially pertinent patents will be made to the Data Interoperability Program Committee members and the Community of Interest simultaneously. The call will also encourage disclosure, where possible, of the existence of pending U.S. patent applications relating to the standard under development, and of any relevant unexpired foreign patents.

- Notification to the Community of Interest of the responses received by the Data Interoperability Program resulting from previous calls for patents.

- Issuance of a press release describing the draft standard, and announcing availability of the document for a 2-month technical review and comment period.

The draft standard submitted for public review will contain a notice that any comments should to be sent to the Data Interoperability Program Committee with a copy to the Community of Interest. The Data Interoperability Program Committee will register every public review comment. Each comment will be sent immediately to the originating Community of Interest for consideration and to the

Community of Interest for information. A formal response must be developed for each comment and approved by the Community of Interest.

Responses to registered comments will include the provision that the commenter has twenty working days from the postmark to reply and indicate if the comment(s) has not been satisfactorily resolved. If no response from the commented is received, the comment will be considered as satisfactorily resolved.

The response may be either a modification to the draft standard, or a statement of the rationale for not making a change. Serious effort should be made to accommodate the comment by correspondence or discussion with the author.

In the case of changes that are editorial only, all comments are resolved, either by changes to the draft standard or by communication with the commenter. The Community of Interest will advise the Data Interoperability Program Committee and provide all pertinent correspondence.

In the case of one or more substantive changes to the draft standard in order to resolve the public review comments, the Community of Interest votes. If the Community of Interest achieves the criteria for approval, the Community of Interest will send the comments, the replies to the comments, ballot results, the revised text, a summary of the changes and rationale to the Data Interoperability Program Committee.

The Data Interoperability Program Committee will advise the Community of Interest that a further public review is required, and will take action to notify the purchasers of the latest draft standard that another public review is necessary. Subsequent public reviews will begin no sooner than thirty days after the mailing of responses to public review comments. Processing returns to the beginning of Milestone 5.

If there are no public review comments during the second (or subsequent) public review, the Community of Interest will forward the document to the Data Interoperability Program Committee for final approval.

7.5.6 Milestone 6 - Data Interoperability Program Committee Approval

If the Data Interoperability Program Committee letter ballot or meeting vote to submit the draft standard passes with no negative votes or comments, the Data Interoperability Program Committee immediately submits the draft standard to the Community of Interest along with all documentation required by the Community of Interest.

When there are negative votes or comments, the voting tally and all comments are sent to the Data Interoperability Program Committee and to the Community of Interest that developed the draft standard. An effort to resolve all expressed objections will be made, and each objector will be advised in writing of the disposition of the objection and the reasons therefore. Any unresolved objections (including all documentation) and any substantive changes made in a proposed standard will be reported to the Data Interoperability Program Committee in order to afford all members an opportunity to respond, reaffirm or change their vote.

If the letter ballot or meeting vote fails due to the number of negative votes, the record is referred to the Community of Interest that developed the draft standard.

If the letter ballot or meeting vote fails due to insufficient affirmative votes and there are no negative ballots cast, the record is referred to the Data Interoperability Program Committee for reconsideration.

If the letter ballot or meeting vote is canceled due to public review comments, the package is returned to the Community of Interest and processing continues at the beginning of Milestone 5.

7.5.7 Milestone 7 - Enterprise Approval

If the Data Interoperability Program operates within a corporation or business, or for example operates within the domain of the Chief Information Officer, then an additional level of approval may be necessary. In that case, upon receipt of the transmittal of the draft standard, the appropriate organization reviews the submittal and processes it according to the established procedures.

Upon notification of the corporate approval, the Data Interoperability Program Committee advises, by individual letter, those Data Interoperability Program Committee members that may have had unresolved negatives that they have fifteen days from the date of the notification letter from the Data Interoperability Program Committee to appeal the approval. Such an appeal would be filed with the appropriate organization within the business.

In case the business disapproves the standard, it is sent back to the Data Interoperability Program Committee for further processing or disposition.

7.5.8 Milestone 8 - Publication

The originating Community of Interest may not convert to Maintenance status until the standard has been published.

7.6 Business Event Summary

This chapter sets out the classes of business events that will commonly occur during within a data interoperability program. Two classes stand out as being more critical than the others: Office appointment, and Community of Interest.

Officer appointment is very crucial because it is the quality of the officers, especially Chair and Editor that determine the overall success of any data interoperability program subgroup. Great care should be expended that these two individuals should have one and only one objective: The achievement of data interoperability standards.

Community of Interest events are also very important. These eight milestones have been chiseled into crispness over a period of 40+ years by the American National Standards Institute (ANSI) and the International Committee for Information Technology Standards (INCITS). It is almost not arguable that the most sophisticated and widely accepted IT standards have been created and are being maintained by these two organizations.

Every business event is a milestone of some sort. Additionally, it may also signify the requirement for some support from the business information systems. For example, the business event, Milestone 1: Approval of the Project Proposal, presumes that the project proposal functions from Chapter 8 have been accomplished by some person occupying a position (Chapter 10) within an organization (Chapter 9). The project proposal should then be constructed according to the format specified in Chapter 11, and should then be entered in the metadata repository system (Chapter 6), and result in some project metadata (Chapter 5). Voting on the project proposal is governed by rules from Chapter 13.

Virtually everything in this book has a role, and is integrated in some way with something else. This integration is not an accident. It is a direct consequence of all those persons and organizations who are acknowledged at the front of this book.

8

Business Functions

There are the following classes of business functions within the Data Interoperability Program:

- General functions.
- Data Interoperability Program functions.
- Community of Interest functions.
- Officer Appointment functions.
- Service Fee Waver functions.
- Appeals procedures.
- Parliamentary functions.

8.1 General Business Functions

The general functions relate to the positions that exist in almost every Data Interoperability Program subgroup. That is,

- Chair.
- Vice Chair.
- Secretary.
- Editor.

8.1.1 Chair

The general duties of every subgroup chair include:

- Preside at meetings.

- Ensure that the Data Interoperability Program work is carried out in a prompt, efficient and an effective manner in accordance with the objectives, policies, and procedures of the Data Interoperability Program.

- Prepare and present Subgroup Annual Report to the Standards Development Board.

- Communities of Interest and Study Groups must prepare and present an annual report to the Standards Development Board.

- Disseminate in writing the 'Call for Volunteers' for officer positions for the Subgroup.

- Ensure that the Administrative Duties (shown under Vice Chair duties) are carried out.

- Provide or arrange for tutorials to membership on procedures.

- Forward to the appropriate subgroup parent timely and complete subgroup documentation.

- Send timely warning letters on endangered memberships.

- Attend required training sessions.

- Represent the body to other committees and organizations.

- Prepare and forward to the Data Interoperability Program Committee press releases and other publicity material about the Subgroup's program of work.

Appoint:

- ♦ Vice Chair.

- ♦ Secretary.

- ♦ Vocabulary Representative.

- ♦ Project Editor(s) for each project, as appropriate.

  - Liaisons.

  - Head of Delegation for each inter-organizational meeting.

  - Other (e.g., ad hoc group Chairs).

- Ensure the Subgroup mailings are reviewed for information, possible action, and redistribution as appropriate.

- Ensure the orderly transfer of any Subgroup documents upon appointment of new officers.

- Schedule Subgroup meetings for a rolling full calendar year; ensure administrative meeting arrangements are addressed: and notify the Data Interoperability Program Committee to update the Meeting Schedule and Calendar.

- Ensure that any coordinating liaison responsibilities are carried out in a timely manner.

8.1.2 Vice Chair

The duties of the Vice-Chair are:

- In the absence of the Chair, perform the duties of the Chair.

- Act as Subgroup administrator with the following duties (unless redistributed, by agreement, among the membership).

- Register, control, and distribute documents, ensuring that the original or a reproducible copy of each is sent to the Data Interoperability Program Committee staff for the permanent file. A complete document register must be sent to the Data Interoperability Program Committee at the end of each calendar year.

- Prepare and distribute meeting notices and agendas in accordance with the Data Interoperability Program procedures and in consultation with the Chair.

- Prepare, distribute, tally, and report the results of letter ballots.
- Maintain mailing lists, record attendance and ballot responses, and notify the Chair of any individual requiring membership jeopardy notice.
- Prepare supporting documentation for submission of proposed standards to the next higher Subgroup level.
- Prepare, for approval, status reports of work as required by the Subgroup.
- Ensure the timely distribution of mailings from the Subgroup pertinent to its work and administration.
- Review documents prior to distribution for legibility, clarity, accuracy, and appropriateness, and modify when appropriate.
- Notify the Data Interoperability Program Committee of changes in the Subgroup membership.
- Attend required training sessions.

8.1.3 Secretary

The duties of the secretary include:

- Record and transcribe meeting minutes in consultation with the Chair and Vice Chair.
- Provide minutes to the Vice Chair so that they can be distributed within four weeks of the meeting.

8.1.4 Editor

The duties of the editor are:

- Maintain documents and make timely changes as agreed by the Subgroup.

- Prepare documents according to the most recent edition of the Community of Interest style manual for preparation of proposed Data Interoperability Standards.
- Submit an electronic version of the standard according to the guidelines for submitting proposed standards in an electronic format.
- Make arrangements for all artwork and engineering diagrams to be prepared and submitted electronically.
- Plan and schedule document preparation, taking into consideration lead times for document transmission, review and approval periods, meeting schedules and target dates established by the Data Interoperability Program and by Communities of Interest.
- Maintain an awareness of the development and approval process, including required lead times.
- Report the status of the document at each meeting.
- Attend required training sessions.

8.2 Data Interoperability Program

8.2.1 Overall

As such, the Data Interoperability Program Committee is required to:

- Serve as the consensus body of the Data Interoperability Program.
- Ensure the efficiency and ethical stature of the entire organization.
- Continually evolve the organization to ensure the highest quality of work and standards development.
- Retain ultimate responsibility for all standards developed and approved by the various Communities of Interest.

- Create and disband its immediate Subgroups and Communities of Interest.
- Elect the Chair and Vice-chair of the Data Interoperability Program Committee, the Chairs of the Standards Development Board and the Standards Policy Board. Elect the Chairs of the Communities of Interest and Data Interoperability Program Committee committees. Recall elected officials, as circumstances require.
- Oversee and coordinate the work of the Standards Development Board and the Standards Policy Board. Harmonize recommendations from all of the Data Interoperability Program Committee Subgroups.
- Approve and determine external distribution of nonstandard documents from the Standards Development Board, the Standards Policy Board and all the Communities of Interest.
- Approve and disseminate organizational collateral.
- Retain and recruit members.
- Approve and fund trade shows, symposiums and seminar opportunities.
- Maintain and approve procedures as necessary.
- Forecast services required for administrative support.
- Ensure a financially viable organization.
- Evaluate and approve recommendations for Data Interoperability Program Committee operating expenses, revenues and special accounts. Approve the three year rolling financial plan.
- Resolve administrative issues.
- Determine which matters can only be considered in Executive Sessions.

8.2.2 Data Interoperability Program Chair

The Data Interoperability Program Chair will carry out the following responsibilities:

- Chair meetings of the Data Interoperability Program Committee providing a neutral viewpoint to facilitate the achievement of the Data Interoperability Program.
- Coordinate with Data Interoperability Program Committee member organizations to ensure the effective meetings. This would include coordination related to meeting room requirements, production of minutes of the meeting, et al.
- The Vice Chairman will support the Chairman as required.

8.2.3 Finance Board

The Finance Board, for a rolling two year plan, shall:

- Review financial results (budget and actual) of the Data Interoperability Program Committee, all Boards, Communities of Interest.
- Make recommendations on the Data Interoperability Program Committee service fees.
- Recommend budgets for the Data Interoperability Program Committee.
- Make recommendations on the finance aspects of acquisition, retention and divestiture of the Communities of Interest assets.
- Make recommendations on and monitor financial aspects associated with new services and requirements.

8.2.4 Procedures Board

The Procedures Board shall:

- Draft and recommend to the Data Interoperability Program Committee the procedures for operation of the Communities of Interest; review Community of Interest operations to ensure that they comply with the Data Interoperability Program policies and procedures.
- Amend the procedures as necessary.
- Respond to requests for additions, changes, deletions, or new developments to the procedures.
- Review procedures changes originated outside of Procedures Board Committee prior to ballot by the Data Interoperability Program Committee.
- Circulate proposed changes, modifications, and enhancements to affected Subgroup(s) for preliminary review and comment.
- Render interpretations on procedural issues. Maintain a record of interpretations. Consider these for future incorporation into appropriate procedure documents.
- Review and submit to the Data Interoperability Program Committee for approval any internal operating procedures developed by Communities of Interest organizational entities to ensure compliance with this document.

8.2.5 Standards Policy Board

The Standards Policy Board initiates activities to accomplish the following:

- Identify and develop methods for rapid inter-organizational adoption of standards.
- Find, facilitate and promote opportunities for inter-organizational collaborative standardization activities that enhance interests.

- Monitor and determine impact of relevant policies and make recommendations accordingly.

- Define and implement methods for the Communities of Interest to collaborate with other organizations on technology policy issues.

- Identify and determine how to form inter-organizational alliances, partnerships, joint projects, etc.

- Create a coexistence strategy with consortia and other standards' organizations.

- Investigate expansion of scope.

8.2.6 Standards Development Board

The Standards Development Board is the most important of the Data Interoperability Program boards. The functions of this board include:

- Standards review.
- Managing the standards process.
- General functions.
- Community of Interest Management.
- Community of Interest Discovery.

8.2.6.1 Standards Review

In carrying out its program of work, the Standards Development Board has the following major responsibilities for standardization within its scope:

- Review and approve proposed standards.

- Develop and maintain the Data Interoperability Program Management Plan.

- Develop and maintain the Data Interoperability Program Integrated Schedule.

- Make recommendations to the Data Interoperability Program Committee regarding the appointment of officers in all Subgroups reporting to the Standards Development Board and any recalls of officers as needed.

- Maintain current approved standards and respond to requests for standardization within its scope.

- Avoid conflicting standards but not preclude development of families of standards.

- Minimize duplication of standards through the creation of appropriate liaison and coordination mechanisms among the standards of the Standards Development Board and with other standard's bodies having common interests.

- Provide the opportunity to participate in the standardization process for all those know to be or who indicate they are directly and materially affected by the Standards Development Board scope.

- Make recommendations to the Data Interoperability Program Committee regarding the creation and disbandment of management groups, Communities of Interest, and other subgroups as may be necessary to accomplish the standards' work of the Standards Development Board and the Data Interoperability Program Committee.

- Maintain the Project Proposal Guide, and Community of Interest Annual Report Guide.

- Maintain a complete list of Communities of Interests, the projects assigned to each, and the standards.

- Maintain the Data Interoperability Program database that lists the officers of each Community of Interest as well as the meeting schedules of the Community of Interest and its Subgroups.

8.2.6.2 Managing the Standards Process

To manage the standardization process, the Standards Development Board shall:

- Perform defect management reviews.
- Perform management reviews (Milestone 5).
- Monitor 5 Year Recommendations for Maintenance.
- Develop and submit maintenance recommendations due for Standards assigned to the Community of Interest.
- Perform first level of response to, and resolve as appropriate, issues of Communities of Interest.
- After Data Interoperability Program approval, request for approval of new projects.
- Approval of project proposals for new areas of work, including evaluating the needs for systems of standards within the scope of the Data Interoperability Program

8.2.6.3 General Functions

The Standards Development Board also has the following general functions:

- Coordinate the training of officers.
- Act as liaison with Communities of Interest.
- Perform the work of any Communities of Interest or other Subgroup when no appropriate Subgroup exists to perform the function or an existing Subgroup is not responsive.
- Analyze and evaluate promptly, including organizing and managing Study Groups as needed, all proposals to the Data Interoperability Program Committee for new or revised standards development projects.

- Organize and manage the processes needed to study, over a short term, closely related topics and to prepare advisory reports for guidance to specific elements of the Data Interoperability Program, as needed.

- Monitor, manage, and validate the initiation and development of all the Data Interoperability Program standards' projects in accordance with Data Interoperability Program Committee direction, assuring there is no overlap or duplication of work, and pro-actively managing project milestones.

- Prepare the charter, scope and program of work for Collaborative Subgroups.

- Manage liaison functions to other standards' organizations projects as necessary to improve working relations and minimize overlap or redundant work

8.2.6.4 Community of Interest Management

The Standards Development Board also exercises the following functions in regard to the general management of the Communities of Interest:

- Effect co-ordination between the Data Interoperability Program Communities of Interest and ensure the effectiveness of the technical groups.

- Make implementation level decisions and perform risk mitigation as necessary.

- Develop and maintain the Data Interoperability Program communication and liaison plan.

- Develop and maintain the Data Interoperability Program vision and scope.

- Develop and maintain any other the Data Interoperability Program Documents as directed by the Data Interoperability Program Committee.

- Provide direction and guidance to the Data Interoperability Program representatives in the Data Interoperability Program.

- Establish and maintain the Data Interoperability Program web site.
- Develop and maintain the Data Interoperability Program work plan.
- Provide support for staffing of Data Interoperability Program management documents.
- Report Data Interoperability Program Community of Interest activities to the Data Interoperability Program Committee.
- Raise issues as necessary for resolution by the Data Interoperability Program Committee.
- Maintain a formal record of all Data Interoperability Program Projects Committee meetings.
- Develop and Maintain the Data Interoperability Program briefings.
- Execute other specific tasks as may be directed by the Data Interoperability Program Committee.

8.2.6.5 Community of Interest Discovery

A critical function of the Standards Development Board is the discovery of communities of interest within the enterprise. The following functions are performed to that end:

a. Establish and manage Community of Interest Infrastructure
   i. Create Prototypical Concept of Operations
   ii. Create Metadata Repository Environment
   iii. Create Methodology for Community of Interest Efforts
   iv. Create Information Exchange Data Model Product Specifications
      (1) Create Development Guides
      (2) Create Metadata Repository Export and Import Templates
      (3) Create Information Exchange Data Model Product Assessment Guides

b. Create Metadata Infrastructure in Metadata Repository

i. Mine and load the 11179 Data Element Metadata Components from the any existing data dictionaries not compliant with ISO 11179
ii. Mine and load, the Specified Data Model Metadata Components from data modeling tools and/or repositories
iii. Acquire and load appropriate Ontologies and Taxonomies into 11179 Data Element Metadata Components
iv. Acquire and load appropriate data management metadata into the metadata repository

c. Discover Communities of Interest
i. Create the Resources of the Enterprise
ii. Create Resource Life Cycles for each Enterprise Resource
iii. Identify inventory of Business Information Systems within the enterprise
iv. Allocate Business Information System to Resource Life Cycle Nodes
v. Identify/Characterize Database Objects within each Business Information System
vi. Allocate non-redundant set of Database objects to the resource Life Cycle Nodes
vii. Allocate a Create-Read-Update-Read indicator to the intersection of Database Object and resource life cycle node
viii. Allocate a Create-Read-Update-Read indicator to the intersection of Business Information System and resource life cycle node
ix. Perform an Affinity Analysis of the Business Information System & Database Object with respect to the resource life cycle node
x. Propose Communities of Interest for the highest affinity levels
xi. Organize Institutional Communities of Interest as those that are organizationally related
xii. Organization Joint Communities of Interest as those that embrace multiple services
xiii. Organization expedient Communities of Interest as those that are not institutional nor joint

d. Establish and Manage Mission Area Communities of Interest
i. Build Enterprise Mission Area metadata within the Metadata Repository
(1) Create Enterprise Mission Area Mission Models
(2) Create Enterprise Mission Area Organization Models
(3) Create Enterprise Mission Area Function Models

        (4) Create Enterprise Mission Area Information Needs Models
        (5) Create Enterprise Mission Area Resource Life Cycle Models
    ii. Interrelate Mission Area metadata with other mission areas
    iii. Evolve and maintain Mission Area metadata

e. Establish and Manage Domain Area Communities of Interest
    i. Build Domain Area metadata within the Metadata Repository
        (1) Create Domain Area Domain Models
        (2) Create Domain Area Organization Models
        (3) Create Domain Area Function Models
        (4) Create Domain Area Information Needs Models
        (5) Create Domain Area Resource Life Cycle Models
    ii. Interrelate Domain Area metadata with other Domain Areas
    iii. Interrelate Domain Area metadata with Mission Area Metadata
    iv. Evolve and maintain Domain Area Metadata

f. Establish and Manage Function-based Communities of Interest
    i. Build Function-based Communities of Interest metadata within the Metadata Repository
        (1) Create Function-based Community of Interest Infrastructure Metadata Models
            (a) Create Function-based Communities of Interest Mission Models
            (b) Create Function-based Communities of Interest Organization Models
            (c) Create Function-based Communities of Interest Function Models
            (d) Create Function-based Communities of Interest Resource Life Cycle Models
        (2) Evolve and maintain Function-based Community of Interest Metadata
        (3) Create Function Area Information Exchange Data Models
        (4) Evolve and maintain Information Exchange Data Models

    ii. Interrelate Function-based Community of Interest metadata with other function area Community of Interest metadata
    iii. Interrelate Function-based Community of Interest metadata with Domain Area Metadata

g. Harmonize Community of Interest Information Exchange Data Model Products
    i. Harmonize Function Area Models with multi-Community of Interest Information Exchange Data Models
    ii. Harmonize Function Area Models with enterprise Information Exchange Data Models
    iii. Harmonize Function Area Models with inter-enterprise Information Exchange Data Models
    iv. Create Policies, procedures, and documentation regarding Communities of Interest
h. Establish and Manage Data Management Communities of Interest
    i. Build Data Management metadata within the Metadata Repository
        (1) Create Information System Models
        (2) Create Business Event and Calendar and Cycle Models
        (3) Create Information System Models
        (4) Create Information System Planning Models
            (a) Create Mission Area Information System Planning Models
            (b) Create Domain Area Information System Planning Models
            (c) Create Functional Area Information System Planning Models
    ii. Interrelate Data Management Metadata with Mission and Domain area metadata
    iii. Evolve and maintain Data Management metadata

8.2.7 Study Groups

The steps involved in every Study Group project include:

- Developing the problem statement, or external statement of the requirement to be satisfied, or existing deficiency in support of identifying the need, or the identification of the deficiency or need to be addressed, or the need for improved performance.

- Performing the requisite analysis includes employing enterprise missions, functions, and organization to frame or focus the analysis. If possible, refine this analysis to the point of specifying the problem space to the appropriate level of detail. Develop an initial data interoperability project planning problem statement. Identify the specific objectives that must be achieved to support mission performance. This is a statement of desired results, with specific, quantifiable, and measurable outcomes that contribute to achievement.

- Configuring Data Interoperability project plans that include work breakdown structures of task statements that support the achievement of the Data Interoperability project. The Data Interoperability project also includes the various goals and objectives that are to be achieved. Alternative approaches are created and evaluated through Proof of Principle Projects that validate the recommended alternative (risk reduction) or validate the specifications (for issuance to the developer).

- Managing the Data Interoperability projects that include the accomplishment of the actual project deliverables. Additionally, it includes monitoring and evaluating the proper use of a created standard, that is, cycling back lessons learned reports, issue resolution reports, or refinement of performance metrics that were employed in the development effort. In the Data Interoperability project, the nature of the technical solution, evaluations via the functional (user) and technical environments are accomplished.

8.3 Community of Interest

The overall business functions of a Community of Interest are really just two, which are:

- Data Interoperability Standard Development
- Data Interoperability Standard Maintenance

In support of these two main functions, the Community of Interest will in general:

- Develop draft standard.

- Submit to the Standards Development Board approved new projects within the Community of Interest's general area of interest.

- Participate technically on behalf of or advise the Standards Development Board on related inter-organizational standards' activity

.

The program of work includes the following functional elements for each assigned project:

- Develop and update the work plan and schedule of target dates for completing the project.
- Collect data needed to develop a standard.
- Develop the outline and table of contents of a standard.
- Draft the standard, appendices, and associated expository remarks.
- Vote until Community of Interest consensus is reached or it is apparent that a consensus cannot be reached.
- Prepare responses to public review and Community of Interest letter ballot comments.
- Recommend defect management actions during a standard's maintenance phase.
- Recommend revisions when experience with a standard so indicates.
- Conduct the required review and recommendation for revision, reaffirmation, designation as an archival standard, or withdrawal.

More detailed processes associated with each data interoperability standard follow:

8.3.1 Data Interoperability Standard Development

Within the development of any data interoperability standard there are four main functions that must be performed by the technical committees within the Community of Interest. These deal with:

- Authoritative Data Sources
- Enterprise Identifiers
- Information Exchange Data Models

- XML data exchanges

While critical for operating interoperable data environments, the means and the method of information exchanges such as intra-net, internet, or any of the supports for these exchanges are outside the scope of this book.

8.3.1.1 Creating Authoritative Data Sources

a. Identify Authoritative Data Source Requirements
    i. Identify Authoritative Data Source Classes

        (1) Identify Requirements for Reference Data Authoritative Data Source
            (a) Identify timeliness requirements
            (b) Identify quality requirements
            (c) Identify distribution alternatives

        (2) Identify Requirements for Actual Fact Authoritative Data Source
            (a) Identify timeliness requirements
            (b) Identify quality requirements
            (c) Identify distribution alternatives

        (3) Identify Requirements for Meta Fact Authoritative Data Source
            (a) Identify timeliness requirements
            (b) Identify quality requirements
            (c) Identify distribution alternatives

    ii. Identify Metadata Requirements for Authoritative Data Source Classes

b. Create Metadata Infrastructure for Authoritative Data Source
    i. Identify Authoritative Data Source Metadata
    ii. Design Authoritative Data Source Metadata Database
        (1) Prototype Authoritative Data Source Metadata database
        (2) Iterate until acceptable
        (3) Implement Authoritative Data Source Metadata database

c. Identify and Acquire Authoritative Data Source instances
    i. Identify location of Authoritative Data Source

   ii. Identify Authoritative Data Source acquisition mechanism
      (1) Physical relocation of Authoritative Data Source
      (2) Virtual relocation of Authoritative Data Source

   iii. Load Authoritative Data Source Metadata Database

d. Create Scenario to transform databases and information systems to use Authoritative Data Source
e. Create Scenario to evolve and maintain Authoritative Data Source
f. Create Scenario to refresh distributed Authoritative Data Source
g. Create Policies, procedures, and documentation appropriate for Authoritative Data Source

8.3.1.2 Enterprise Identifiers

a. Create Metadata Infrastructure for Enterprise Identifiers
   i. Identify Enterprise Identifier Metadata
      (1) Identify Enterprise Identifier Seed Metadata
      (2) Identify Enterprise Identifier Increment Metadata

   ii. Design Enterprise Identifier Database
      (1) Prototype Enterprise Identifier database
      (2) Iterate until acceptable
      (3) Implement Enterprise Identifier database

b. Identify Enterprise Identifiers
   i. Determine Initial set of Enterprise Identifier seeds
   ii. Determine IT Assets that will contain Enterprise Identifier incrementors
   iii. Load Enterprise Identifier Database
      (1) Acquire and Load Enterprise Identifier Seed Data
      (2) Acquire and Load Enterprise Identifier Incrementor Data
   iv. Estimate Effort to Accomplish all Enterprise Identifier Assignments
   v. Develop Enterprise Identifier Assignment Work Plan

c. Create Enterprise Identifier Generation and Maintenance Environment
   i. Create Seed Generator

ii. Create Incrementor Generator
iii. Prototype Enterprise Identifier Generator and Maintenance Environment
iv. Iterate until Acceptable
v. Implement Enterprise Identifier Generator and Maintenance Environment

d. Create Enterprise Identifier Assignment Environment
  i. Create IT Environment Modification Scenarios
  ii. Create Scenario to Modify Databases and Business Information System that can accommodate modification
  iii. Create Scenario to "Bolt-on" Enterprise Identifier translators to Databases and Business Information System that cannot handle modification
  iv. Prototype Scenarios and iterate until successful
  v. Implement IT Environment Modifications

e. Create Asset Discovery for Enterprise Identifier Assignment Scenario
  i. Identify how to discover assets
  ii. Identify how to access assets
  iii. Identify how to affix Enterprise Identifier to asset
  iv. Identify how to record asset Enterprise Identifier into Databases and Information Systems

f. Create Enterprise Identifier Employment Scenarios
  i. Create Agents to traverse Databases and Information systems for Enterprise Identifier based assets
  ii. Create supporting Information Exchange Data Models for each Enterprise Identifier search
  iii. Create strategies for Asset Assembly presentations

g. Create Policies, procedures, and documentation regarding Enterprise Identifiers

8.3.1.3 Information Exchange Data Models

a. Create Information Exchange Data Model
  i. Import Operational Data Models

ii. Employ and/or Modify Mission, Organization, and Function Models
iii. Employ and/or Modify Information Needs Models
iv. Employ and/or Modify Resource Life Cycle Models
v. Identify common information needs
vi. Inventory Community of Interest Member Business Information Systems
    (1) Identify Community of Interest Member Business Information systems that are related to Community of Interest Resource Life Cycle Nodes
vii. Build Community of Interest Business Event, Calendar, and Cycle Information
viii. Create Information Exchange Data Model Implemented Data Model
ix. Inductively build Information Exchange Data Model at the Implemented Data Level based on Information Needs of the Community of Interest
x. Resolve any Implemented Data Model table column conflicts for Operational Data Model Schemas
xi. Fully develop database object models
xii. Map Implemented Data Model to Resource Life Cycle Model
xiii. Create, Map, or Modify Specified Data Model
    (1) If Create or Map, then perform Specified Data Model changes
    (2) If Update, then harmonize with other Community of Interest owners of Specified Data Model
xiv. Create, Map, or Modify 11179 Data Element Metadata
    (1) If Create or Map, then perform 11179 Data Element Metadata changes
    (2) If Update, then harmonize with other Community of Interest owners of 11179 Data Element Metadata
    (3) Build the ISO 11179 Data Element upper layer metadata
    (4) Determine the value domains for all ISO 11179 Data Elements
    (5) Determine the value domains for all attributes, columns, and DBMS columns
    (6) Resolve value domain conflicts
xv. Create, Map, or Modify data integrity rule models
    (1) If Create or Map, then perform Data Integrity Rule Model changes
    (2) If Update, then harmonize with other Community of Interest owners of Data Integrity Rule Models

xvi. Generate the Information Exchange Data Model Operational Data Model from its Implemented Data Model
xvii. Generate Prototype application to validate Information Exchange Data Model
xviii. Validate and Iterate Information Exchange Data Model
xix. Create Business Event Models
xx. Create View Models for Information Exchange Data Model to Business Information System import and export
xxi. Formulate complete Information Exchange Data Model Report
xxii. Audit Information Exchange Data Model
xxiii. Cycle Lessons Learned

b. Create Information System Plans for the Information Exchange Data Model
   i. Identify the view models for intersecting Community of Interest member system with the Information Exchange Data Model System
   ii. Identify the Business Event, Business Cycle, and Calendar Cycles models required for the Information Exchange Data Model to successfully operate
   iii. Create specification for the Export and/or Import of Community of Interest member Business Information System process to/from the Information Exchange Data Model
   iv. Create the specification of the Import and/or Export from the Information Exchange Data Model to the Community of Interest member Business Information System
   v. Review and revise all Business Event, Business Cycle, and Calendar Cycles models across all the Community of Interest member Business Information Systems to ensure that there is proper data synchronization

c. Evolve and maintain Information Exchange Data Models
   i. Receive requests for change
   ii. Evaluate change requests
   iii. Accomplish change requests if possible
   iv. Update all Information Exchange Data Models
   v. Republish Information Exchange Data Model Report
   vi. Configuration manage Information Exchange Data Model use across its lifecycle
   vii. Audit Information Exchange Data Model

viii. Cycle Lessons Learned

d. Create Policies, procedures, and documentation regarding Information Exchange Data Model

8.3.1.4 Creation of XML Data Exchanges

a. Create Metadata Infrastructure for XML

i. Support XML Schema Catalog data
   (1) Identify metadata infrastructure requirements for metadata catalogs
   (2) Design metadata repository changes
   (3) Prototype metadata repository changes
   (4) Iterate until acceptable
   (5) Implement metadata repository changes

ii. Support XML schemas
   (1) Identify metadata infrastructure requirements for metadata
   (2) Design metadata repository changes
   (3) Prototype metadata repository changes
   (4) Iterate until acceptable
   (5) Implement metadata repository changes

iii. Support XSLTs
   (1) Identify metadata infrastructure requirements for metadata
   (2) Design metadata repository changes
   (3) Prototype metadata repository changes
   (4) Iterate until acceptable
   (5) Implement metadata repository changes

iv. Support Generation of XML wrapped data
   (1) Identify metadata infrastructure requirements for metadata
   (2) Design metadata repository changes
   (3) Prototype metadata repository changes
   (4) Iterate until acceptable
   (5) Implement metadata repository changes

v. Support Generation of other types of tag wrapped data
   (1) Identify metadata infrastructure requirements for metadata
   (2) Design metadata repository changes
   (3) Prototype metadata repository changes
   (4) Iterate until acceptable
   (5) Implement metadata repository changes

b. Identify requirements for programs to generate metadata catalog data
   i. Create Scenario for metadata catalog generation
   ii. Create prototype
   iii. Iterate until acceptable
   iv. Plan for Enterprise-wide implementation

c. Identify requirements for programs to automatically create XML schemas for every Information Exchange Data Model
   i. Create Scenario for metadata catalog metadata generation
   ii. Create prototype
   iii. Iterate until acceptable
   iv. Plan for Enterprise-wide implementation

d. Create requirements to assess effectiveness and utility of XML implementation
e. Create Policies, procedures, and documentation appropriate for XML

8.3.2 Maintenance of Data Interoperability Standards

Upon the Community of Interest approval of standard that document is automatically assigned to a maintenance project.

A maintenance project retains that status until experience indicates a need for revision, reaffirmation, or withdrawal, or has been converted to status as a stabilized standard.

On the four-year anniversary of the standard's approval a determination is made whether the standard is to be revised, reaffirmed, or withdrawn.

During the maintenance phase, experience in using and implementing a standard may cause questions to arise. These questions are processed under the procedures for defect management.

The Community of Interest responsible for the standard will use the voting procedures to process the response to a report of an alleged defect.

8.3.2.1 Revision

Whenever it is determined that a revision of the standard is needed, a project proposal for the revision will be developed by the Community of Interest in accordance with the provisions in the Community of Interest, Project Proposal Guide. After approval by the Community of Interest, the Project Proposal will be submitted to the Data Interoperability Program Committee. Processing continues at Milestone 1.

If a revision is planned or underway, but not completed by the four-year anniversary of either the approval or the last reaffirmation of the standard, the Community of Interest must determine whether the standard being revised will be reaffirmed or withdrawn while the revision is being developed, and make a recommendation to the Standards Development Board.

NOTE: If the revision process extends for four years beyond a previous reaffirmation, this process will be repeated. The effect of this is that the Community of Interest must forward to the Standards Development Board by the above mentioned four-year or nine-year anniversary, either a completed revision to the standard, or a recommendation for reaffirmation or withdrawal.

8.3.2.2 Reaffirmation/Withdrawal

If it is determined that the standard should be reaffirmed or withdrawn, the Community of Interest will forward a package that includes all of the following:

- A recommendation of reaffirmation or withdrawal.
- The final tally of the Community of Interest vote recommending reaffirmation or withdrawal with a copy of any unresolved negative votes, and the Community of Interest response to each.

The Community of Interest package is forwarded to the Data Interoperability Program Committee and the Data Interoperability Program Committee initiates the public review of the Community of Interest recommendation.

- If comments are received as a result of the public review, these comments are forwarded to the Community of Interest that made the recommendation and the Community of Interest will consider these comments at their next meeting, provide a response to each commenter, and forward final Community of

Interest recommendation to the Data Interoperability Program Committee for final action. The final Community of Interest recommendation will contain a copy of each comment and the Community of Interest 's response to each, in addition to the information contained in the package.

- If there are no comments, the Data Interoperability Program Committee will initiate a Data Interoperability Program Committee letter ballot for approval of the Community of Interest recommendation. If there are any negative votes on the Data Interoperability Program Committee Letter Ballot, a 15-day reconsideration ballot will be issued. At the completion of the letter ballot process, if the Data Interoperability Program Committee letter ballot passes, the Data Interoperability Program Committee submits the recommendation to Board of Standards Review for a Data Interoperability Standard.

If the Data Interoperability Program Committee letter ballot fails, for lack of affirmative votes, and there are no negative votes, final action is taken by the Data Interoperability Program Committee at its next meeting.

If the Data Interoperability Program Committee letter ballot fails based on the number of negatives, the recommendation is returned to the Community of Interest that originated it for further deliberation.

8.3.2.3 Amendments and Supplements

Amendments are separately processed documents that modify a standard with technical changes or additions, or with changes in what it means to conform to the standard. If it is determined that one or more amendments are needed prior to the revision of the standard, such amendments, other than Defect Management, will be processed in the same manner as standards, e.g., initiated with a project proposal.

8.3.2.4 Defect Management

These procedures are for the Standards falling under the following conditions:

- The rapid amendment of standards for which proper use is dependent upon the rapid promulgation of errata or amendments as defects are detected.

- The rapid promulgation of commentary consisting of clarifying interpretations without technical amendment of the standard.

The submission of the report of an alleged defect may result in one or more of the following:

- Erratum to a standard.
- Amendment to a standard.
- Interpretation of a standard.
- Response to the submitter explaining why an erratum, amendment, or interpretations will not be issued.

Each of these, except the last is discussed in turn. For the Standards, the concepts in this section generally apply except where indicated.

8.3.2.4.1 Erratum

A standard may be modified with corrigenda to:

- Correct a typographical error.
- Insert a missing word, sentence, paragraph, figure, example, table, or clause.
- Delete an extraneous word, sentence, paragraph, figure, example, table, or clause.

Any such modification of the standard will not introduce technical changes or changes in what it means to conform to the standard.

8.3.2.4.2 Amendment

Any modification of the standard that introduces technical changes or changes in what it means to conform to the standard will be treated as an amendment to the standard.

8.3.2.4.3 Interpretation

An interpretation is a clarifying commentary on the standard that does not introduce either a technical change or a change in what it means to conform to the standard.

8.3.2.5 When the Community of Interest No Longer Exists

If the Community of Interest responsible for the standard no longer exists, the Data Interoperability Program Committee is responsible for dealing with reaffirmation, revision, or withdrawal of the standard. The Data Interoperability Program Committee will also process any defect management documents associated with the standard.

If, by the four-year anniversary of the approval or last reaffirmation of a standard, the Community of Interest responsible for the standard has not forwarded a proposed revision to the standard or a recommendation for reaffirmation or withdrawal of the standard, the Data Interoperability Program Committee will take action during the fifth year to approve reaffirmation or withdrawal of the standard.

8.3.2.6 Alleged Defect

8.3.2.6.1 Action by the Data Interoperability Program Committee

If the Data Interoperability Program Committee receives a report of an alleged defect, the Data Interoperability Program Committee will forward the report to the Community of Interest responsible for the standard.

8.3.2.6.2 Action by Community of Interest

Upon receipt of a report of an alleged defect, the Community of Interest Chair or designee will:

- Enter the report in a permanent register of defect reports.
- Distribute the report to all Community of Interest members within two weeks of receipt.
- Send an acknowledgment of receipt to the submitter within thirty calendar days of receipt of the report.
- Place the report on the agenda for the next meeting of the Community of Interest, if the meeting is scheduled within two months of receipt of the alleged defect; in this case the submitter of the report will be invited to participate in discussion of the report.

If a meeting of the Community of Interest has not been or cannot be conveniently scheduled no later than two months after receipt of the report of the alleged defect by the Community of Interest Chair or designee, the Community of Interest Chair or designee, in consultation with the Data Interoperability Program Committee, will appoint a group of experts to expedite the preparation of a recommendation to the Community of Interest. In this case, the submitter of the request is not necessarily involved.

If the Community of Interest determines that an erratum, amendment, or interpretation will not be issued, the submitter of the report will be advised why no further action is expected to be taken.

8.4.2.6.3 Processing of Responses

The Community of Interest will forward a package to the Data Interoperability Program Committee that will include all of the following:

- A letter recommending the action to be taken.
- The final tally of the Community of Interest vote recommending the action with a copy of any unresolved negative votes and the Community of Interest response to each.

The Community of Interest package is reviewed by the Standards Development Board, which recommends action to the Data Interoperability Program Committee as appropriate. If the Data Interoperability Program Committee agrees with the Community of Interest recommendation, processing continues as specified in the following sections.

8.4.2.6.3.1 Erratum

If the Community of Interest determines that the response will be processed as an erratum to the standard, the Data Interoperability Program Committee will forward the report, response, and erratum for a Data Interoperability Program Committee Letter Ballot and concurrently to the Community of Interest for any required the Community of Interest public review. The submitter of the report will be advised of this action by the Data Interoperability Program Committee. Processing will continue at Milestone 5.

8.4.2.6.3.3 Amendment

If the Community of Interest determines that the response will be processed as an amendment to the standard, the Data Interoperability Program Committee will forward the report, response, and amendment for a concurrent Data Interoperability Program Committee Letter Ballot and the Community of Interest public review. The submitter of the report will be advised of this action by the Data Interoperability Program Committee. Processing will continue at Milestone 5.

8.4.2.6.3.4 Interpretation

If the Community of Interest determines that the response will be processed as an interpretation of the standard, the Data Interoperability Program Committee will forward the report, response, and interpretation for a Data Interoperability Program Committee Letter Ballot. If the Data Interoperability Program Committee Letter Ballot results in the approval of the interpretation, the submitter of the report will be advised of this action and the interpretation is published by the Data Interoperability Program Committee as the Community of Interest interpretation bulletin.

At the discretion of the Community of Interest, approved interpretations can be collected and published by the Data Interoperability Program Committee. Interpretations will be published within two years of their approval.

8.3.2.7 Stabilized Standards

Whenever it is determined that a standard has ongoing validity and effectiveness, but is mature and unlikely to require maintenance of any sort, it can be designated as a stabilized standard, that removes the requirement for periodic reaffirmation.

In order for a standard to be declared a stabilized standard, at least five years must have passed since the previous reaffirmation, without any modifications.

If it is determined that the standard should be designated as a stabilized standard, the Community of Interest will forward a package that includes all of the following:

- The rationale for the recommendation.

- The final tally of the Community of Interest vote recommending status as a stabilized standard with a copy of any unresolved negative votes and the Community of Interest response to each.

The Community of Interest package is forwarded to the Data Interoperability Program Committee and the Data Interoperability Program Committee initiates the public review of the Community of Interest recommendation.

- If comments are received as a result of the public review, these comments are forwarded to the Community of Interest that made the recommendation and the Community of Interest will consider these comments at their next meeting, provide a response to each commenter, and forward final Community of Interest recommendation to the Standards Development Board for review and subsequently to the Data Interoperability Program Committee for final action. The final Community of Interest recommendation will contain a copy of each comment and the Community of Interest 's response to each, in addition to the information contained in paragraphs above.

- If there are no comments, the Data Interoperability Program Committee will initiate a Data Interoperability Program Committee Letter Ballot for approval of the Community of Interest recommendation. If there are any negative votes on the Data Interoperability Program Committee Letter Ballot, a 15-day reconsideration ballot will be issued. At the completion of the letter ballot process, if the Data Interoperability Program Committee Letter Ballot passed, the Data Interoperability Program Committee submits the recommendation to Board of Standards Review.

If the Data Interoperability Program Committee Letter Ballot failed, for lack of affirmative votes, and there were no negative votes, final action is taken by the Data Interoperability Program Committee at its next meeting.

If the Data Interoperability Program Committee Letter Ballot failed based on the number of negatives, the recommendation is returned to the Community of Interest that originated it for further deliberation.

The Data Interoperability Program Committee will maintain a list of stabilized standards. Besides providing status of the standards, this list will be used by the Data Interoperability Program Committee to:

- Report to the Community of Interest on reaffirmation of the Standards that the standard is reaffirmed, without requiring a Community of Interest ballot or public review.

- Report to Data Interoperability Program Committee on reaffirmation of ISO standards for which a Community of Interest holds the Technical Advisory Group, that the standard is reaffirmed, without requiring a Community of Interest ballot or public review.

In either case, the Data Interoperability Program Committee will post the action on the Community of Interest web site and respond to the authority requesting the reaffirmation.

If a new work proposal is generated and adopted against a stabilized standard, the standard will revert to maintenance status.

8.3.2.8 Introductory Statements for the Response

An introductory statement will be included in the response to a report of an alleged defect in a standard. Thereafter, the response will include one or more of the following responses depending on type:

- Erratum
- Amendment
- Interpretation

8.3.2.8.1 Erratum

An erratum is issued in response to questions that have been raised regarding certain specifications contained in the standard. The erratum will identify the affected standard, the Community of Interest preparing the erratum, the problem specifications, the approach to a solution, and the erratum solution itself. The erratum will be created as quickly as possible so as to avoid any unnecessary rework on the part of standard adopters.

This erratum is to be considered as part of the standard and must be used in conjunction with that standard. Any subsequent revision, erratum, or amendment to the standard may or may not reflect the contents of this erratum.

8.3.2.8.2 Amendment

An amendment is issued in response to questions that have been raised regarding certain specifications contained in the standard. The amendment will identify the affected standard, the Community of Interest preparing the amendment, the problem specifications, the approach to a solution, and the amendment solution itself. The amendment will be created as quickly as possible so as to avoid any unnecessary rework on the part of standard adopters.

This amendment is to be considered as part of the standard and must be used in conjunction with that standard. The amendment may alter the meaning of the standard. Any subsequent revision, erratum, or amendment to the standard may or may not reflect the contents of this amendment.

8.3.2.8.3 Interpretation

An interpretation is issued in response to questions that have been raised regarding certain specifications contained in the standard. The interpretation will identify the affected standard, the Community of Interest preparing the interpretation, the problem specifications, the approach to an understanding of the standard. The interpretation will be created as quickly as possible so as to avoid any unnecessary rework on the part of standard adopters.

This interpretation, while reflecting the technical opinion of the Committee responsible for maintaining the standard, is intended solely as supplementary information to users of the standard. The standard is not altered by the issuance of this interpretation. Any subsequent revision, erratum, amendment, or interpretation to the standard may or may not reflect the contents of this interpretation.

8.4 Officer Appointment

8.4.1 Election Procedures

At the time an elected officer position becomes vacant or within six months prior to an incumbent officer's term expiring, a thirty-day call for volunteers for candidates to fill the officer position will be issued to the Chair of the Subgroup with the vacancy. The Subgroup Chair will expeditiously forward this call to the Subgroup membership.

In order to be considered, candidates must apply within the time frame specified in the call for volunteers. The incumbent may also apply unless this would cause a violation of the term limitations for the office.

For the Data Interoperability Program Committee and Subsidiary Boards, a candidate for an officer position must be a principal representative of a voting member of the Data Interoperability Program Committee.

For all other subgroup, the candidate must be a principle or alternate representative of a voting member of the Subgroup.

In the event of two or more officer positions from a Subgroup being filled at the same time, the Data Interoperability Program Committee will stagger the Subgroup officers' appointment process for those offices (i.e., conclude one election before closing the call for another position) in order to allow candidates to apply for more than one vacancy.

When a new Subgroup is formed, the Data Interoperability Program Committee will appoint a convener and issue the call for volunteers for candidates to fill the officer positions. The call will be issued to the convener of the Subgroup who must expeditiously forward it to the Subgroup membership. Until a Chair has been elected, the convener will continue to assume the Chair responsibilities.

Each volunteer candidate, whether for appointment or reappointment, must submit to the Data Interoperability Program Committee the following documentation in support of their candidacy:

- A statement of experience, indicating the volunteer's expertise in the Subgroup's program of work, voluntary standards' efforts, and leadership abilities .

- A statement of management support acknowledging the additional workload, financial resources, and duties required of an officer over and above that of a technical participant.

Statements of management support on behalf of officer candidates must be submitted from those organizations that are affected by the additional workload and financial resources required. Letters of management support should indicate a commitment for at least one year, although commitment for the full term of office is preferred.

The Data Interoperability Program Committee will review the documentation to determine if it satisfies all of the procedural requirements and review the membership records of the Subgroup involved to determine if the candidate(s) is a principal or an alternate in good standing in the Subgroup.

The Data Interoperability Program Committee is the officer appointment body for Chair positions in all Communities of Interest. When there is more than one qualified candidate applying for the position, the Data Interoperability Program Committee will provide the Chair of the Community of Interest, an advisory, thirty-day letter ballot with a request that it be distributed to the Community of Interest membership for completion. This letter ballot will contain the names of all qualified candidates with a request to indicate the candidate the member prefers fill the vacant position. The letter ballot will be returned to the Data Interoperability Program Committee by the individual Community of Interest members and the results of the letter ballot will be provided to the Data Interoperability Program Committee as information in the appointment process.

Letter ballots received by the Data Interoperability Program Committee after the close of the ballot period may not be processed depending upon the postmark. The results of Community of Interest letter ballots are confidential and are only advisory to the Data Interoperability Program Committee in the appointment process.

The Data Interoperability Program Committee will furnish the Data Interoperability Program Committee the documentation provided by the candidates and the summary of the results of the advisory Community of Interest letter ballot. The Data Interoperability Program Committee will take final appointment action in executive session. When Data Interoperability Program Committee appointment action is completed, the Data Interoperability Program Committee will advise the Community of Interest and the candidates. The individual appointed will assume the officer position upon completion of the term of the incumbent, or, if the officer position is vacant or the incumbent's term has expired, the individual appointed will assume the officer position immediately.

8.4.2 Terms of Elected Officers

Terms of elected officers normally end at their designated termination dates or by resignation of officer, termination of the body, termination of officer's membership, or by recall, whichever occurs first. In the event that the issuance of a call for candidates prior to the designated termination date is delayed, the term will be extended either until the election of a successor is completed, or the call is issued and closed with no response, whichever occurs first.

8.4.3 Officer Recall Procedures

When circumstances require, it is the responsibility of the Data Interoperability Program Committee to recall the Chair, elected Vice-chair of a Subgroup. Recall is a very serious responsibility discharged with utmost regard to confidentiality and due process.

For all matters considered by the Data Interoperability Program Committee, the following procedures apply:

- Formal consideration of corrective action or recall begins with a written communication between a concerned party and the staff of the Data Interoperability Program Committee. The matter is discussed in an executive session at the next Data Interoperability Program Committee meeting at that time the Data Interoperability Program Committee decides whether sufficient grounds exist to investigate it.

- If it is decided to investigate the matter, the Data Interoperability Program Committee will notify in writing the officer involved. A Data Interoperability

Program Committee member is designated to follow up on the original communication to the Data Interoperability Program Committee, discuss the matter with the officer involved, gather other information and opinions, as appropriate, and make a report in an executive session at the next Data Interoperability Program Committee meeting. At that time, the Data Interoperability Program Committee decides whether to take no further action, to continue its investigation or to recall the officer involved. In any case, the officer involved is notified in writing.

8.5 Service Fee Waiver Procedures

Any organization believing there is justification to obtain a full or partial waiver of the Data Interoperability Program Committee service fee may apply in writing to the Data Interoperability Program Committee. The requester should provide documentation that would enable the Data Interoperability Program Committee to make a recommendation for final action. Waiver requests will be handled in strict confidence. Results of the request are conveyed directly to the requester and are not reported to any other individual or group.

8.6 Appeals Procedures

8.6.1 Introduction

The provision for appeals is important for the protection of directly and materially affected interests and of the standard's developers. An appeals mechanism is required as a part of due process by the Data Interoperability Program.

8.6.2 Right of Appeal

Directly and materially affected interests who believe they have been or will be adversely affected by a Standard or any action or inaction relative thereto within the Data Interoperability Program Committee 's jurisdiction have the right to appeal such actions or inactions of the Community of Interest subgroup or the

Data Interoperability Program Committee in accordance with the following procedures.

The Community of Interest will not normally hear an appeal of an action or inaction by a Subgroup or its Data Interoperability Program Committee until the procedures provided by the Community of Interest have been completed as prescribed below. Such appeals will be directed to the Community of Interest in accordance with the procedures of the appropriate the Community of Interest entity (e.g., Board of Standards Review, Executive Standards Council, or standards boards).

8.6.3 Criteria for Appeals Mechanism

It is the intention of the Data Interoperability Program Committee that the following general criteria are encompassed in these appeal's procedures:

- Appeals will be addressed promptly and a decision made expeditiously.
- The right of the involved parties to present their cases will not be denied.
- These procedures will provide for participation by all parties concerned without imposing an undue burden on them.
- Consideration of appeals will be fair and unbiased and will fully address the concerns expressed.
- Records of appeals will be kept and made available upon request. The Data Interoperability Program Committee may levy a nominal charge to cover the cost of reproduction, handling and distribution for requests received from other than the involved parties.

8.6.4 Appeals

The appellant will file a formal complaint with the Data Interoperability Program Committee within thirty calendar days after the date of notification of the action being appealed or at any time with respect to inaction. The complaint will state the nature of the objection(s) including any direct and material adverse effects, the section(s) of these procedures or the standards that are at issue, actions or inactions that are at issue, and the specific remedial action(s) that would satisfy the appellant's concerns. Previous efforts to resolve the objection(s) and the outcome of each will be noted.

Within thirty calendar days after receipt of the complaint, the Data Interoperability Program Committee will respond by correspondence to the appellant, specifically addressing each allegation of fact in the complaint to the extent of the respondent's knowledge.

If the appellant and the Data Interoperability Program Committee are unable to resolve the complaint informally in a manner consistent with these procedures within fifteen calendar days, the Data Interoperability Program Committee will schedule a hearing with an appeal's panel on a date agreeable to all participants but within forty-five calendar days, giving at least ten calendar days notice. If there is not a mutually agreeable date, the Data Interoperability Program Committee will set the date and time for the appeal hearing. Should any party of interest not be present at the meeting, the decision of the appeal's panel will be based on the written submissions and any presentations made by the parties.

The appeal's panel will consist of three individuals who have not been directly involved in the matter in dispute. At least two members will be acceptable to the appellant and at least two will be acceptable to the Data Interoperability Program Committee. The appeal's panel members will be selected as follows:

- The appellant selects one.

- The Data Interoperability Program Committee selects one.

In the event the appellant does not wish to select a panelist or a third panelist cannot be agreed upon, the Data Interoperability Program Committee will appoint these individuals to the panel in order to hold a hearing. The appeal's panel will convene at a mutually agreed site is selected.

The appellant has the burden of demonstrating adverse effects, improper actions or inaction, and the efficacy of the requested remedial action. The Data Interoperability Program Committee has the burden of demonstrating that the Community of Interest and the Data Interoperability Program Committee took all actions in compliance with these procedures and that the requested remedial action would be ineffective or detrimental. Each party may adduce other pertinent arguments, and members of the appeal's panel may address questions to individuals.

The appeal's panel will render its decision in writing within thirty calendar days, stating findings of fact and conclusions, with reasons therefore, based on a preponderance of the evidence. Consideration may be given to the following positions, among others, in formulating the decision:

- Finding for the appellant, remanding the action to the Data Interoperability Program Committee for remedy by the Community of Interest with a specific statement of the issues and facts in regard to that fair and equitable action was not taken.
- Finding for the Data Interoperability Program Committee with a specific statement of the facts that demonstrate fair and suitable treatment of the appellant and the appellant's objections.
- Finding that new, substantive evidence has been introduced, and remanding the entire action to the Data Interoperability Program Committee for appropriate reconsideration.

If, for whatever reason(s), the appellant chooses to forego the process detailed above, the Data Interoperability Program Committee will forward the appeal action to the Community of Interest. Included in the materials forwarded to the Community of Interest will be all documents pertaining to the Data Interoperability Program Committee 's attempts to resolve the matter at hand.

8.6.5 Further Appeal

If the appellant gives notice to the Data Interoperability Program Committee that further appeal is intended, a full record of the complaint, response, hearing, and decision will be submitted by the Data Interoperability Program Committee to the appropriate organization within the business.

8.7 Parliamentary Procedures

On questions of parliamentary procedure not covered in these procedures, Robert's Rules of Order.

8.8 Business Functions Summary

Business functions are those activities performed by "humans." If they were just the functions that are inside the IT boundary, then there would be many processes missing from this book. All critical processes should be described in sufficient detail that different groups of persons would ultimately produce the same products according to the same standards for quality and completeness.

Different collections of functions may produce the same overall results. That is perfectly acceptable. The architecture of the processes in Chapter 6 that build the products of Chapter 5, can fully support multiple collections of functions that are effectively equivalent.

Business functions also have a many-to-many relationship with business events. This is quite important because then business events can be generalized and used to serve multiple purposes.

The business functions that are more critical than others are those related to the data interoperability program, community of interest, and officer appointments.

A key function of the data interoperability program is how to discover the need for a community of interest. Critical too are the four key functions within communities of interest that support the construction of the four technology pillars of data interoperability: Authoritative data sources, enterprise identifiers, information exchange models, and XML data exchanges.

Necessary as well within the set of functions are the processes for standards maintenance including revision, affirmation, and withdrawal.

A very necessary component of any data interoperability program are service fees. Standards are very costly to create and if fees are not imposed there will likely be no feeling of ownership or perceived value.

9

Organizations

9.1 Data Interoperability Program Organization Structure

The Data Interoperability organization is divided among two classes of organizations:

- Data Interoperability Program Committee
- Communities of Interest

In the event there is just one data interoperability community of interest, then these two levels can be collapsed into just the single level community of interest. As more Communities of Interest arise then the additional levels should be created to ensure that there is consistency and consensus semantics across the communities.

9.2 Data Interoperability Program Committee

The overall architecture of the Data Interoperability Program is based on a top-down and bottom-up approach. Figure 23 shows the composition of the Data Interoperability Program Committee.

The Data Interoperability Program itself consists of policy, guidance, procedures, methodologies, courses, workshops, and a metadata repository software tool support which are engineered, tested, and administered. The roles, functions and duties of the main committee and the boards that report to the committee are provided in the sections that follow.

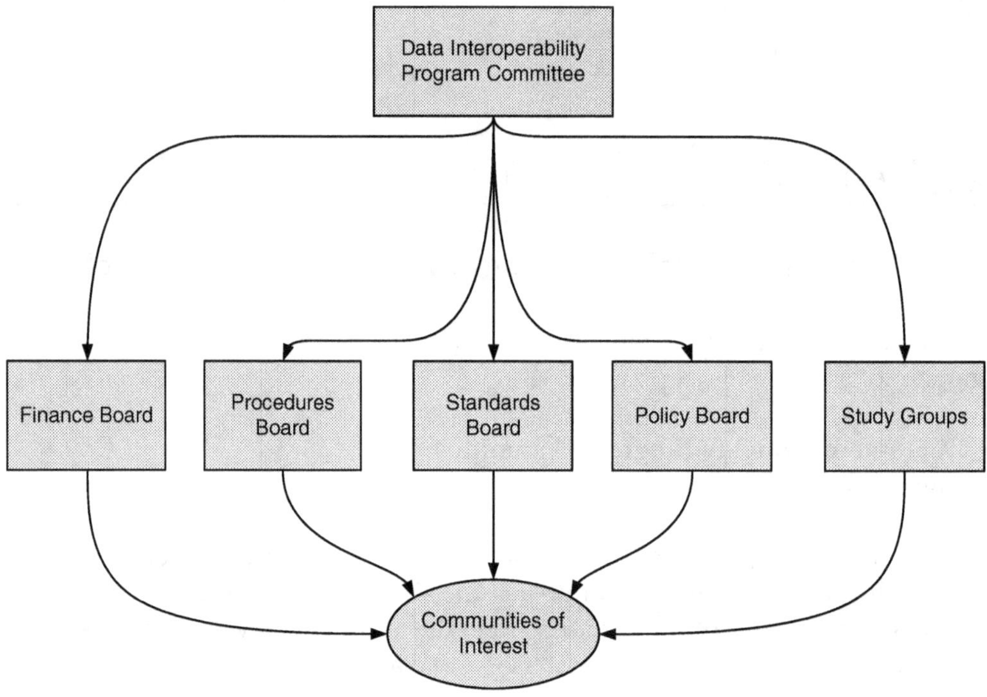

Figure 23. Data Interoperability Program Committee subgroups.

The top-down components, the Data Interoperability Program Committee provides guidance and facilitation. The Data Interoperability Program is accomplished through Communities of Interest throughout the enterprise to ensure both vertical and horizontal semantics integration. The data represented through the Information Exchange Data Models created by these committees are made trustworthy through authoritative data sources for all critical reference data. The data is guaranteed uniqueness through enterprise identifiers. Finally, data exchanges occur through highly managed XML definitions and exchanges. The bottom-up components, the Communities of Interest, provide empowerment to the ultimate creators, owners and users of the data interoperability's centerpiece, the Information Exchange Data Model. The Information Exchange Data Model and all other required metadata products reside within Communities of Interest and are manifest in a federated metadata environment. The

Information Exchange Data Model products across Communities of Interest are harmonized.

The governance of the Data Interoperability Program is through policy, guidance, and Communities of Interest data goals assessments. Supporting the guidance is a myriad of workshops, white papers, seminars, and software tool sets. These collectively assist staff as they develop, publish, integrate, and maintain all Data Interoperability Program work products within and across Communities of Interest.

The designation of a Chairman and Vice Chairman of the Data Interoperability Program Committee is by election of the Data Interoperability Program Committee members.

9.2.1 Data Interoperability Program Committee Membership

Membership on the Data Interoperability Program Committee is mandatory at all membership levels and gives the entity a right to vote on all matters before the Data Interoperability Program Committee. If the Data Interoperability Program is such that participants outside of an organization are of value, then other Business, Government and Standards Development Organizations level memberships may be allowed to request to be a member of the Standards Development Board and/or the Standards Policy Board at no additional charge. User Groups, Academics, Consortia members and Advisory level memberships may also be allowed to be members of the Standards Development Board and/or the Standards Policy Board for an additional fee.

9.2.2 Data Interoperability Program Committee Voting Rights

Only members in good standing can vote on Data Interoperability Program Committee matters. Similarly, only members in good standing can vote on subgroups.

9.2.3 Data Interoperability Program Committee Leadership

When multiple leadership positions are open, elections will be conducted in the following non-overlapping priority sequence.

- Data Interoperability Program Committee Chair
- Standards Development Board Chair
- Standards Policy Board Chair
- Data Interoperability Program Committee Vice-chair
- All Data Interoperability Program Committee committees.

This permits all interested parties to respond to a call for volunteers for the positions and minimizes the possibility of facing more than one term expiring at the same time. The Data Interoperability Program Committee Chair, Vice-chair and the Chairs of the Standards Development Board and Standards Policy Board are elected by the Data Interoperability Program Committee for a three-year term with a limit of two consecutive terms. A single person may not occupy two of the above positions.

9.2.4 Data Interoperability Program Committee Activity

The Data Interoperability Program Committee is the consensus body and has the ultimate responsibility for all standards developed and approved by the Communities of Interest.

The Data Interoperability Program Committee accepts recommendations from the Standards Development Board and the Standards Policy Board, which are responsible for the day-to-day operations of the Data Interoperability Program. The Data Interoperability Program Committee has final approval authority for recommendations from the Standards Development Board, Standards Policy Board and the Data Interoperability Program Committee committees.

The Standards Development Board and Standards Policy Board only provide consensus recommendations. The formal vote on all such consensus recommendations is taken at the Data Interoperability Program Committee level; therefore, none of the voting requirements (criteria and approval) apply to the Standards Development Board and Standards Policy Board.

There are two Committees reporting directly to the Data Interoperability Program Committee that are responsible for developing operational positions with respect to the Community of Interest. These subcommittees make recommendations directly to the Data Interoperability Program Committee, which has final approval authority. Chairs for these Committees are elected by the Data Interoperability Program Committee for a three-year term and may serve for an unlimited number of terms.

The current Data Interoperability Program Committee chair, Data Interoperability Program Committee Vice-chair and the Standards Development Board and Standards Policy Board Chairs may not serve in these offices. These two subcommittees are:

- Finance Board
- Procedures Board

.

The Data Interoperability Program Committee also has two subsidiary Boards:

- Standards Development Board
- Standards Policy Board

.

Both Subsidiary Boards operate in an advisory capacity to the Data Interoperability Program Committee.

Membership on these subsidiary Boards has a prerequisite of being a Data Interoperability Program Committee member.

9.2.5 Finance Board

The Finance Board operates under the auspices of the Data Interoperability Program Committee.

The Finance Board is advisory to the Data Interoperability Program Committee and is responsible for making recommendations to the Data Interoperability Program Committee on all matters pertaining to the finances of the Data Interoperability Program.

The Finance Board consists of a Chair, Vice Chair, an Editor, and a Secretary. Additional members are those determined necessary by the Data Interoperability Program Committee.

9.2.6 Procedures Board

The Procedures Board operates under the auspices of the Data Interoperability Program Committee.

The Procedures Board Committee is advisory to the Data Interoperability Program Committee and is responsible for making recommendations to the Data Interoperability Program Committee on all matters pertaining to the Communities of Interest.

Each Board consists of a Chair, Vice Chair, an Editor, and a Secretary. Additional members are those determined necessary by the Data Interoperability Program Committee.

9.2.7 Standards Policy Board

The Standards Policy Board addresses all policy matters related to the standards' work of the various Data Interoperability Committees. This Board makes recommendations, for Data Interoperability Program Committee approval, that affect Communities of Interest standards. Such recommendations will always have a focus on policies to support improving the market relevance of the Community of Interest.

Each Standards Policy Board consists of a Chair, Vice Chair, an Editor, and a Secretary. Additional members are those determined necessary by the Data Interoperability Program Committee.

9.2.8 Standards Development Board

The general responsibilities of the Standards Development Board are:

- Identify, engineer, plan, and evaluate the accomplishment of standards that are to be accomplished by Communities of Interest.
- Adopt and promote externally developed specifications.
- Enable collaboration with other standards' organizations.
- Create and agree to methodology for new work identification.

The Standards Development Board program of work is segmented into "projects," each related to the development of a specific standard. In addition, in the management of operations, the Standards Development Board manages the standardization process within Communities of Interest.

Each Data Interoperability Projects Committee consists of a Chair, Vice Chair, an Editor, and a Secretary. Additional members are those determined necessary by the Data Interoperability Program Committee.

9.2.9 Study Groups

The Data Interoperability Program Committee, Standards Development Board or Standards Policy Board may establish Study Groups to investigate a general subarea of information processing technology, to assess trends and relationships, and to provide advisory study reports to its parent body. While study groups have a finite duration they are formally constituted. Once their final report is completed with respect their charter, the study group dissolves.

A Study Group may also be established to conduct a study of a proposal for a standard's development project, or group of related projects, or for similar projects leading to a standard. When the mission of a Study Group is to examine an assigned proposal(s) in light of the requirements delineated in the Project Proposal Guide, the Study Group will submit a report, upon completion, to its parent body recommending:

- Support for introduction of a project, or
- Objections against the Community of Interest initiating the proposed project, or
- When a consensus cannot be reached, the report includes both the supporting and dissenting recommendations.

The Data Interoperability Program Committee or the Standards Development Board may alternatively request the study of a project proposal by an existing Community of Interest, if related to the Community of Interest's assigned projects. Each Study Group is established for a specific study. Upon completion and acceptance of its report by the parent body, the group is disbanded.

Each Study Group consists of a Chair, Vice Chair, an Editor, and a Secretary. Additional members are those determined necessary by the Data Interoperability Program Committee.

9.2.9.1 Study Group Charter

The parent body prepares a scope and program of work as the charter for a Study Group. The charter may contain additional guidance or constraints, as appropriate. The program of work contains the expected time schedule for completion and submission of the Study Group report and recommendation for (or against) a proposed project. At its organizational meeting, the Study Group reviews its scope and program of work, and may then or later recommends modification(s) to its parent body.

9.2.9.2 Study Group Project

Study group project planning begins with a problem statement that is taken through a rigorous functional and technical analysis process, resulting in a feasible solution for the Data Interoperability requirements.

9.2.9.3 Study Group Report and Project Recommendation

The Study Group report should be submitted to the parent body with a transmittal letter including the following:

- Reference to the meeting at which the report was approved.
- The Study Group vote on the report.
- Brief history of the study, showing the date of first meeting, the number of meetings, the extent of general agreement or disagreement, a brief summary of major issues considered, and the rationale for not accepting significant possible alternatives.
- The final report or recommendation.

- Any minority view(s) or supplemental statements provided by members of the Study Group.
- Membership mailing list.

9.2.10 Ad Hoc Groups

An ad hoc group may be established by the Chair of any formal committee within the Data Interoperability Program for one or more specific tasks to be completed not later than the end of the second following meeting of the parent body. Ad hoc groups are thus very different from Study Groups which are formally constituted and last until their study area final report is completed.

Ad hoc groups may consist of one or more persons. Its function is to do a specific job and report back. Upon completion of its report, or at the second meeting of the parent body following the ad hoc group's establishment, the group is dissolved.

Since an ad hoc group is limited in duration and scope, its business may be conducted informally. The principal record-keeping effort should be the documentation of its report. However, when the ad hoc group meets between scheduled meetings of its parent group, then the requirements for meeting notices and agenda will be followed. Results of such meetings may be documented in minutes or the final report to the parent committee.

9.3 Communities of Interest

The technical work of the Data Interoperability Program is distributed among a number of Communities of Interest. Upon completion of all currently assigned tasks and acquiescence by the Data Interoperability Program Committee, they may:

- Assume inactive status until required to resume activity for the required five-year review of published standards.
- Provide interpretations of their standards.
- Undertake new project assignments.

All work of the Communities of Interest is subject to approval of the Data Interoperability Program Committee. Each Community of Interest consists of a Chair, Vice Chair, an Editor, and a Secretary. Additional members are the Chairs and Vice Chairs from each contained technical committee. Each Community of Interest may determine if additional members are appropriate considering that virtually all the work of a Community of Interest is to be accomplished by Community of Interest Technical Committees.

The technical scope of each Community of Interest comprises the scope of its assigned projects. A Community of Interest may also develop proposals for new Data Interoperability projects related to its existing work, following the requirements and guidance of the Project Proposal Guide.

9.3.1 Establishment/Disbandment

New Communities of Interests are established only upon approval of the Data Interoperability Program Committee. A Community of Interest 's status will be reviewed, and the Community of Interest may be disbanded upon a vote of the Data Interoperability Program Committee if:

- The voting membership of the Community of Interest is not sufficient to meet quorum requirements.
- After two calls for officer candidates, no candidate has been identified.
- The Community of Interest program of work has been eliminated.
- Any other conditions that preclude the effective functioning of the Community of Interest in accordance with the policies and procedures of the Data Interoperability Program.

If any projects of the Community of Interest are transferred to another Community of Interest, members in good standing who maintain an interest in the projects may apply for membership in the Community of Interest accepting the transferred projects. Voting privileges begin with the first meeting attended, providing that the member attends one of the next two meetings of the Community of Interest. The member will be credited with any fees paid for membership in the disbanded Community of Interest.

9.3.2 Maintenance Communities of Interest

When a Community of Interest has completed all of its standards' development and standards' revision projects, these projects become maintenance projects. The duties that continue are:

- Recommend defect management actions during the standard's maintenance phase.
- Recommend revisions when experience with the standard so indicates.
- Conduct the required review and recommendation for revision, reaffirmation, designation as an archival standard, or withdrawal.

The Community of Interest may decide, however, that it can perform these specific duties in a less formal manner than that required of active Communities of Interest. To carry out its standards' maintenance duties without remaining a fully active Community of Interest, the Community of Interest may elect to revert to the status of Maintenance Community of Interest.

A Maintenance Community of Interest is relieved from the following requirements levied on Communities of Interest engaged in standards' development activities:

- Maintenance Communities of Interest do not need to hold at least one meeting a year.
- Members of Maintenance Communities of Interest do not have to pay service fees.
- No document distribution by the Data Interoperability Program Committee is provided unless it is specifically addressed to the Maintenance Community of Interest.

Technical Committees under the Community of Interest are automatically terminated when a Community of Interest changes its status to Maintenance Community of Interest.

To attain the status of Maintenance Community of Interest, the Community of Interest must approve, by Community of Interest letter ballot, a recommendation to the Standards Development Board for a change in status. A Super Majority of those voting must agree to the change in status in order for the recommendation to be approved. The approved recommendation is forwarded to the Data Interoperability Program Committee by the Standards Development Board for final approval action.

The officers and membership of the Community of Interest of record in the Data Interoperability Program Committee at the time the letter ballot is taken are the officers and membership of the Maintenance Community of Interest. The officers' appointments are indefinite and they are not subject to the three-year election process required of other Communities of Interest.

When it becomes necessary for an officer of a Maintenance Community of Interest to resign, the Maintenance Community of Interest Chair will so notify the Data Interoperability Program Committee, a call for candidates for the officer position will be issued by the Data Interoperability Program Committee.

Members of Maintenance Communities of Interest may lose their membership by failure to respond to two out of three successive ballots, in which case the membership will be terminated if the next ballot is not returned. Applications for membership will be by correspondence to the respective Chair or to the Data Interoperability Program Committee for forwarding. Membership becomes effective after the return of one letter ballot. However, that member's vote will not be counted in that ballot.

The Chair will continue to provide an Annual Report for the Standards Development Board. This report does not need to be delivered in person.

Should circumstances dictate that a Maintenance Community of Interest change its status back to an active Community of Interest, a recommendation will be made to the Standards Development Board using the same voting procedure as indicated above. The Data Interoperability Program Committee will take final approval action on this Standards Development Board recommendation, or the Data Interoperability Program Committee may initiate the action itself.

When changing status from Maintenance Community of Interest to an active Community of Interest, the Community of Interest will be bound by all of the procedures required of an active Community of Interest. Upon change of status from Maintenance Community of Interest to an active Community of Interest, the rules relating to meetings and service fees will apply only after the approval of the change in status of the Community of Interest.

Membership of the maintenance Community of Interest becomes the membership of the reactivated Community of Interest. In addition, attendees at the first meeting following activation will also attain voting rights.

9.3.3 Community of Interest Projects

Community of Interest projects are mainly about the specification, development, and evolution of Data Interoperability standards. In general, every Data Interoperability Standard includes subprojects that deal with:

- Metadata Infrastructure,
- Information Exchange Data Models
- Evolution, Maintenance and Support.

9.3.4 Community of Interest Technical Committees

As depicted in Figure 24, each Community of Interest is broken into five technical committees which are:

- Operational Technical Committee
- System Engineering Technical Committee
- Data Modeling Technical Committee
- Test and Evaluation Technical Committee
- Configuration Control Technical Committee.

9.3.4.1 Operations Technical Committee

The Operations Technical Committee is the technical committee performing the operational modeling discipline in the Community of Interest with support from the other technical committees.

The Operations Technical Committee consists of a Chair, Vice Chair, Secretary, and Editor. There are at least four additional members to assist in the accomplishment of the work that is set forth in the committee's work plans.

It is the responsibility of the Operations Technical Committee to make a report of its activities to the Community of Interest as appropriate.

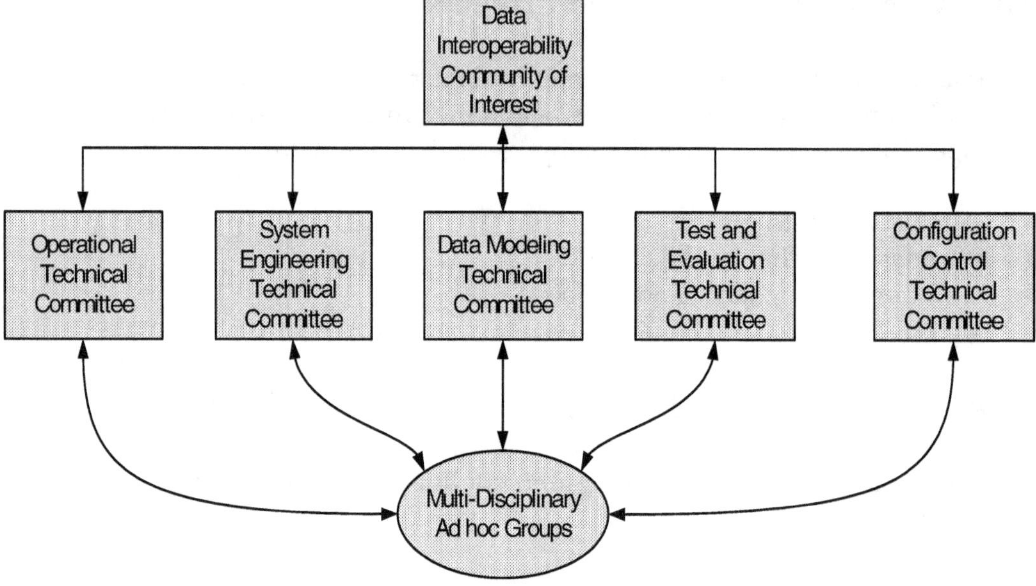

Figure 24. Data Interoperability Community Of Interest Technical Committees.

9.3.4.2 Systems Engineering & Architecture Technical Committee

The System Engineering and Architecture Technical Committee is the technical committee performing the system modeling discipline in the Community of Interest with support from the other technical committees.

The System Engineering and Architecture Technical Committee consists of a Chair, Vice Chair, Secretary, and Editor. There are at least four additional members to assist in the accomplishment of the work that is set forth in the committee's work plans.

9.3.4.3 Data Modeling Technical Committee

The Data Modeling Technical Committee is the technical Committee defining the data architecture and a common data model for interoperability.

The Data Modeling Technical Committee consists of a Chair, Vice Chair, Secretary, and Editor. There are at least four additional members to assist in the accomplishment of the work that is set forth in the committee's work plans.

9.3.4.4 Test and Evaluation Technical Committee

Test and Engineering Technical Committee provides the overall framework for the Community of Interest testing and evaluation. In addition, it conducts all tests regarding a given information exchange data model so as to certify its trustworthiness, reliability and performance sufficiency.

The Test and Evaluation Technical Committee consists of a Chair, Vice Chair, Secretary, and Editor. There are at least four additional members to assist in the accomplishment of the work that is set forth in the committee's work plans.

9.3.4.5 Configuration Control Technical Committee

The Configuration Control Technical Committee specifies a common set of procedures, methods and processes for controlling the standard's configuration. The Configuration Control Technical Committee also provides configuration control advice to all other technical committees on an as required basis. It also makes a report of its activities to the Community of Interest as appropriate.

The Configuration Control Technical Committee consists of a Chair, Vice Chair, Secretary, and Editor. There are at least four additional members to assist in the accomplishment of the work that is set forth in the committee's work plans.

9.3.4.6 Multi-disciplinary Committee

Multi-disciplinary Committees are short lived and ad-hoc in nature. They exist to address problems that span technical committees, or that are specially commissioned by the Community of Interest. In that regard, the Community of Interest officers initiate Multi-disciplinary Committees, define their scope and program of work, identify the various Community of Interest technical committees that must supply members to participate in the Multi-disciplinary effort, and set out the initial work plan, deliverables, and schedule that should be met by the Multi-disciplinary Committee. Data Interoperability Multi-disciplinary Committees:

- Address specific subjects or groups of subjects usually requiring a multi-disciplinary approach.
- Bring results back to the tasking Communities of Interest for further action and directions while the group members report the results back to their parent communities of as appropriate to keep their peers up to date on current efforts and results.
- Integrate with other Community of Interest Technical Committees as necessary.
- Integrate with other data interoperability Communities of Interest as necessary.

Each Multi-disciplinary Committee consists of a Chair, Vice Chair, Secretary, and Editor. Additional members from other technical committees assist in the accomplishment of the work that is set forth in the committee's work plans. Upon completion of its work, the Multi-disciplinary Committee dissolves.

9.3 Organization Summary

There are the traditional set of organizations within the data interoperability program except for the technical committees. These special technical committees are depicted in Figure 24 and are described within Section 9.3.4. Special care should be paid to these technical organizations to ensure that they are sufficiently funded and staffed. These committees are the "work-horse" committees. Without them the whole data interoperability program will fail.

10

Positions

Positions within a Data Interoperability Program are critical to its success. There is real work to be done, some of it is bureaucratic, some of it is planning and management, but most of it is the specification, implementation, and maintenance of the data models, process models, software specifications that comprise the entire data interoperability environment. There is also all of the information technology aspects with the real implementation of the databases and database oriented information systems that bring interoperable data environments alive and that enable them to be evolved and maintained.

This chapter concentrates exclusively on the positions that are necessary for the engineering, specification, and maintenance of the specifications of interoperable data environments rather than on the actual information technology aspects for implementation, operation, and evolution.

10.1 Membership Classes

Membership within the Data Interoperability Program is open to all members of an organization. There are, in general, three classes of membership: Full, Associate, and Observer. There are also liaison and ex officio memberships as well. In addition to classes of membership there are special memberships to the Data Interoperability Program Committee, its subcommittees, and subsidiary boards, to the Data Interoperability Program Projects committee, and finally to Communities of Interest.

10.1.1 Full Members

A Full Member is an organization that commits to support the collaborative development of succeeding versions of the Data Interoperability Program interoperability solution. Full Members undertake to be represented in Communities of Interest and must be prepared to expend the resources required to develop and sustain the Data Interoperability Program solution. A Full Member must be involved in and contribute actively to the decision-making process throughout the specification and development cycle. Full Members have voting and access rights at all meetings.

A full member may appoint no more than one principal representative to each subgroup. A full member may also appoint one or more principal member alternatives who can participate in any subgroup's activities. In all subgroup actions that require a vote, only full members can vote.

10.1.1.1 Requirements

Only an organization is eligible to become a Full Member. Before an organization becomes eligible for Full Membership, it must first be an Associate Member, it must agree to the program and scope of work of the overall Data Interoperability Program. The organization applying for full membership must have a data interoperability interest, that is, one or more Business Information Systems either available, or in the planning or development stage that would be involved in one or more data interoperability solutions, and inform the Data Interoperability Program Committee accordingly.

10.1.1.2 Application

The official request will be made by formal written proposal to any of the Data Interoperability Program Full Member organizations through the Data Interoperability Program Committee. This proposal must contain a statement indicating the organization's commitment to the Data Interoperability Program, and its agreement to conform to current baseline documents, architecture, configuration and employment concepts. The request must also acknowledge commitment to the Data Interoperability Program administrative requirements.

10.1.1.3 Acceptance

Acceptance as a Full Member to the Data Interoperability Program requires super majority agreement of all the Data Interoperability Program Full Members at a Data Interoperability Program Committee meeting.

10.1.2 Associate Members

Associate Members include organizations showing an interest in this program, which have been granted Associate Member status by the Data Interoperability Program Committee. Associate Members enjoy all the rights and privileges of a Full Member as agreed by the Data Interoperability Program Committee except Associate Members do not have any voting rights at meetings. Associate members need to attend all Data Interoperability Program Committee meetings and need to be represented in at least one Community of Interest at all the Community of Interest meetings.

10.1.2.1 Requirements

Organizations wishing to become Associate Members to the Data Interoperability Program must meet the following requirements:

- Be sponsored by a Data Interoperability Program Full Member.
- Be involved with a Business Information Systems either at an organizational or inter-organizational level.
- Agree to abide by the decisions of the Data Interoperability Program Committee.

10.1.2.2 Application

The official request will be made by formal written proposal that must be endorsed by a current the Data Interoperability Program Full Member. This Full

Member becomes the sponsoring member and assumes the responsibility for forwarding the endorsed application to all other Full Members.

The application must include a statement on the status of involvement in a Business Information Systems in one or more data interoperability solutions, the nature of interest in the Data Interoperability Program, and an agreement to abide by Data Interoperability Program Committee.

The Data Interoperability Program Committee as an empowered body will, at the next available opportunity, consider the application for membership as presented by the sponsoring member. On super majority agreement, the Data Interoperability Program Committee will issue direction to the host member to extend an invitation to the applicant to attend the next Data Interoperability Program Committee.

10.1.2.3 Associate Member Restrictions

Associate Members do not have any voting rights at meetings.

10.1.2.4 Associate Member Privileges

Associate Members will have full access to information within the Data Interoperability Program. Associate members should:

- Attend and participate in Data Interoperability Program Committee and one or more Community of Interest meetings.
- Be represented in at least one Technical Committee at all Community of Interest meetings.

At their discretion, they may engage in any of the following activities:

- Access all the Data Interoperability Program documentation.
- Participate in testing, including provision of staff, facilities and equipment.
- Host Data Interoperability Program meetings.
- Make proposals for the Data Interoperability Program agendas.

- Submit Change Proposals to the Data Interoperability Program specifications and program documents.
- Register concerns for discussion at the Data Interoperability Program Committee and Community of Interest levels.

10.1.3 Observers

Observers are not members, but are representatives from organizations with a cooperation and/or coordination relation to the Data Interoperability Program and may participate in an observer status in meetings of Communities of Interest. The coordination and/or cooperation relations are established through the Data Interoperability Program Committee. Privileges for observers are determined on a case-by-case basis, but observers will have no voting rights.

Observers can attend Community of Interest meetings only when invited by a Full Member. The invitation for attendance must receive a majority vote of all Full Members. After attending the first meeting, the observer must then apply for observer status through a written application, declaring their interest in the Data Interoperability Program to the Data Interoperability Program Committee Chairman.

10.1.4 Liaison Members

A Liaison member of a Community of Interest is someone who is a full member of different Community of Interest or a Community of Interest Technical Committee but desires to represent that different Community of Interest's position to the Community of Interest to which they are a liaison. Liaison members must be approved by the Data Interoperability Program Committee.

Liaison members may attend meetings, speak, and submit contributions. Liaison members receive meeting notices, draft agenda and minutes, and draft standards, and Study Group reports being voted upon by letter ballot. Other documents are not required to be distributed to liaison members.

10.1.5 Ex Officio Members

Ex officio members of the Data Interoperability Program's Committee or any of its subgroups may attend meetings, speak, and submit contributions. Ex officio members may also present motions; such motions require no second. Ex officio members may receive, if they request, meeting notices, draft agenda and minutes, and draft standards, and Study Group reports being voted upon by letter ballot. Other documents are not required to be distributed to ex officio members.

The Chairs of the Data Interoperability Program Committee, Standards Development Board, Standards Policy Board, and Communities of Interest are eligible to be ex officio members of the committee or board they formerly chaired.

10.2 Data Interoperability Program Committees

10.2.1 Data Interoperability Program Committee

Full Member status, that is, voting membership, in the Data Interoperability Program Committee is open to organizations directly and materially affected by the scope of the Community of Interest that are willing to participate regularly and that have paid the designated service fee.

A representative of a prospective voting member will initially attend a meeting without voting privileges and reaffirm interest in the work of the Community of Interest. Voting privileges become effective immediately with attendance at one of the next two successive meetings and upon receipt by the Data Interoperability Program Committee of applicable fees for the membership year. Failure to attend one of those two successive meetings constitutes withdrawal of the application for voting membership.

An organization with voting membership will appoint one and only one principal representative and may appoint one or more alternate representatives.

No representative will have more than one vote except in the case where two or more organizations appoint the same individual to represent them (as principal or alternate representative). An individual so designated may cast a separate vote for each organization represented. Each organization will confirm in writing to the Data Interoperability Program Committee that it is aware of the multiple role of the individual and will accept the results of the arrangement. Representation of more than one organization by the same individual will require the approval of the Data Interoperability Program Committee.

10.2.2 Data Interoperability Program Committee Subcommittees and Boards

Data Interoperability Program Committee contained subcommittees and boards develop recommendations for the Data Interoperability Program Committee to approve. Membership is achieved at the start of the first meeting at ended.

Voting membership is open to any organization with voting membership on the Data Interoperability Program Committee that is willing to participate regularly and has paid the appropriate service fee(s).

Voting rights are achieved when Data Interoperability Program Committee membership is achieved and all designated service fees have been paid.

10.2.3 Study Groups

Voting membership in Study Groups is open to all directly and materially affected parties that meet attendance and voting requirements and pay the designated service fee(s).

A representative of a prospective voting member will initially attend a meeting of the Study Group without voting privileges and reaffirm interest in the work of the Community of Interest or Study Group. Voting privileges become effective with attendance at one of the next two successive meetings and receipt by the Data Interoperability Program Committee of the applicable fees for the membership year. For a new Subgroup, all attendees at the formation meeting or second meeting will be considered voting members.

An organization with voting membership will appoint one and only one principal representative and may appoint one or more alternate representatives.

10.2.4 Ad Hoc Groups

There is no formal voting in Ad Hoc Groups.

10.3 Community of Interest Membership

Applications for membership to a Community of Interest will be by correspondence to the Data Interoperability Program Committee. Applicants will state their organization's reasons for interest.

Applications for or notifications of membership will be in writing to the Data Interoperability Program Committee and the Committee Chair. A representative of a prospective voting member will initially attend a meeting of the Community of Interest without voting privileges and reaffirm interest in the work of the Community of Interest. Voting privileges become effective with attendance at one of the next two successive meetings and receipt by the Data Interoperability Program Committee of the applicable fees for the membership year. For a new Community of Interest, all attendees at the formation meeting or second meeting will be considered voting members.

10.4 Limitations on Organizational Memberships

All directly and materially affected parties will have the opportunity for fair and equitable participation in the Data Interoperability Program.

Data Interoperability Program Committee and its subgroups will not be dominated by any single interest category, individual or organization. Unless it is claimed in writing by a directly and materially affected party that a single interest category, individual or organization dominated the standards development process, no test for dominance is required.

10.4.1 Single Federal, State, or Local Government Agency

When a Data Interoperability Program is wholly contained within a single Federal, State, or Local Government agency, there will be only one voting membership for separate government subdivisions within that agency, whether it is a Federal, State, or Local Government. A separate government subdivision is defined as an entity that reports to its parent executive, legislative, or judicial branch of government.

10.4.2 Multiple Federal, State, or Local Government Agencies

When a Data Interoperability Program extends across multiple Federal, State, or Local Government agencies, there will be only one voting membership for each separate government subdivisions or agencies, whether it is a Federal, State, or Local Government that is represented on the subgroup. A separate government subdivision or agency is defined as an entity that reports to its parent executive, legislative, or judicial branch of government.

However, in the case of the U.S. Department of Defense, it allowed a maximum of four votes from separate and unrelated entities such as the Department of Army, Department of Navy, Department of Air Force, Defense Logistics Agency, Defense Mapping Agency, etc. This exception is due to the unique nature of the DoD and is, therefore, not considered a precedent for any further exceptions.

10.4.3 Single Corporation or Company

When a Data Interoperability Program is wholly contained within a single Corporation or Company, there will be only one voting membership for each separate subdivision within that Corporation or Company. A separate subdivision is defined as an entity that reports to its parent executive.

10.4.4 Multiple Corporations or Companies

When a Data Interoperability Program spans multiple Corporations or Companies, there will be only one voting membership for each separate Corporation or Company. A separate Corporation or Company is defined as an entity that reports to its parent executive.

10.4.5 Mixed Data Interoperability Program Organizations

When a Data Interoperability Program subgroup spans Governments and Corporations or Companies, there will be one voting member for each separate government subdivisions or agencies, whether it is a Federal, State, or Local

Government that is represented on the subgroup. A separate government subdivision or agency is defined as an entity that reports to its parent executive, legislative, or judicial branch of government.

However, in the case of the U.S. Department of Defense, it allowed a maximum of four votes from separate and unrelated entities such as the Department of Army, Department of Navy, Department of Air Force, Defense Logistics Agency, Defense Mapping Agency, etc. This exception is due to the unique nature of the DoD and is, therefore, not considered a precedent for any further exceptions.

Further, there will be only one voting membership for each separate Corporation or Company. A separate Corporation or Company is defined as an entity that reports to its parent executive.

Members from academic communities such as Universities or University related institutions or corporations will have only one voting membership for each separate educational institution. A separate educational institution is defined as an entity that has a controlling body, such as a Board of Regents.

Finally, if membership is requested by Standards Development Organizations, User Groups, or Consortia, then only one member from each such organization will be allowed. Because those members are voting the interests of the Standards Development Organizations, User Groups, or Consortia, the principal and alternate representatives may be employed by other organizations who have voting memberships.

10.5 Executive Sessions

For those matters considered by the Data Interoperability Program Committee which require consideration in Executive Session, participation in Executive Session is limited to the Committee membership plus anyone invited by the Committee.

10.6 Membership Status Review Process

Whenever a Full Member is of the opinion that a Member is not fulfilling their obligations toward the Data Interoperability Program, it may bring it to the attention of the Data Interoperability Program Committee and request a formal review of the efforts of the Member concerned. The Data Interoperability Program

Committee review takes in consideration the arguments of the Member under review and may decide to give that Member an official warning.

After an official warning has been issued, the Data Interoperability Program Committee Chairman will request the Data Interoperability Program Committee Chairman for a Data Interoperability Program Committee review at a future Data Interoperability Program Committee meeting, leaving ample time for the Member under review to reinstate its commitment to the Data Interoperability Program.

The Data Interoperability Program Committee will hear the Member concerned and decide on possible implications for that member, if any.

In this review process the Data Interoperability Program Committee is the only management body that may apply consequences to a Member or that may grant a waiver to a Member regarding its responsibilities toward the Data Interoperability Program.

Whenever a Full Member is of the opinion that an Observer is not any more beneficial to the Data Interoperability Program, the same procedure is applied.

Members of the Data Interoperability Program Committee and subgroups will be terminated by the Data Interoperability Program Committee for failure to pay appropriate service fees within the time specified by the Data Interoperability Program Committee.

An organization that has had its voting membership terminated may reestablish it. If this membership is reestablished within the same billing period and the organization has paid its fee, no new service fee will be accessed.

Members of the Communities of Interest or Study Groups will be terminated under the following conditions:

- The principal and all alternate representative(s) will be warned in writing upon failure of the organization to:

  - Attend two out of three successive meetings, in that case the membership will be terminated if not represented at the next meeting; or

  - Return two out of three successive non accelerated letter ballots if the next non accelerated letter ballot after the warning is not returned, An organization fails to perform an above action when none of the organization's representatives performs the action.

- Voting and advisory memberships will be canceled by the Data Interoperability Program Committee for failure to pay appropriate service fees within the time specified by the Data Interoperability Program Committee.

Communities of Interest or Study Groups may vote to continue the membership despite failure of the member to comply with the attendance and/or ballot criteria.

An organization that has had its voting membership terminated may reestablish membership. If this membership is reestablished within the same billing period and the organization has paid its fee, no new service fee will be accessed.

10.7 Membership Withdrawal

A Full Member, an Associate Member or an Observer may withdraw at any time from the Data Interoperability Program upon written notification to the Data Interoperability Program Committee. Any Full Member or Associate Member that has withdrawn from participation in the Data Interoperability Program and requests reinstatement must re-apply in accordance with the Data Interoperability Program Membership procedures.

Members of the Data Interoperability Program Committee and Subgroups will be terminated by the Data Interoperability Program Committee for failure to pay appropriate service fees within the time specified by the Data Interoperability Program Committee.

An organization that has had its voting membership terminated may reestablish it. If this membership is reestablished within the same billing period and the organization has paid its fee, no new service fee will be accessed.

10.8 Community of Interest Officers

10.8.1 Chair

For each Subgroup, the Chair is responsible for presiding at meetings and ensuring that the program of work for that body is carried out in a prompt, efficient, and effective manner. Chairs are either elected or appointed.

Unless otherwise stated, appointed chairs have an indefinite term of office and elected chairs have a three-year term of office.

Chairs of the Data Interoperability Program Committee, the Standards Development Board and the Standards Policy Board are elected positions from the principal or alternate representatives of voting members on the Data

Interoperability Program Committee. They may not serve for more than two consecutive terms nor may a member provide more than a single elected officer on these three boards.

Chairs of the four Data Interoperability Program Committee Boards are elected positions from the principal or alternate voting representatives of members on the Data Interoperability Program Committee. They may not serve for more than two consecutive terms.

Chairs of Study Groups, Communities of Interest are elected by the Data Interoperability Program Committee from their constituency on a recommendation from that constituency. There is no limitation on number of terms.

All other Chairs are appointed by the Chair of their parent bodies. Their term is indefinite except for ad hoc Chairs, who are limited to the duration of the ad hoc subgroup.

10.8.2 Vice Chair

For each Subgroup, the Vice-chair (if one exists) performs the duties of the Chair, in the absence of the Chair. Vice-chairs may vote and participate according to membership rules.

Except for the Data Interoperability Program Committee, the Vice-chair of those groups with a Vice-chair is considered the chief administrative officer and is responsible for the administrative duties.

The Vice-Chair of the Data Interoperability Program Committee is an elected position from the principal or alternate representatives of members on the Data Interoperability Program Committee. If a member's representative is elected as Data Interoperability Program Committee Vice-Chair, that member may not provide another elected officer on the Data Interoperability Program Committee, Standards Policy Board or Standards Development Board.

For all other subgroup, the Vice-chair is appointed by and serves at the pleasure of the Chair of the parent body.

10.8.3 Secretary

The Secretary is responsible for the recording and transcribing of meeting minutes. The Secretary may also be responsible for other administrative as required by the Chair of a Subgroup.

The Secretary of a Subgroup is appointed by the Chair of that Subgroup. The Data Interoperability Program Committee Secretary serves at the pleasure of the Chair of that Subgroup.

10.8.4 Editor

The Editor is responsible for maintaining the data interoperability products, i.e., making timely and accurate changes as approved by the group. The Project Editor will report the status of each product at each meeting of the group.

Editors are appointed by and serve at the pleasure of their respective Chairs with no limitation on terms.

10.8.5 Other Positions

Chairs may appoint members to other positions (e.g., meeting coordinator, Committee librarian, etc.) with titles and responsibilities as required.

These other positions are appointed by and serve at the pleasure of their respective Chairs with no limitation on terms.

10.9 Position Summary

Positions within the data interoperability program are mainly by organization versus by individual. That is because it is mainly organizations that have systems that are required to interoperate.

The various memberships are formally identified and described. Different membership classes have different responsibilities, duties, and authorities.

Described also are the methods of constructing data interoperability programs that consist of organizations from different corporate structures.

11

Documents and Guidance

There are a number of documents that are created and comprise the everyday business of a Community of Interest. These include:

- Project Proposal Guide
- Annual Report
- Data Interoperability Standards
- Change Proposals
- Standing Documents
    - Procedures
    - Guidelines for Proposals
    - Letter Ballots
    - Ballot Comments
    - Guidelines for hosting meetings

11.1 Community of Interest Project Proposal Guide

The Community of Interest Project Proposal Guide defines the information to be submitted by any person, organization, or group as a proposal to initiate a project to develop a new or revised the standard.

The person, organization, group, or the Community of Interest Community of Interest initiating a standard development project proposal is asked to provide, in as complete a manner as possible and practicable, the information indicated. If supplementary material is required for presenting the proposal to pursue the activity, this should also be supplied.

Proposals should be uploaded to the Data Interoperability Program server. Alternatively, proposals should be emailed to:

DataInteroperabilityProgram@Organization.Com

Or finally, it should be mailed to the Data Interoperability Program address, which is:

> The Data Interoperability Program
> <Street Address 1>
> <Street Address 2>
> <City, State Zip>

During the review by the Data Interoperability Program Committee, and in developing its recommendation, the proposal will be examined to determine whether:

- A rational purpose and substantive goal exists.
- There is a need, an interest is evident, and the economic benefits are obtainable.
- The proposed standard development is technically feasible.

In preparing the recommendation, the definition of the standard development project in the original proposal may be augmented or modified. If the recommendation is that no Community of Interest activity be undertaken, the reasons for this negative decision will be appended. It must be kept in mind that Community of Interest recommendations are based on current judgment, and reconsideration of proposals may be appropriate in the event of changes in the conditions examined during the review.

The time and effort expended in the preparation of a well-researched and well-documented proposal will generally reduce the time and effort required to develop the recommendation for a standard's development and the recommendation to start that process.

Proposal for Project to Develop a New or Revised Standard		
Section	**Title**	**Description**
1.	**Source of the Proposed Project**	
1.1	Title	Provide a descriptive subject matter title.
		The date should be the date of submission of the proposal to the Data Interoperability Program Committee.
1.3	Proposer(s)	If the proposer is not an existing Community of Interest, identify the individual who will serve as the acting chairman until a new Community of Interest has been established.
2.	**Process Description for the Proposed Project**	
2.1	Project Type (Development or Revision)	Indicate "D" if DEVELOPMENT will be done within a Community of Interest and the expected result in the standard. Indicate "R" if the project proposal describes a proposed REVISION to a standard.
2.2	Definitions of Concepts and Special Terms	Provide definitions of key concepts and special terms (if any) needed in developing and understanding the standard.
2.3	Expected Relationship with Approved Reference Models, Frameworks, Architectures, etc.	Identify relevant reference models, frameworks, architectures, etc., that are being used to conceptualize the relationships among the various information technologies and this project, and any known or anticipated areas of conformance or conflict.

Proposal for Project to Develop a New or Revised Standard		
Section	**Title**	**Description**
2.4	Recommendation regarding a Community of Interest (Existing or New)	Indicate a preference for assignment of the proposed project to a particular existing Community of Interest, or propose creation of a new Community of Interest. Creation of a new Community of Interest must include the rationale. Include a description of available resources, that is, at least four organizations which are capable of the Community of Interest work effort and interested in the subject matter to assure that adequate resources exist to accomplish the proposed program of work. Indicate which are members of the Community of Interest.
2.6	Anticipated Frequency and Duration of Meetings	Estimate of the anticipated frequency and duration of meetings.
2.6	Target Date for Initial Public Review (Milestone 4)	Estimate the target date for releasing the draft standard for public review (See Milestone 4).
2.7	Estimated Useful Life of Standard	Estimate the useful life of the standard.
3.	**Business Case for Developing the Proposed Standard**	
3.1	Description	Describe the technical information that will be covered by the standard.
3.2.	Existing Practice and the Need for a Standard	Identify why a standard is needed, rather than another kind of solution. Describe existing practice in the area of a proposed standard to aid in judging timeliness and appropriateness of the project. Address the expected stability of the proposed standard with respect to both current technology and potential technological advances.

Proposal for Project to Develop a New or Revised Standard		
Section	**Title**	**Description**
3.3.	Implementation Impacts of the Proposed Standard	Address the potential impacts of the proposed standard. To the extent possible, address the following implementation considerations:
3.3.1	Development Costs	Provide an overall estimate of the technical development costs for this standard. Include labor costs for technical editor(s), logistical costs for meetings, work between meetings, and any other significant costs.
3.3.2	Impact on Existing or Potential Markets	Provide a cost/benefit statement (qualitative or quantitative) on the impact on users and suppliers, should this standard be implemented.
3.3.3	Costs and Method for Conformity Assessment	What testing environment is appropriate for this technology (e.g., suppliers' declaration, accreditation of testing laboratories, certification bodies)? Will this standard contain the necessary and sufficient testing information for assessing conformity to this standard? If not, how will this information be developed, and what are the associated development costs?
3.3.4	Return on Investment	What is the estimated ROI for development of this standard and the conformity assessment costs associated with it?
3.4	Legal Considerations	Address the following legal consecrations:
3.4.1	Patent Assertions	Identify assertions of patent rights in accordance with the relevant the Community of Interest. Is the proposer aware of any patent assertions that may be made? If so, describe. How will the possible extent of patent rights be determined and redetermined during the life of the development of the standard?

Proposal for Project to Develop a New or Revised Standard		
Section	**Title**	**Description**
3.4.2	Dissemination of the Standard	Identify how drafts of this standard will be disseminated electronically. How will the final standard be disseminated. Is the proposer aware of any intellectual property rights assertions that will hinder this distribution? If so, describe?
4.	**Related Standards Activities**	
4.1	Existing Standards	Identify existing standards including but not limited to the particular Community of Interest that may affect or be affected by the proposed project.
4.2	Related Standards Activity	Identify projects under development, including but not limited to the Community of Interest, that may affect or be affected by the proposed project. For each project identified, indicate if the liaison arrangements have been made with these activities.
4.3	Recommendations for Close Liaison	Recommend which Communities of Interest should be identified as close liaisons. Close liaisons require an exchange of information, but the work of one is not dependent upon the work of the other Communities of Interest
5.	**Units of Measurement used in the Standard**	**Indicate units of measurement used in the standard.**

Table 10. Format for standard's development project.

11.2 Subgroup Annual Report

11.2.1 Format/Period Covered

All Subgroups are required to produce an Annual Report. The Annual Report covers the period from the previous Report to the date the current Report is being prepared.

11.2.2 Report Schedule

The Annual Report must be provided electronically to the Subgroup's parent Subgroup in a format suitable for posting to the Data Interoperability Program web site. The Annual Report is due one month in advance of the Data Interoperability Program Meeting at which the report is scheduled for discussion. Communities of Interest provide their annual report to the Data Interoperability Program Committee.

11.2.3 Validation of Data Interoperability Program Databases

Most of the material related to a subgroup's work activities should be maintained on a regular basis in the Data Interoperability Program Committee 's projects' database. Approximately one to two months prior to the scheduled presentation of the Annual Report, the subgroup should ensure that the Projects database accurately reflects the current status of the subgroup's work.

In addition, the Subgroup Chair will validate the Membership database no less often than annually and certify that the membership database is up-to-date when the annual report is presented.

11.2.4 Oral Presentation

The Annual Report must be presented orally by the subgroup's Chair (or designee) according to the subgroup's parent's reporting schedule. Chairs of maintenance Communities of Interest do not need to provide oral reports.

The scheduled oral presentation by a Community of Interest concentrates on projects that did not reach the projected Milestone during the year and on administrative and procedural issues of concern. Other aspects of the Annual Report may also be covered as agreed upon by a Community of Interest Chair.

11.2.5 Format And Required Contents

Section	Title	Description
1.0	Annual Report for:	Name of the Subgroup
2.0	Covering the Period from [ ] to [ ]	Start date and end date
3.0	Title of the Subgroup's main work effort	Name of the main work effort chartered to the subgroup
4.0	Links:	• Subgroup's web site (if applicable) • Executive summary • Link to Subgroup's area on the Data Interoperability Program Committee 's Projects Database • Significant accomplishments • Significant challenges • Expected challenges • Previous year's meetings • Next year's meetings • Liaison activities • Membership and Officers • Future Trends • Other administrative information
5.0	**Informal Description of Work**	
5.1	Executive Summary	The Executive Summary should address the overall status of the subgroup areas such as the current level of participation, general reasons for any delays in progressing standards activities, and any overall administrative or procedural matters of note. This section should be written to provide the Data Interoperability

Section	Title	Description
		Program committee an overview of the current situation within the subgroup.
5.2	Significant Accomplishments	This section should address significant accomplishments since the previous annual report. This should be free form and not exceed a page. It should include a list of significant publications during the past year. A significant publication is one that, in the Chairman's judgment, contains information that could be useful to someone desiring descriptive background information not incorporated in the subgroup's work.
5.3	Significant Challenges	Significant challenges since previous annual report. What problems have been faced? Are the issues resolved? If not, what is the plan for resolving the issues? If approved milestones exist, status should be in terms of these milestones. Any delays should be explained and future plans highlighted.
5.4	Expected Challenges	Expected challenges in the next twelve months. Is controversy expected for approving a subgroup's work? Is there likely to be a huge mass of public comments?
6.0	**Committee Activities**	
6.1	Previous Year	This should be a list that shows the dates and locations for each meeting held during the previous 12-month period, i.e., between reports. If the activity uses number designations for meetings they should be included.
6.2	Next Year	Same as above, except for the forthcoming year. Include full twelve months, if known.
7.0	**Membership and Officers**	
7.1	Officers:	The title, name and address of each person that

Section	Title	Description
		held an office during the year. If an office was held by more than one person, list each and indicate dates in office. Include the date each officer last attended a training course held by the Data Interoperability Program Committee.
7.2	Membership:	Names, organization, and contact information (phone, fax and email address) of all members, associate members, and observers.
8.0	Future Trends and Related Technical Activities	This section allows for comment on the market relevance of this area of the subgroup's work. Areas that should be addressed are the number of organizations participating in the activity, new members attracted to this area of work, and survey data regarding the economic impact of this area of standardization should be cited. The subgroup should prepare a brief analysis of technical trends leading to future work needs and how this may affect its program of work. In the interest of more proactive and strategic planning, insights on trends surrounding the standard should be shared. In considering related technical activities, it is helpful if the report included a description of where this subgroup's work fits within the realm of Information Technology. To aid you in the response to this future trends section these kinds of questions should be considered: a. What is your vision of the technology for the subgroup? b. What are the emerging technologies or user requirements that might require some level of standardization?

Section	Title	Description
		c. Where is the work growing and possibly linking (e.g., bindings, profiles) with or requiring close coordination with other the subgroup? The subgroup should report on its future standardization plans and briefly describe probable project proposals.
9.0	Requested changes to subgroup procedures.	The Chair will submit any internal procedures or changes to the Standards Development Board for approval through inclusion in the annual report.
10.0	Other Administrative Information	At a minimum, this needs to include a financial statement for any funds collection. The report should also identify any administrative matters the subgroup feels should be brought to the attention of its parent subgroup. Examples might be: reports on letter ballots taken, voting patterns, document processing, or preparation issues. This section can also be used to provide the reporting of any procedural matters the subgroup feels should be brought to the attention of its parent subgroup. Examples might be: issues raised by the Community of Interest interaction with other Communities of Interest, or compliance with the standards. This section can also be used to make a recommendation to the Data Interoperability Program as a result of the subgroup's experiences during the year. The subgroup will include a financial statement. This report will indicate - total receipts, receivables outstanding, total disbursements, debts outstanding and current balance of the fund. If the subgroup does not collect funds, a note to that effect should be

Section	Title	Description
		included in the Annual Report.

Table 11. Subgroup annual report format.

11.3 Data Interoperability Standards

Every data interoperability standard should consist of at least the information contained in the table that follows.

Data Interoperability Standard Format		
Section	**Section Title**	**Description**
1.0	Standard Admin-istration Information	This section should contain the identifying standard identifying number, name, title, version and effective date. There should also be Community of Interest title, and list of officers and full and associate members who contributed to the creation of the standard. Included as well is the standard's scope.
2.0	Normative References	This section contains references to other standards that are used as a basis for some sections of this standard.
3.0	Definitions, notations, and conventions	This section contains a complete set of definitions in the form of a glossary, any notations such as symbols that have special meaning within the standard. Conventions would include for example, the form for informative notes and whether they are part of the standard or not, the sequence and format of sections and subsections within the standard. For example, function then format, then syntax rules, then access rules, then general rules, then leveling rules.
4.0	Concepts	This section contains a complete list of all the concepts and their detailed definition. The definitions should be detailed to the extent that there should be little or no ambiguity in the understanding of the concepts or how these concepts are applied within any of the technical components of the standard.

Data Interoperability Standard Format		
Section	**Section Title**	**Description**
5.0	Parts of the Standard	The names and descriptions of the various parts of the standard that provide information such as the Enterprise Architecture, business information systems, and data model components comprise the total specification of the standard.
6.0	Enterprise Architecture	The Enterprise Architecture part of the standard should includes all relevant regarding the missions, organizations, functions, information needs analysis resource life cycles, and database objects. Included also are all the cross references among these enterprise architecture components.
7.0	Business Information Systems	The Business Information Systems part of the standard includes all relevant metadata about the business information systems involved in the creation of a database based on the standard's Information Exchange Data Model. Included as well are all the business events, calendars, and business event calendars involved in acquisition, staging, transforming and loading data into any database that is to act as an Information Exchange database. Included also are all the cross references among these business information system components and their relationship to the enterprise architecture components.
8.0	Data Models	The Data Model data includes all relevant metadata regarding the data element models, specified, implemented, operational, and view data models necessary to fully understand the data interoperability standard. The data element model metadata includes concepts, conceptual value domains, value domains, data element concepts, and data elements. Specified data model metadata includes all subjects, entities, attributes, and relationships of all data model templates employed in the development of the Information Exchange Data Model. Similarly, the implemented data model metadata includes all the schemas, tables, columns, and relationships involved in any database related to the development of the Information Exchange Data Model.

Data Interoperability Standard Format		
Section	**Section Title**	**Description**
		Also included from the Operational Data Models are the metadata included in the DBMS Schemas, DBMS Tables, DBMS Columns, and relationships involved in any database application that is employed in the acquisition and staging of data for the Information Exchange Data Model based database. Finally included are all necessary Views that are the interconnection between database metadata and business information system metadata. Included also are all the cross references among these data model components and their relationship to the enterprise architecture and business information system components.

Table 12. Format for an annual standard's report.

11.4 Change Proposals

Change proposals advance the program and scope of work of Communities of Interest subgroup more than do the work of any other subgroup within the Data Interoperability Program. After all, if there are no change proposals, why meet? There's no agenda. It is critical that a strawman base document exists if at all possible before a Community of Interest starts its activities. By base document, the following should be specified with respect to the Community of Interest:

- Missions
- Organizations
- Functions
- Business Information Systems
- Database Domains

These should all exist and hopefully be part of the Community of Interest's project proposal. It is on the basis of a collection of organizations wanting to have shared data across a mission with business information systems which are ready as sources for the shared data that forms the basis for the Community of Interest. Without these there is no "community." From the missions the database domains, which are high level specifications of the shared data, can be created. These metadata should all be collected and made available to those organizations willing to participate in the Community of Interest.

Once the Community of Interest is created and started, several meetings should occur to refine these base document materials. The mechanisms of refinement are change proposals. The general format of a change proposal should follow the guidelines established by the Community of Interest that is set out in one of its standing documents.

11.5 Community of Interest Standing Documents

Every Community of Interest should have a set of standing documents that contain commonly employed guidance and instructions. The list of standing documents that follow represents the key standing documents from a very successful IT Community of Interest. Four of these standing documents are further detailed in later sections of this chapter.

- Procedures
- Guidelines for Submission of Proposals
- Letter Ballots
- Ballot Comments
- Guidelines for Hosting Meetings

Community of Interest Standing Documents		
Document Title	**Responsibility**	**Description**
Standing Documents List	Chair	This document contains the list of standing documents, the officer responsible for each, and a short description. Each document also contains its own introduction and description of contents. Standing documents are created and are placed on the next meeting's agenda for review and if appropriate approval. All standing documents are retained for historical purposes.

Community of Interest Standing Documents		
Document Title	**Responsi-bility**	**Description**
Documents Log	Secretary	This document contains a listing of documents that the committee has considered and taken action on during a calendar year.
Procedures	Vice Chair	This document contains the set of procedures under which the committee operates. These procedures cannot be in conflict nor more strict than the procedures set down by the Data Interoperability Program committee for Communities of Interest.
Projects and Standards	Chair	This document contains a list of all the current standards under maintenance, revision, and/or development.
Projects Schedule	Editor	This document contains the current schedule for processing standards. This document also identifies the current milestone for each standard and the expected time anticipated to achieve the next milestone.
Participants List	Chair	This document lists the current membership of the committee including members, associate members, and observers. Provide with each member's listing is contact information.
Meetings Schedule	Chair	This document contains the meeting schedule for the community of interest and all its technical committees. The schedule should be extend out at least one year.
Guidelines for Submission of Proposals	Editor	This document contains guidelines for the submission of technical proposals. These guidelines may contain mandatory checklists that ensure that a proposal that

Community of Interest Standing Documents		
Document Title	**Responsi-bility**	**Description**
		changes a standard has been carefully crafted to ensure that it changes the standard in a way that does not introduce "bugs."
Directions for Posting and Downloading Papers	Editor	This document contains the instructions for uploading and downloading papers to and from the standards server via FTP.
Template for Submission of Letter Ballot Comments	Editor	This document contains the template for constructing comments about a standard during a formal letter ballot process. The resulting document is then able to be consolidated into a single document used by the editor to present a committee's position on a standard.
Guidelines for Hosting Meetings	Vice Chair	This document contains the set of guidelines that a host should follow for obtaining suitable space, table sizes, electrical outlets, and meeting refreshments for attendees.
Attendance	Vice Chair	This document contains the attendance log for the committee so that a member's standing with respect to attendance can be determined.

Table 13. Community of Interest standing documents.

11.5.1 Procedures

A key standing document is the one containing procedures of the Community of Interest. These procedures are supplemental to those overall procedures that govern the operation and behavior of all subgroups within the Data Interoperability Program. Each subgroup may need to have its own set of additional procedures because its mission and mode of operations are slightly different.

The procedures that follow are those for a Community of Interest, which is the main "action committee" of any Data Interoperability Program. These procedures were adapted from the ANSI INCITS H2 Technical Committee on Database's procedures. Each Community of Interest should review and adapt these procedures to meet their own needs.

11.5.1.1 Meetings

Meetings of the Community of Interest will be conducted in accordance with the latest edition of Robert's Rules of Order, with the following two exceptions.

First, Robert's Rules will not apply when strict adherence would conflict with Community of Interest procedures, with the objectives of Community of Interest as set forth in its Scope and Program of Work, or with any governing Data Interoperability Program rules.

Second, at the discretion of the Chair, discussion may be conducted informally, especially on technical matters, unless any member objects. Members are given the opportunity to make a presentation of their Change Proposal or Working Paper at the appropriate point in the agenda. After the member concludes the presentation, the Chair will solicit questions from the committee, and the presenter of the paper will have the opportunity to respond to those questions. Debate is not allowed during the question period.

At some point, a member may request that the Change Proposal be "moved," or the Chair may solicit the membership to "move" the Change Proposal. Once the Change Proposal has been moved, the Chair will solicit a "second." Once moved and seconded, the Change Proposal may be debated (questions are still allowed). The person seconding a motion will not represent the same organization as the person who made that motion.

A Change Proposal may be amended by the presenter prior to it being moved and seconded. Once moved and seconded, the proposal "belongs to the body" and cannot be withdrawn or modified without general consent or a motion. An amendment can be amended; however, an amendment to an amendment cannot be amended. A member will not address a motion and "call the question" (request a vote) in the same turn.

11.5.1.2 Documents and Distribution

11.5.1.2.1 Change Proposals

Proposals to modify a prospective standard will be made in the form of Change Proposals that specify deletions, additions, or changes to the current Base Document for the prospective standard. Change Proposals are the mechanism by which progress is made in advancing the current Base Document towards becoming a standard.

The Editor has the right to refuse to process a Change Proposal if the instructions regarding the changes to the current Base Document are incomplete or unclear, or if the Change Proposal is not written against the current Base Document. In particular, the Editor may refuse to process a Change Proposal that fails to cite the number and title of the document being changed, the proper Clause and/or Subclause numbers and titles affected, or the Rule numbers and partial text of Rules that are changed. In such cases, the Editor will bring the Change Proposal back the Community of Interest for revision.

Members are referred to the Standing Document, Guidelines for Submission of Proposals. For Change Proposals written for the purpose of defect management (such as an erratum or an amendment to a standard, or an interpretation of a standard), there may be additional requirements. Generic requirements relating to Change Proposals written against Defect Documents are summarized below:

- If a Change Proposal affects parts of a Standard that have already been changed in a Defect Document, then those parts of the Change Proposal are required to be written against the appropriate parts of the Defect Document. Those parts of the Change Proposal that do not touch areas that have been changed in the Defect Document should be written against the Standard.

- Change Proposals are required to include a brief Rationale section for inclusion in the Defect Document.

- If a Change Proposal is written against the Defect Document, it may be necessary to alter the Rationale section in the Defect Document.

11.5.1.2.2 Working Papers

A Working Paper is a technical document, other than a Change Proposal, that is distributed for consideration by the committee. Generally, a member will solicit informal feedback from the committee regarding the advisability and desirability of the content of the Working Paper. Working Papers do not cause any changes to the current Base Document. Members should keep in mind that feedback (including straw votes) obtained on a Working Paper may not necessarily correspond to the vote that may take when the Working Paper is followed up by a Change Proposal.

11.5.1.2.3 Electronic Distribution

The Chair will designate a document server site and an electronic mailing list (reflector) server. All documents will be posted to this server, preferably in PDF format, although other common usage formats are also acceptable. Electronically posting a document also requires sending an email message to the reflector, notifying Community of Interest members of the posting. Members are responsible for obtaining copies of the electronic documents. If, for some reason, the Chair has not designated an official server, electronic posting will not be a valid document distribution method.

11.5.1.2.4 Documents Eligible for Disposition

Documents to be considered at a meeting will be properly numbered and made available to members (i.e., electronically posted) at least two weeks before the meeting. Specifically, change proposals and working papers must be available on the same day of the week on which the meeting will commence two weeks prior to the meeting week; e.g., on the 2nd Monday before a meeting starting on Monday, the 2nd Tuesday before a meeting starting on Tuesday, etc.

Documents distributed after the two-week deadline defined above may be considered only if there is no objection from any voting member. Such an objection can be made at any time before the document is considered at the meeting, but must be made prior to the start of debate on the paper. That is, a member may object any time prior to or during presentation of and questions about a late paper, but the member cannot object after a motion is on the floor and debate has started. The Chair will ask if there are any objections before entertaining a motion to act on a late paper.

11.5.2 Guidelines for Proposals

Proposals to be accepted into any part and any version of the standard should be written in such a way that allows readers to quickly understand the proposals (in the context of the standard, of course) and that allows the Editor to readily apply the proposals in a manner that satisfies the intent of the proposal author and of the approving body.

In addition, all proposals for changes to any and every part and any and every version of the standard should be subjected to scrutiny for completeness and lack of ambiguity. In short, all proposals must be formulated to reassure the reader that all relevant material has been considered and addressed.

There are a number of guidelines for writing proposals that are maximally friendly both to proposal readers and to the Editor. There is also a checklist of criteria that must be satisfied by every change proposal's author so that the editor can know what should be done with the proposal's content should the proposal be approved by the committee.

11.5.2.1 Text Changes

The main form of the "data" that comprises the standard is to be records that reside in the metadata repository. Changes to any text should be specified such that the editor can quickly and easily find the text that is to be changed and then via a "cut and past" strategy change the actual text in the repository presentation layer window. It is additionally critical that the impact of any such changes be fully explained in the change proposal.

11.5.2.2 Information Exchange Data Model Changes

In the case of metadata for one or more components within the Information Exchange Data Model, the change proposals must include not only the addition, deletion, or modification of any data model component but also any changes that would be required to any related data model component.

Since the Information Exchange Data Model is the heart of the overall standard, then any changes that impact business information systems that would provide data to an Information Exchange Data Model based database must also be thoroughly analyzed to ensure that complete database integrity continues. This extends also to business events and their associated business event calenders.

11.5.2.3 Change Proposal Format

11.5.2.3.1 Title Section

This section of the change proposal should contain the change proposal's administrative information. That is, the change proposal document number, its date, the submitting organization, the author and coauthors if any. This section should provide a clear title and abstract of the change proposal so that any informed reader can quickly know the purpose of the proposal and the sections of the standard that are to be affected by the change.

11.5.2.3.2 Discussion Section

It is helpful to the reader if the discussion part makes quite clear why the proposal is being made. It also helps if any approaches that were considered and rejected are also mentioned, together with the reasons for their rejection.

Proposal writers should strive to describe all changes and their implications in the discussion part. Readers should not have to proceed through the detailed changes to understand the consequences of the change.

11.5.2.3.3 Proposed Changes

The following are critical to the understanding of the proposed changes.

- Every separate item of the proposal should be numbered.
- When referring to a specific section of the standard, or to a metadata item within the repository that is to be changed, always specify both section

number and exact sequence of steps that the editor will have to take to quickly and accurately locate the component that is to be changed.

- When inserting, deleting, or replacing text in the standard, specify the precise set of steps that the reader and editor will have to perform to then add, delete, or replace the text.

- Where only a few words of existing text are to be changed, it is clearer both to the reviewer and the Editor to flag differences in some way, e.g., by striking out deleted text and underlining new text or setting new text in boldface. Whatever convention is used should be explained. The use of color to distinguish between existing text, new text, and deleted text is also encouraged; it is quite helpful to proposal readers and to the Editor, especially when proposals are read and used in PDF (as opposed to a printed) form.

11.5.2.4 Use of Notes

Change proposals often must draw the proposal reader's attention to some detail or explanation. This is best done by means of a note starting off with "Note to proposal reader:".

Similarly, change proposal sometimes need to call the Editor's attention to some detail, such as the need to assign a value to a value domain values set. This is best done by means of a note starting off with "Note to the Editor."

However, there is also the need for change proposals to insert notes into the text of the document that they modify, so that the reader of the resulting standard has access to the note text. This is best done by specifying something like "NOTE nnn: text of the note."

11.5.2.5 Quality Proposal Checklist

Every proposed change to a component of the standard should be assessed against all possible related components. This is best done by examining the complete repository meta model and determining all related components to those that are being changed. The checklist that should be in the proposal therefore should list all these related components, and via the repository report writer print out the before change state and the after change state of the repository so that the proposal reader can assess that the change is acceptable. Any effect on any related component needs to be fully explained and justified.

11.5.3 Letter Ballots

Letter ballots beyond those called for in a Community of Interest for some important business item are almost always employed to cause a focus on those areas of a standard that need work before proceeding to the next stage of a standard. The stages are commonly committee draft, final committee draft, draft standard, and standard. Each letter ballot is designed to force members of a Community of Interest to formally identify what parts, sections, and specific aspects of a standard need additional work. The table that follows provides the general form for a letter ballot. If there are multiple parts of a standard that are being voted, then there would be additional columns to the right of the second column. The header would then identify which part the vote applies to.

Suggested Format for a Letter Ballot	
Vote: I vote as follows: (check one only)	**<Identification Information of Standard>**
Approve the draft as presented	
Approve the draft with comments given in the attached document	
Disapprove the draft for reasons given in the attached document.	
Abstain from voting on the draft for reasons given in the attached document	
Name:____ Organization:______________________________________ Full Member Primary (___) or Alternate (___) Date:_____ / ______ / ______	

Table 14. Letter ballot format.

11.5.4 Ballot Comments

The table below provides the general format for recording comments regarding the standard that requires work. The table after that contains definitions for each of the columns.

Seq Number	Com-ment Id	See Also	Severity	Ref-erence	Descrip-tion	Addres s-ed By
<number>	<for-matted string>	<for-matted string>	One of four choices	<for-matted string>	Text descrip-tion and if available, a solution	<for-matted string>

Table 15. Ballot comment columns.

Ballot Comment Column Definitions	
Sequence Number	This is a permanent sequence number once a consolidated comment from all Community of Interest full members has been created. This number is created by the editor once all ballot comments have been received.
Comment Id	This is completed by each Community of Interest member organization submitting a comment. The format of the values in this column should be abc-P##-seq# or nbc-T##-seq#, where: abc is an abbreviation assigned to the submitting organization, P## is the part number of the standard if it is a multi-part standard. Else it is 00. Seq# is the sequence number that the Community of Interest member organization has assigned to the comment.
See Also	This enables a submitting organization to reference other comments.

Ballot Comment Column Definitions	
Severity	This is a four value severity assigned to the comment. The codes are: Major Technical, Minor Technical, Major Editorial, Minor Editorial. In general a Major classification represents something that must be changed before the standard can proceed to the next stage. A Minor classification represents something that should be changed. The initial classification is at the discretion of the submitted. The final classification is voted by the entire Community of Interest.
Reference	This identifies the specific document to which the comment applies and to the location in the document to which it applies.
Description	This contains two sections. The first, starting immediately at the beginning of the column, should be a textual description of the comment being submitted. This text may be in any form, with WYSIWYG aspects if required to get the message of the comment to the reader, and with multiple paragraphs if so required. It should be followed by a line with the word "Solution" After that line, the submitted may choose to insert additional text specifying the solution to their comment; alternatively, the text "None supplied with comment" may be inserted.
Addressed By	This should normally be left blank. However, if the submitted has provided a solution with their comment, they should put the string "See Comment" or "See comment" into the Addressed By column. If the submitter has provided a separately numbered paper containing a proposal that addresses the comment, they are encouraged to put that paper's number into the Addressed By column.

Table 16. Ballot comment column definitions.

11.5.5 Guidelines for Hosting Meetings

The following are guidelines for hosting a Community of Interest meeting. Generally it involves:

- Finding a Hotel
- Financial Arrangements
- Contractual Arrangements
- Other Considerations
- Meeting Room and Hotel Facilities
- Food service
- Meeting Announcement
- At the Meeting

11.5.5.1 Finding Hotels

One of the easiest ways to locate hotels suitable for our meeting is to contact the Visitor's Bureau, the Convention Bureau, or the equivalent in the city in which the meeting is planned. This office will take the necessary information (dates, meeting size, etc.) and can pass along that information to the hotels. The hotels themselves will then send proposals directly to you.

11.5.5.2 Financial Arrangements

One goal in negotiating hotel accommodations is to minimize the cost of sleeping rooms in order to allow all participants to stay in the hotel where the meeting is held. Ask about the availability of rooms at government per-diem rates. When the room rate is much higher than the corporate rates at co-located hotels, members have been known to stay at those hotels. Make sure the hotel knows that this will occur. If possible, call hotels to find out what their corporate rates are.

Many hotels will offer you a "free" meeting room and adjust the price of the sleeping rooms upward accordingly. Community of Interest members would rather pay a higher meeting fee than a higher sleeping room rate. Indicate that hotel proposals must separate the cost of meeting rooms and the cost of sleeping room. Ask the hotel for the attendance level above or below which fees for the meeting rooms would be affected (upward or downward), if applicable. E.g., booking 75 sleeping room nights for a three-day meeting might qualify for a reduced meeting room price, or booking less than 60 meeting room nights for a three-day meeting might result in a higher per day meeting room price. Just ensure that as host you understand any such relationships/dependencies between the cost of sleeping rooms and meeting rooms.

11.5.5.3 Contractual Arrangements

The following are the key points from the guidelines of the ANSI INCITS H2 Technical Committee on Database that are used by H2 members when making contractual arrangements of a Committee of Interest meeting at a commercial hotel.

- The Community of Interest will not enter into legal commitments; i.e., the Community of Interest will not sign a hotel contract. Therefore the meeting host should be prepared to either sign the contract individually or as a representative of their organization, or convince the hotel that no contract signature is necessary (which usually is not acceptable to hotels).

- Most hotels will offer a contract with various penalty clauses. Don't sign such a contract unless you or your employer are prepared to honor it. You may be asked to provide the hotel with an advance deposit for the meeting space, if so, the Community of Interest can agree to a reasonable deposit (typically $500) at time of contract signing.
- Some hotels will accept a credit card to serve as guarantee for the deposit - the Community of Interest does not have credit card, but some member hosts have used their own credit card for this - but such is the decision of the individual host and the hotel they are working with.

- If the hotel doesn't want to do business on terms that are mutually agreeable to them and the Community of Interest, then consider another hotel or even another city.

- In most cases, you can strike the penalty clauses or at least negotiate them downward, and the hotel will agree.

- Many hotels will request a signing of a "letter of intent." Many hosts have signed these. To reassure the hotel representatives, you can point to the fact that this committee has been meeting six times a year for twenty years and has always met its financial obligations.

- You may occasionally be asked for previous hotel names to serve as references - if so, contact the Community of Interest chair and references will be furnished. Indicate for example that the Committee of Interest, to date, has never cancelled a meeting. When adjustments had to be made, e.g., change the date, the committee has always provided more than two months notice. Inform the hotels that we will pay them by cash and check at the end of the meeting.

- Some hotels have difficulty differentiating the organizational reason for the meeting, that is, the specific name of the Community of Interest, from the corporate hosting organization such as NCR, Oracle, IBM, etc. These names are typically used by hotel reservations staff when making sleeping room reservations to ensure affiliation with the correct hotel group function, and that you get quoted the correct sleeping room prices and options. Thus, you should consider listing the meeting both under the Community of Interest name and your corporate organization name.

11.5.5.4 Other Considerations

Some hotels will want you to coordinate in some way the sleeping room arrangements. You might volunteer to send reservation cards with the meeting announcement, brochures, etc., but ensure that the hotel understands and that the contract states all arrangements for sleeping rooms (e.g., guarantees for late arrival, etc.) are solely between the individual attendee and the hotel.

We may finish our meeting before the scheduled adjournment date. Some members may wish to leave before the meeting is over. There should be no commitment to pay for sleeping rooms that are vacated early. It's also desirable to be able to cancel the meeting room and avoid payment for any final, unused days (but this is not required). However, the Community of Interest will not pay for food service that we cancel with sufficient notice (e.g., > twelve hours notice).

11.5.5.5 Meeting Room and Hotel Facilities

The meeting should be held at the hotel where members are sleeping. The Community of Interest does not meet at a host company's facility. The committee has been averaging about 25 people. As a guideline, a minimum room size of approximately 50′ x 30′ is typically sufficient for the Community of Interest meeting of 25 persons. Such rooms can usually be configured to comfortably seat up to 28-30 persons.

Tables in the larger meeting room should be arranged in an "open rectangle" or similar fashion. There must be 3 to 4 linear feet per person. The tables should also be 30 to 36 inches deep. In addition, one or two extra tables should be set up at a side in the meeting room for papers and documents brought to the meeting. A diagram might be helpful to hotels to give them an idea of our needs.

The meeting room should be reserved for 8 a.m. to 8 p.m. except on the last day, when it should be reserved until 5 p.m. Rooms should be accessible overnight. Keeping the room overnight is known as a "24 hour hold."

No ashtrays, podium, projectors, or microphone should be provided in the meeting room. Lighting in the meeting rooms should be ample for business work, reading, writing, using the laptop computers. The lighting suitable for an evening social function is insufficient for a technical working meeting. Trash cans should be available in the meeting rooms.

The hotel must be made aware that we cannot hold a meeting while, for example, a sales meeting with microphones, applause, loud music, etc., is being held in an adjacent meeting room. It has been learned the hard way that an adjacent meeting with even only a microphone is sufficient to interfere with committee work. The hotel must ensure that no such meetings will be scheduled in the rooms adjacent to ours.

The meeting room should have extension cords and power strips as almost all members bring laptop computers. The committee requires power strips for approximately 20-25 laptops, spaced at intervals around the inside of the table arrangement. Check on the hotel charges for use of such power strips, some hotels have such priced these quite expensively, while others will provide these reasonably or even without additional charge.

Touch-tone phone facilities should be available in both the meeting room area and in the individual sleeping rooms. The sleeping rooms should be equipped with modular jacks for computer laptops and modem use.

Meeting rooms are more pleasant with windows and/or direct outdoor access. The hotel should provide copy services and fax services at a reasonable charge. Note that fax charges may include separate charges for incoming and outgoing fax transmissions. The hotel should be asked to indicate its charges for these services beforehand. As we have found out, they can be either reasonable or exorbitant. As host, you should attempt to locate in advance off-site copy and fax services, which tend to be much less expensive.

11.5.5.6 Food Service

The Food Service should include:

- Water service.

- Continental Breakfast. Generous portion continental breakfast including coffee, tea, decaffeinated coffee, decaffeinated tea, juice, soft drinks (regular and diet), and rolls. It has been suggested that a variety of rolls, both sweet (e.g., Danish), and not so sweet (e.g., croissants or muffins) be included. Bagels and cream cheese usually go over very well. A fruit plate is also standard. The breakfast service should be set up by 8:00am each meeting day.
- Throughout the meeting day the hotel food service staff will check with the meeting host for any additional needed items, or leave a phone number to call when special service is needed.

- At approximately 10:00 a.m. and 1:30 p.m., coffee, tea, decaffeinated coffee, and soft drinks should be checked for restocking. A smaller restocking check should be made around 3:00 - 3:30pm. No late afternoon service should be scheduled on the last day unless it is known that the meeting will last long enough on that day to make such service desirable. If it is consistent with hotel policy, "continual replenishment" rather than "specific time" service is preferred.

- Afternoon food service is optional, but popular with members. This can include cookies or other light dessert type items (brownies), and should be arranged for 2:00- 2:30 PM setup.

11.5.5.7 Meeting Announcement

You should send out a meeting announcement as soon as possible after the preceding meeting. According to our rules, e-mail no later than four weeks prior to the meeting - and preferably six weeks in advance to give members the best opportunity at lowest airfares, etc. The earlier, the better. The meeting announcement is to be emailed to the Community of Interest email distribution list. The announcement should include:

- Meeting dates.

- Hotel information including name, location, phone number, and the rates you've arranged, including government rates; i.e., sufficient information to make reservations.
- Complete hotel information - name, address, phone, fax, website if available.
- Information on transportation from the airport(s), and additional information such as availability and price of limousines, public transportation, and parking fees at the hotel.
- You might also wish to include information about the area; e.g., maps, tourist sites, list of restaurants, and so on. A call to the local Chamber of Commerce or Visitor's Bureau will usually get you all the copies you need.

11.5.5.8 At the Meeting

As soon as possible, introduce yourself to the hotel's catering/meeting/banquet (whatever) staff. Let them know that you will be their point of contact. Check the meeting rooms as soon as possible upon your arrival to ensure they will meet the Community of Interest meeting requirements. In addition, be prepared to spend some time with the hotel staff straightening out any problems that might occur (Murphy's law). One of Murphy's laws is that you can never find what you need in Robert's Rules. Similarly, one of Robert's rules is that Murphy's Laws are always out of order.

11.6 Standard Motions for Inter-Community of Interest Meetings

Whenever a Community of Interest participates in an inter-Community of Interest meeting there commonly are only delegates from each participating Community of Interest. Those delegates should be instructed as to the types and kinds of authority they have on behalf of their "home" Community of Interest. Each Community of Interest appoints delegates to the meetings.

Delegate instructions are given during a Community of Interest meeting shortly before the multi-Community of Interest meeting. There are two such motions that are provided here as template for delegate instructions.

- Delegate behavior on non-"Home" Community of Interest motions and proposals when not instructed and not unanimous.

  Motion (mover, seconder, Vote: tally) that the delegates to the <meeting name> abstain on all motions and change proposals for which they have not been given explicit direction by a "home" Community of Interest decision, unless the delegates to the meeting agree unanimously to vote "Yes" or "No" on the motion or change proposal under consideration.

- Delegate behavior regarding "Home" Community of Interest proposals not previously approved by the "home" Community of Interest.

  Motion (mover, seconder, Vote: tally) that the delegates to the <meeting name> will not make visible to any person or persons other that "home" Community of Interest participants any paper (change proposal, discussion paper, position paper, etc.), unless the delegates to the meeting agree unanimously that the paper is acceptable to make visible.

11.7 Document Summary

Documents within a data interoperability program are very important. It is through formally constituted documents that subgroups are determined, established, brought into existence, and of course, operate.

All data interoperability standards are started as a consequence of a standard's proposal document. If this document is not properly created, then the standard's effort just does not even start. Along the way, and at the end of the standard's process, the standard itself must be able to be generated as a properly formatted document that is exact, unambiguous, and "votable."

All through the life of a standard, the progress of the committee occurs because of change proposals. These documents are not only essential to the operation of the committee, the impact or consequence of change proposals can be in the 10s of millions of dollars.

Decisions by committees are made by ballots. Hence there is a document format for ballots, and another document format for ballot comments. Ballots are focusing mechanisms, and ballot comments are the specifications of the focus. Entire meetings are devoted to reviewing and determining the proper set of words in each ballot comment. That is because the technical work that then has to follow to resolve the ballot comment can only be based on those words.

Other classes of documents include subgroup annual reports, meeting minutes, agendas, document registries, and standing documents that provide the current status of various subgroup topics.

There is even a document that suggests the appropriate way to find a location for a meeting. At any meeting, if it lasts for a whole week, and has 25 persons in attendance can have a cost of about $150,000. The staff costs of those attending the meeting can be upwards of $100,000. Travel and hotel costs for the staff can easily be another $40,000. And finally, the costs for the hotel's meeting room and refreshments can be another $5,000. That's a grand total of about $150,000 per meeting. Consequently, meeting locations and arrangements should be carefully accomplished.

12

Projects

Data Interoperability Program projects fall into these categories:

- General projects.
- Data Interoperability Program projects.
- Community of Interest Projects.

12.1 General Projects

There are five types of Data Interoperability Program projects that are general in nature. These are:

- Annual report projects.
- Special event projects.
- Administrative procedure projects.
- Membership procedure projects.
- Standards' development projects.

Annual Report projects engineer the content and procedures for Data Interoperability Program subgroup preparation of annual reports.

Special Events projects define the contents and procedures necessary for the creation and presentation of the business plans associated with special events.

Administrative Procedures projects examine the processes that every subgroup performs on a regular basis for meeting planing and scheduling, the conduct of meetings, the development of minutes, and the content and format of data interoperability standards for the Information Exchange Data Models.

Membership Procedures projects determine the rules and processes for identifying individuals and organizations to participate in all the Data Interoperability Program subgroups.

Standards' development projects determine the detailed processes that are to be performed to create Information Exchange Data Models and all the supporting products necessary to fully define data interoperability standards.

12.2 Data Interoperability Program Projects

Data Interoperability Program projects that are to be accomplished in support of some aspect of the overall program. Thus, there are projects related to the program's architecture, governance, and components. Each project has a firm goal, specific objectives, a work plan, metrics, deliverables, and a schedule that must be accomplished. All deliverables must fit within the overall set of all deliverables from all the other Data Interoperability Program projects

- Component Architecture projects, which are specifically targeted at the engineering, design, deployment, and long-term evolution and maintenance of the components within the Data Interoperability Program. Components of the Data Interoperability Program include its overall process, specific standards, metrics, project management, the technical components of Data Interoperability Program such as Enterprise Identifiers, Authoritative Data Sources, Information Exchange Data Models, XML (as appropriate for data transport), and finally the metadata repository system that creates, holds, and interrelates all products within and across all Communities of Interest. Each component architecture project would be scoped, its work plan developed, resource loaded and staffed, and managed during its accomplishment.

- Concept of operations projects address either the Data Interoperability Program in general, or specific components of the Data Interoperability Program architecture. Thus, there would be concepts of operations documents addressing process, standards, metrics, project management, Data Interoperability Program technical components, and the federated metadata repository environment. Each project would be scoped, its work plan developed, resource loaded and staffed, and managed during its accomplishment.

- Data Interoperability Program planning environment projects are generally in three areas: metadata management, the ongoing evolution of the environment's functionality, and extensions to the Data Interoperability Program planning.

- Training and awareness projects are those that cause the creation of various presentations, workshops, courses, and support services such as hot-line, on-line tutorials, and the like.

- Methodology projects are created so that different organizations produce the same set of deliverables from the same or similar requirements. The methodology is to be at least one or more levels more detailed than the actual management of the work. Methodologies have well-engineered deliverables and metrics for work efforts. Methodologies are accompanied by training, workshops and as needed, consulting. Methodologies may address any aspect of the data management program effort. Ultimately, methodologies are procedural guidance that enables quality products to be developed.

- Technical support projects are those engineered to make experts available to those performing a project.

A key type of Data Interoperability Program project are those accomplished by the Standards Development Board. These projects identify and implement strategies that achieve objectives of data interoperability across the enterprise, and attain interoperability capabilities. First and foremost these projects are the development of action plans.

The Standards Development Board's projects do not actually effect the creation and/or evolution of Information Exchange Data Models. Rather, their projects are to identify, plan, and manage standards accomplishment. Key areas that are addressed by these Standards Development Board projects are the:

- Data model(s) .

- Data integrity rules that govern the definition, production, storage, ownership, management, exchange formats, and replication of data, based on data.

- Data interoperability efforts and issues that relate to accomplishing the organization's mission(s).

To eliminate the possibility of stovepipe Information Exchange Data Models, a certain class of Information Exchange Data Models projects may need to create products in the areas of mission, event, information systems, function, and organization so that the various Information Exchange Data Models can be set within their proper contexts thus ensuring proper integration across all other Information Exchange Data Models of the enterprise, within a community of interest and/or across Communities of Interest.

To illustrate, a primary focus of an Information Exchange Data Models project within data management planning may be to model data and create the specification of how data will be acquired, stored, transferred and managed. Thus, an Information Exchange Data Model may state that a person's name is related to the person's Social Security Number (SSN). Just an Information Exchange Data Models is not sufficient to specify that the SSN is Privacy Act data and must be protected from unauthorized access, nor will it say how the Person Identifier is created, assigned, physically stored in databases, and formatted for data exchange. These additional rules are part of other Information Exchange Data Models products that might be created in other projects. Because there exists an integrated metadata repository that would contain all these products, they could be available for use by all. Simply put, the purpose of data management planning is to create and manage an environment within the enterprise that enables the development of data assets that are flexible, interoperable, and evolvable. Anything short of that is failure.

Data Interoperability Program planning projects begin with a problem statement that is taken through a rigorous functional and technical analysis process, resulting in a feasible solution for implementation at the appropriate level, ranging from specific, pair-wise, database-to-database exchanges up to enterprise level data sharing in a "virtual, distributed single database" environment. Data management planning projects result in the identification of specific projects.

12.3 Community of Interest Projects

The projects associated with Communities of Interest are:

- Metadata Infrastructure,
- Information Exchange Data Models
- Evolution, Maintenance and Support.

12.3.1 Metadata Infrastructure

Metadata infrastructure subprojects are divided into three classes: enterprise architectures, data element metadata, and specified data model projects.

Enterprise architecture projects are those that cause the creation of the necessary and sufficient metadata to support contextually accurate Data Interoperability Program projects. Included are the creation of mission, organization, function, business information systems, and business event metadata, as well as required supporting metadata such as data types, DBMS, classes of Data Interoperability Program projects, and the like.

Data element metadata is created either top-down, bottom-up, or through time, evolved. Data element metadata consists of all the metadata components from the information systems standard 11179 for data element metadata, for example, concepts, conceptual value domains, value domains, data element concepts data element classifications, derived and compound data elements, and all associated data stewardship information.

Specified Data Models represent engineered collections of attributes within entities within narrowly constructed subjects. Specified Data Models can be used as data model templates for use within Implemented Data Model construction. Examples include the set of attributes for a person's name, for personnel skill information, for a standard requisition, disposition, or payment.

12.3.2 Information Exchange Data Model Projects.

Information Exchange Data Model projects may include the following subprojects:

- **Enterprise identifier projects**. Enterprise identifier projects involve the creation of IT independent identifiers for all instances of the real or abstract assets necessary to be tracked by the enterprise. Enterprise identifiers are employed as the immutable identifiers for these assets in all IT systems, and where possible, on the assets themselves. Included within this project are the identification of all the materials that represent the definition of the enterprise identifier, the requirements for an effective enterprise identifier solution, and the materials that define the enterprise identifier's solution. These projects include materials related to various designs, alternatives, analysis of the alternatives, and the selected solution. Identified also are the classes of data structures that should and should not be supported by enterprise identifiers.

Contained as well are the policies and procedures for the creation and deployment of enterprise identifier seeds (asset classes) and incrementers (asset class instances). Contained too are the detailed procedures for locating enterprise identifier sources and their effective use. Finally contained are any IT assets that assist developers in the proper use of enterprise identifiers within IT systems and database, and database management systems.

- **Authoritative Data Source Projects**. Authoritative Data Source projects are designed to create the existence of data structures that represent data that is authoritative in nature. These data structures likely will contain an Enterprise Identifier so that the authenticity of the data's use can be tracked. Authoritative data sources are commonly one of two types: reference data or multi-column data structures.

    - The reference-data project is generally employed to represent coded values and meanings. Reference data may, however, be more robust and thus represent entire tables or collections of tables. For each, the data structure requirements, and the requirements for value recasting over time must be created, including establishing the precise mapping strategy from one value set to the next. All reference data level data elements must be interrelated with enterprise level data elements.

    - A multi-column data structure is one or more tables of data from an Information Exchange Data Model that has been identified as an authoritative data source. For example, the authoritative value set of a person's name, address and telephone number or the definitive specifications of a weapon system's component. In either case, the overall process causes the creation of the mission, organization, function, data element, conceptual, logical, physical, and view models. Built also are the various information systems and event models so that a complete specification can be generated. The SQL DDL is also created so that a DBMS can create the actual database. Authoritative data source data can either be centrally stored or distributed under a very controlled update environment.

- **Data Transport (e.g., via XML) Projects**. Data Transport (e.g., via XML) projects address the creation of the necessary set of XML schemas and/or XSLT that enable XML tagged data from databases to be exchanged with other databases. The overall process creates XML objects that are squarely based on view data models generated from physical database schemas. Managing the XML Data Transport layer is the overall process of creating, evolving and maintaining a high quality and effective environment of data transport. Included in data transport are all forms, which range from technology bound data exchanges through to generalized data exchanges such as those included in XML.

- **Information Exchange Data Model Projects.** Information Exchange Data Model Projects represent collections of data that is commonly shared by multiple database applications.

  - The overall process presumes the existence of mission, organization, function, data element, specified, implemented, operational, and view data models for an existing set of database applications. From the operational databases the process causes the discovery of shared data structures. From this discovery, a common schema at the Implemented Data Model level is created that maps to the shared data of the database applications. Then information systems are specified including events set within business and calendar cycles so that users of the information exchange standards specification can know when the Information Exchange Data Model would be updated by the "put" information systems.

  - Data integrity rules are contained in the Information Exchange Data Model if and only if they are common across all uses of the Information Exchange Data Model. Data integrity rules that are common across a subset of business information systems are specified in an SQL View on that Information Exchange Data Model. Finally, data integrity rules unique to a particular business information system are specified in the business information system. Regardless of the containment layer for a data integrity rule, all data integrity rules must be centrally defined and managed to ensure they are nonredundant and that there are zero semantic conflicts across the data integrity rule set.

12.3.3 Evolution, Maintenance and Support Projects.

Participation in evolution and maintenance efforts include both the evolution and maintenance of all the metadata associated with specification of the Information Exchange Data Model, that is, the modification of its design, implementation, etc., the management of the Information Exchange Data Model itself, that is, the quality of its content, and finally all the associated discovery metadata associated with the Information Exchange Data Model. Consequently, a quality engineered Information Exchange Data Model consists of its view data models, its Operational Data Models, its Implemented Data Models, the source data model templates, and the source enterprise level data elements. All these must be completely interrelated across all classes of Information Exchange Data Models.

The evolution and maintenance of Information Exchange Data Model metadata includes determining the requirements for such metadata and instituting the policies and procedures that ensure that all Information Exchange Data Model metadata relates to the same overall comprehensive set of enterprise-wide metadata. It is critical that individual Information Exchange Data Model metadata be discriminating across the complete set of Information Exchange Data Models, be reliably produced, and validly represented.

The evolution and maintenance of specific Information Exchange Data Models include the discovery of new and/or changed requirements either on a specific Information Exchange Data Model or across an entire class of Information Exchange Data Models, the modification of any data structures, the identification and modification of any data acquisition and/or maintenance systems, the modification of any information system ancillary supports, and the like.

Managing Information Exchange Data Model quality and content involves use of standards established for all Information Exchange Data Model contained data elements, timeliness of all relevant data, and quality across all value domains. Information Exchange Data Model quality is focused both on the form of construction (e.g., third normal form for tables, or SQL view derived XML schemas), and the quality of the content (e.g., only two gender codes and that all stored person gender data conform to these values).

Information Exchange Data Models do not exist in isolation. Supporting each includes all the metadata associated with the Data Element layer via the ISO 11179 standard for data element metadata.

This Information Exchange Data Model support also includes the creation of the specified data model templates that can be employed within and across Information Exchange Data Model tables as a way of standardizing the precision, synchronization, and granularity of data within the enterprise's Information Exchange Data Models.

12.4 Projects Summary

Projects are not explicitly identified in the Knowledge Worker Framework depicted in Figure 1. Projects exist implicitly as collections of performed functions by groups of individuals within organizations that set out to achieve some aspect of a mission. That is, build a standard, create a metadata infrastructure environment, and the like.

Every project ultimately consists of a work plan, a budget, a set of deliverables, and is set within an organizational construct. In this book, while the project classes are identified in this chapter, the functions, organizations, positions, processes, and product specifications for every project are defined in their respective chapters.

To charter a project, it's class must be identified, and its description and rationale set out. Once approved, then the project's work plan would be developed from tasks in the function's chapter. The organizations that are to participate will have been identified in the organization's chapter. Project products will be identified from within the object's chapter. Once all this is assembled, then an estimate can be made of the resources needed to carry out the project. All the project's "metadata" is recorded in the area of the metabase that is equivalent to Figure 19. The task and deliverable template entities, along with the actual task and deliverable entities exist so as to preserve the actual project's history. As the project is accomplished, the products that are built are identified and the resources that are expended are recorded in other entities found on Figure 19.

If possible, all project metadata should be integrated with other data interoperability program metadata so that there can be consolidated reporting. Additionally, as projects are accomplished, some of the resulting metadata products could well impact the resource estimates of other projects. By having all the project metadata integrated, those impacts can easily be employed to re-estimate other projects.

13

Rules

The rules contained in this chapter relate generally to all Data Interoperability Program subgroups except when specifically stated. All actions by any Data Interoperability Program subgroup are governed by Robert's Rules of Order except where specifically noted. The rules relate to:

- Meetings
- Voting
- File Retention
- Officer Training
- Fees
- Reports and Review
- Finance Management
- Membership in Good Standing

• 13.1 Meetings

- Rules for meetings relate to:

- Schedule
- Notice and Draft Agenda
- Document for Action
- Quorum
- Minutes

13.1.1 Schedule of Meetings

The Data Interoperability Program subgroups meet regularly. The schedule is governed as follows:

- The Data Interoperability Program Committee normally meets four times per year.
- The Standards Development Board and Standards Policy Board normally meet at the same venue as the Data Interoperability Program Committee.
- All Communities of Interest and Study Groups will meet at least once a year.
- Maintenance Committees will meet as required.
- The Data Interoperability Program Committee committees will meet as required.

All meetings are held at the call of the Chair and within the frequencies indicated. Each agenda should include a standing item for review and confirmation of the date and location of the next meeting(s). Periodically, the schedule should be extended to a nine- to eighteen-month period ahead, with "tentative" indications when appropriate.

A duly called meeting is one for which the meeting notice and draft agenda are issued at least 4 weeks of the start date of the meeting.

When a quorum is not met at such a duly called meeting or fewer than the number of voting members required to approve an action, the members who are present may propose actions for submission to the entire membership for letter ballot or action at the next meeting. They may conduct all business not requiring voting action. For Communities of Interest, Study Groups and Technical Groups, a duly called meeting will count in determining the members' attendance record.

13.1.2 Meeting Notice and Draft Agenda

The meeting notice and draft agenda will be distributed no closer than four weeks before the meeting.

13.1.3 Documents for Action (Two-Week Rule)

Documents should be distributed at least two weeks prior to the meeting. Recommendations that come from the Standards Development Board and

Standards Policy Board to the Data Interoperability Program Committee and vice-versa are exempted from the two-week rule.

Any documents sent later may be considered, but final action may only be taken in the absence of an objection by any voting member present or by suspension of this rule by vote of the Data Interoperability Program Committee; otherwise, they must be acted upon by letter ballot or deferred until the next meeting.

Documents may be revised during the meeting and still be considered to have met the two-week rule if the original document met this requirement. Note that this provision is intended to provide a means for discussing the document and advancing the progress of the work, and is not intended to permit the introduction of new or orthogonal material.

Project Proposals not posted to the Draft agenda two weeks prior to the meeting must be acted upon by letter ballot or deferred until the next meeting.

13.1.4 Quorum

Quorum for all subgroups is defined accordingly:

- For the Data Interoperability Program Committee and the Subsidiary Boards, quorum is a majority of the voting membership.
- For Study Groups there is no minimum attendance required for a quorum.
- For Communities of Interest and contained subgroups, a quorum is one-third of the voting membership with at least four members present.

13.1.5 Minutes

All subgroups, except ad hoc groups, are required to produce minutes of their meetings. Minutes will be distributed within four weeks after the adjournment of the meeting. When prepared by someone other than a member of the Data Interoperability Program Committee staff, the draft minutes will be reviewed by Data Interoperability Program Committee staff prior to distribution to the Committee.

The required contents of minutes are as follows:

- Date(s), location(s), Chair, Secretary, hour of opening and adjournment.
- Summary of significant actions taken.
- List of all attendees.
- Approved agenda (or approved changes to draft agenda).
- Approval of previous meeting minutes.
- Each motion seconded and not withdrawn, identifying maker of the motion, the fact of a second, and the voting results.
- Future meeting schedule.
- List of action items assigned to members.

Individual remarks or detailed transcripts need not to be recorded; however, any specific statement should be recorded when requested by the Chair or a member. Records of discussions and actions taken pertaining to any topic for which attendance is restricted will not be included in the minutes, except to record that a position was developed.

13.2 Voting

Voting can only occur by subgroup members in good standing. There will be only one voting membership per organization. An alternate representative may vote only if the principal representative fails to vote. In all subgroup actions that require a vote, only full members can vote.

Voting by proxy will not be permitted. A written vote on an issue to be acted upon at the meeting may be submitted by correspondence by an absent voting member provided it is received by the Chair prior to the point when the issue is brought to a vote.

13.2.1 Voting Practice

13.2.1.1 Types of Voting Positions

Three types of voting positions are allowed:

- Affirmative
- Negative
- Abstention

13.2.1.2 Method of Voting and Criteria for Approval

Five voting methods are permitted. These are:

- Letter ballot
- Roll call vote
- Show of hands
- Voice vote
- Unanimous consent

With the exception of letter ballots, all of the above votes are taken at a meeting. The method of meeting votes is at the discretion of the Chair unless otherwise specified in this document. However, a roll call vote may be requested by any voting member on any action that this document permits be handled by a meeting vote. For a roll call vote, the voting position of each member will be recorded in the minutes.

Letter ballot votes are authorized by any of the following methods:

- Majority vote of those present at a meeting.
- The Chair.
- The Data Interoperability Program Committee.
- This document.
- Written request to the Chair from five or more voting members of the Subgroup.

13.2.1.2.1 Letter Ballots

Affirmative votes may include comments. Negative votes must include reasons for the negative and, if possible, recommend specific modifications necessary to change the negative position to an affirmative position. Abstention votes will include the reason for not taking a position.

For purposes of determining a member's voting record, negative and abstention votes cast without reasons will be counted as non-responses and may place the member in jeopardy for failure to vote.

The voting period for letter ballots is usually thirty days. The duration period for all letter ballots commences on the date of issue of the letter ballot. An extension may be granted by the Data Interoperability Program Committee when warranted and when the extension does not cause undue problems, such as failure to submit an inter-organizational vote on time.

13.2.1.2.2 Letter Ballot Reconsideration Procedure

A copy of the letter ballot notification will be sent to the Principal and all Alternate representatives of every Voting Member.

If the letter ballot resulted in any negative votes, the comments that accompanied the votes will be circulated to the Data Interoperability Program Committee membership along with the letter ballot voting tally. All Data Interoperability Program Committee members who returned a ballot on the issue have ten days to reconsider their vote and change it, if applicable, based on the new information provided in the comments accompanying the votes. The Data Interoperability Program Committee will prescribe the form to be used to change a vote.

13.2.1.3 Default Ballots

Default ballots are used when lack of objection presumes approval. A default ballot fails in the presence of any objections. The voting period for default ballots is thirty days unless otherwise specified on the ballot.

13.2.1.4 Accelerated Letter Ballots

The Data Interoperability Program Committee may approve an accelerated letter ballot with a voting period of less than thirty days. An accelerated ballot may not be issued for final approval of a draft standard. Failure to vote on an accelerated letter ballot will not affect membership privileges where voting is a requirement for membership.

13.2.1.5 Report of Final Letter Ballot Results

The final result of voting on letter ballots will be reported to the membership of the Committee that conducted the ballot immediately upon completion of the letter ballot action. Although negative votes without comments are not counted in determining whether the ballot passed, these votes will be recorded in the report of results. During the balloting period, all votes will be a matter of confidence between the Chair and whoever is tallying the votes.

The report of voting on personnel ballots will only state that the candidate has (or has not) received the required approval.

No tallies will be given, no reconsideration ballots will be conducted, no negatives will be distributed, and no members will be placed in jeopardy for failure to respond where voting is a requirement for membership.

13.2.2 Definition of Criteria for Approval

The following definitions apply to subgroups.

13.2.2.1 Majority

For meeting votes, a majority is defined as approval by more than half of the members voting; abstentions are excluded when determining whether a majority has been satisfied. For letter ballot votes, a majority is defined as approval by more than half of the members eligible to vote, excluding abstentions.

13.2.2.2 Super Majority Voting Rule

The super-majority voting rule is defined as:

- Approval by at least two-thirds of those voting YES or NO, and
- Approval by a majority of the voting membership. That is, the threshold is not affected by the number of members present at the meeting for a meeting vote.

13.3 File Retention

The Data Interoperability Program Committee and all contained subcommittees and boards share a document register. All other subgroups maintain their own document registers. Owners of Document Registers must register, control, and distribute documents. The original, full-size reproducible copy, or electronic copy of each membership list, minutes, or document will be submitted to the Data Interoperability Program Committee for file retention.

At least annually, a copy of each Subgroup's document register must also be sent to the Data Interoperability Program Committee for file retention.

Records concerning new, revised or reaffirmed standards will be retained for one complete standard's cycle, or until the standard is revised. Records concerning withdrawn standards will be retained for at least five years from the date of withdrawal.

13.4 Training

13.4.1 Officer Training

Training of Data Interoperability Program Committee chairs, elected Vice-chairs, and project editors is mandatory within one year of appointment. Officers of Maintenance Communities of Interest who have already received this training need not be trained again. Under certain circumstances, training may be waived for experienced officers. Requests for such a waiver should be sent to the Data Interoperability Program Committee for consideration. The Data Interoperability Program Committee, in consultation with the Data Interoperability Program

Committee, may choose to waive the training requirement after consideration of conditions including the following:

- The officer has attended training at least once.
- The officer has served at least one term and demonstrates an exceptional knowledge of, and compliance with, the procedures; e.g., by conducting training sessions, etc.
- The Data Interoperability Program Committee records confirm compliance with the administrative requirements within this document (e.g., membership updates, complete Community of Interest archives, etc.).
- There have not been significant changes in the relevant procedures, or the officer has demonstrated a thorough knowledge of the significant changes.

The Data Interoperability Program Committee will develop the training materials, and schedule and provide the training sessions. Prospective officers and other interested parties are also encouraged to attend these sessions.

13.4.2 Community of Interest Training

Each newly formed Community of Interest will establish time on its first agenda prior to conducting any technical business for presentation of an overview on the Community of Interest and its procedures. A representative from the Data Interoperability Program Committee will provide this presentation.

Additionally, all Communities of Interest are encouraged to arrange periodically (e.g., every two years) for training by a representative from the Data Interoperability Program Committee. Arrangements for this training should be made in conjunction with scheduled Community of Interest meetings.

13.5 Fees

13.5.1 Service Fees

Service fees are those fees necessary for the good order and operation of the entire Data Interoperability Program.

The Data Interoperability Program Committee service fees are not refundable. Members of Maintenance Communities of Interest are exempted from paying service fees.

The Data Interoperability Program Committee will determine the required service fees that will be required to operate the entire Data Interoperability Program. These services fees will be allocated to the various subgroups of the Data Interoperability Program as the Data Interoperability Program Committee deems appropriate. Timely payment (90 days from invoiced service-fees) will be required to continue membership in any Data Interoperability Program subgroup.

13.5.2 Subgroup Fees

13.5.2.1 General Rules

If a Subgroup finds it necessary to collect funds to pay for services to progress the work of the Subgroup, the Subgroup members will agree in advance to the collection of such a fee. Fee amounts will be subject to Subgroup approval. Any changes to set fees also will be approved by the Subgroup. All such fees are required to be approved by the Data Interoperability Program Committee.

13.5.2.2 Reporting Requirements

A financial report will be made a standing agenda item of the Subgroup and be included in the meeting's minutes if any Subgroup fees are assessed to the membership of the Subgroup. The financial report will include a statement of funds received, disbursed, outstanding debits and receivables, and the current balance. Each report will have an attachment that itemizes each individual collection and disbursement for the service(s) rendered and lists the individual(s) or organization(s) providing the agreed to service(s).

As a part of its annual report, the Subgroup will include a financial statement providing a summary of the total receivables, total disbursements, and the current balance for the reporting period.

13.5.3 Document Distribution Subscription Fees

Subgroups may make their documents available to their members through the Document Distribution Program that entails the assessment of subscription fees. In order to participate in the program, the Subgroup Chair will follow the policy established by the Data Interoperability Program Committee.

13.6 Reports and Review

13.6.1 Annual Reports

In order to maintain the management continuity of the entire Data Interoperability Program, and to keep the Standards Development Board informed on matters pertaining to the overall organization, membership, management, and policy, Subgroup Chairs will submit an annual report. This Annual Report Guide will be delivered to the Standards Development Board for review on a time schedule developed by the Standards Development Board.

13.7 Finance Management

13.7.1 Approved Uses of Subgroup Funds

Several of the subgroups may find it necessary to collect funds to pay for services to progress work. This section sets forth the policy for subgroups to establish, collect, disburse, maintain and account for such funds.

Funds collected under this policy are restricted to the following use(s):

- Meeting room rental.
- Meeting refreshments.

- Current meeting document reproduction.
- Per meeting rental of audio-visual, computer and/or office equipment rental.
- Contracting for professional meeting planner.
- Bonding fees for Subgroup Chair and Treasurer.
- Purchase of durable goods (e.g., projectors, LANs, peripherals, etc.).

All purchased items must be approved by the Data Interoperability Program Committee in advance of purchase.

13.7.2 Establishment of the Subgroup Fee

A subgroup will only establish a subgroup fee by issuing a letter ballot that explains the need for and use of a fee, along with the initial fee to be charged. The letter ballot establishing the fund will also document the subgroup procedures for collecting, disbursing and administering these funds. The letter ballot will pass by a super-majority vote for the subgroup fee to be established.

13.7.3 Participation

Because subgroup fees can only be instituted to support meeting-related expenses, fees should be determined based on the number of persons participating. If a member has not paid all authorized subgroup fees for all principal and alternate members desiring to participate in a meeting, the member will be considered to have failed to attend the meeting. The member's voting privileges would be subject to the rules for membership in good standing. The subgroup may grant exceptions by subgroup super-majority vote. If the subgroup fee is established for the purchase of durable goods, the fee will be paid by all voting members. The total purchase amount should be divided equally among all voting members.

13.7.4 Changes to the Fee

Changes to the fee amount will be approved by a majority vote of the Subgroup at least thirty calendar days in advance of the assessment of any revised fee.

13.7.5 Subgroup Fund Administration

13.7.5.1 Treasurer Appointment

Any subgroup establishing a subgroup fee will have a Chair-appointed Treasurer. The Chair will not serve as the Treasurer.

13.7.5.2 Reporting Requirements

13.7.5.2.1 Subgroup Reporting

The Treasurer will prepare a report following each meeting to be distributed with the minutes of that meeting. This report also will be a standing agenda item of the subgroup. This report will include:

- Names of individual Subgroup members (and any other applicable parties) who have or have not paid their assessed fees.
- All disbursements made, including the name of the individual(s) and/or organization(s) receiving payments.
- Debts outstanding.
- Receivables outstanding.
- The current balance of the Fund.

13.7.5.2.2 Annual Report

As part of its Annual Report, the subgroup will include a financial statement containing the following items:

- Total receipts.
- Receivables outstanding.
- Total disbursements.
- Debts outstanding.
- Current balance of the Fund.

The Annual Report will also include a copy of the procedures for administering the fund.

13.7.5.3 Account Management

- Bank accounts will be established for accrued funds that exceed $500.00. Note: If funds are collected for a one-time purchase of durable goods, this is not considered an accrual of funds and establishing a bank account is not necessary.

- Accrued funds will not exceed $25,000.00.

- Bank accounts will have the Treasurer and an elected officer as signatory authority. Only one signature may be required for banking purposes.

- Bank accounts being established will use the Data Interoperability Program Committee tax ID number for the account.

- Subgroups that are not required to establish a bank account will institute procedures for handling any surplus funds remaining at the end of a meeting.

13.7.5.4 Treasurer Duties

The Treasurer will be responsible for the following:

- Collection, disbursement and accounting of the Subgroup funds.
- Where appropriate, establish and maintain an account at a full service bank that is federally insured by the FDIC.
- Maintain a file of all receipts, bank statements, invoices, interest and other pertinent documents. The period of retention for this file will be five years. The file will be made available for inspection by any member of the subgroup, the subgroup's parent's officers, or the Chair of the Data Interoperability Program Committee upon request.
- Durable goods purchased on behalf of the subgroup, including maintaining an inventory of durable goods and reporting the inventory to the Data Interoperability Program Committee.

13.7.5.5 Bonding

Any persons with signature authority over a subgroup bank account will be bonded in the amount of $25,000.00 each. Subgroups not using bank accounts may also have their Treasurer bonded. Bonding will be obtained through the Data Interoperability Program Committee prior to the collection of any funds. Bonding fees will be reimbursed from the subgroup funds.

13.7.6 Dissolution of the Subgroup Fund

A fund will be dissolved in one of two ways:

- By a subgroup Letter Ballot receiving super-majority approval; or
- Disbandment of the subgroup.

In either case, a final financial statement will be distributed to the subgroup members and the Data Interoperability Program Committee. Any remaining balance in the fund will be signed over to the Data Interoperability Program Committee by the subgroup Chair and/or Treasurer for deposit into the Data Interoperability Program equity account. If any durable goods are held by the subgroup, the Treasurer will turn them over to the Data Interoperability Program

Committee. If the subgroup dissolved the fund but did not disband, it may request to retain the durable goods; otherwise, the Data Interoperability Program Committee may retain the durable goods, offer the goods to other Data Interoperability Program subgroups, or may dispose of the goods as it sees fit. Any proceeds will be deposited in the Data Interoperability Program equity account.

13.7.7 The Community of Interest Equity Account

The Data Interoperability Program equity account serves as a financial fund into which excess revenues (derived primarily from Data Interoperability Program Committee Dues and Fees) over expenses could be deposited. Periodic review of the account is done through reports by the Data Interoperability Program Committee. The funds held in this account are to be used for such purposes as meeting expenses when such expenses exceed revenues in any given fiscal year(s), not anticipated within the current fiscal year budget. Use of the Equity Account funds will require prior approval by the Data Interoperability Program Committee. No set figure is required to be maintained within the Equity Account. However, if the account exceeds six months of the Data Interoperability Program Committee operating expenses or the account is depleted to a balance below two month's operating expenses, the equity account should be reexamined by the Data Interoperability Program Committee in light of the current Service Fees.

13.7.8 Special Events

13.7.8.1 Business Plan

In order for the Data Interoperability Program subgroup to evaluate and grant its sponsorship of a subgroup special activity/event, a business plan containing the following information must be provided.

Item	Business Plan Component	Example Response
1	Sponsoring the Subgroup	Database Study Group
2	Additionally involved	Other Subgroups having an interest in object-

Item	Business Plan Component	Example Response
	Subgroups	oriented systems standards. The Chairs of the H2, Database, and X3T3, ODP, have indicated that their Communities of Interest are planning to participate.
3	Title of the activity/event	Objects in Data Management
4	Activity/Event date	January 14-15, <calendar year>
5	Activity/Event location	Grand Hotel, Anaheim, CA
6	Type of activity/event (e.g., symposium, conference, publication, database)	Conference
7	Description and purpose of the activity/event	The conference will bring together representatives of subgroups, other standards groups and developers of object-oriented database management systems. Through formal presentations of input papers, general discussion sessions and ad hoc groups, the participants will compare the directions of the various standards bodies relative to technological advances. Areas of potential divergence will be investigated and recommended actions will be identified.
8	Type and number of participants anticipated	Approximately 100 standards developers, implementors and users of object-oriented database systems.
9	Expected benefits to participants	The conference will provide the opportunity for individuals to present their contributions on object-oriented database technology and standardization, provide a forum for exchange of information and generally raise the participants awareness of current and planned standardization activities.
10	Expected benefits to the Community of Interest in	In addition to the benefit of having the Community of Interest's name associated with

Item	Business Plan Component	Example Response
	sponsoring this activity/event	this conference, the conference will bring together various Community of Interest representatives (both from the Community of Interest and other groups) to share plans, etc.
11	What benefits/opportunities missed if the Community of Interest does not sponsor/authorize this activity/event	As the conference is intended to investigate areas of potential conflict among standards developing groups, this information, which could help avoid future problems in the standards approval process, would not otherwise be available.
12	Who will oversee the planning of the activity/event	The XYZ Corporation has volunteered to oversee the planning, which includes making hotel arrangements, providing a conference coordinator prior to and during the conference, handling registration, processing input papers and publishing the proceedings of the conference. A letter from XYZ Corporation indicating their sponsorship of this event is attached.
13	One-time or anticipated recurring event? (Note: A separate business plan and approval will be required for each occurrence)	This is a one-time event. Future conferences may be planned on related or other topics based on the success of this conference. It is understood that separate business plans and approval will be required for any future events.
14.	Financial and Staffing Considerations	The cost of meeting rooms, refreshments and copying at the meeting are the anticipated expenses. XYZ Corporation has agreed to cover other associated costs, e.g. conference coordinator, publication of proceedings, etc.
14.1	What expenses are anticipated for this activity/event	The cost of meeting rooms, refreshments and copying at the meeting are the anticipated expenses. XYZ Corporation has agreed to cover other associated costs, e.g., conference coordinator, publication of proceedings, etc.
14.2	Will this be a profit, loss or	The event is intended to be break-even; however,

Item	Business Plan Component	Example Response
	break-even event	subsequent sales of the proceedings could generate a profit.
14.3	Who will fund the costs for this activity/event: (i.e., How much of the costs will be borne by the participants and how did you calculate this number? Do you request Data Interoperability Program Committee funding? Do you have other funding?)	The meeting expenses are intended to be covered by a registration fee. The meeting expenses will be negotiated so that they can be covered by a registration fee of not more than $100. The exact fee will be determined at the hotel registration cut-off date approximately two months prior to the event.
14.4	Is the Data Interoperability Program Committee time and personnel necessary for the activity/event	No. However, arrangements will need to be made for the on-going sale of the proceedings after the conference.
14.5	If "YES", provide rationale for staff involvement (include estimate of staff time and travel expense)	Not applicable
14.6	Are there any provisions to cancel activity/event due to lack of interest	At the time of the hotel registration cut-off date, a final decision will be made on holding the conference. The hotel will be made aware of this during arrangement negotiations.
14.7	If proceedings are published, what is the publication plan? (i.e., Who will print them? Who will sell them? Who will hold the copyright?)	XYZ Corporation will print the proceedings. It is anticipated that the Data Interoperability Program will hold the copyright and handle the sale and distribution of the proceedings through a currently utilized (or new) service bureau. The Data Interoperability Program Committee should determine the best means for handling the sales and distribution.

Table 17. Subgroup event business plan components.

13.8 Membership in Good Standing

A member of a subgroup is in good standing if and only if they are current on their service fees, their subgroup's fees, attendance rules, and letter ballot voting.

Members are warned if any fee is unpaid beyond 30 days of invoice tender. A member's standing is in jeopardy if the fee is unpaid between 60 and 90 days. A member is terminated from voting privileges if a fee is unpaid after 90 days.

Members are warned if they miss two out of three successive meetings. If they miss the next meeting then their voting privileges are terminated.

Members are warned if they fail to return two out of three letter ballots. If they miss the next letter ballot then their voting privileges are terminated.

13.9 Rules Summary

Rules are bought out only when there is no other choice. At least that is the intention of the rules contained in this chapter. Because the impact of the cost of a standard is so significant, then the actions of a committee regarding standard's development must be above reproach. All meetings, change proposals, voting, the application of changes to a standard must all be very carefully governed so that in the event of a dispute it can be quickly resolved not only to the satisfaction of the majority but also to the organization that has brought the dispute forward.

Index

www.ingramcontent.com/pod-product-compliance
Lightning Source LLC
LaVergne TN
LVHW061218100826
845148LV00004B/796

* 9 7 8 0 9 7 8 9 9 6 8 0 2 *